French Menu

Concise Dictionary of French Food

T. William Walker

Copyright © 2015 by T. William Walker
ISBN-13:978-1511666862

All rights reserved.

Printed by CreateSpace™
  4900 LaCross Road
  North Charleston, SC 29406
  USA

You must not circulate this book in any other binding or cover and you must impose the same condition on any acquirer.
No part of this book may be reproduced, stored in a retrieval system, or transmitted in any form or by any means, electronic, mechanical, photocopying, recording, or otherwise, without the prior permission in writing of the author, who may be reached at: frenchfooddictionary@gmail.com

The author has made every reasonable effort to ensure that the information contained in this dictionary is both accurate and complete.

Caveat: given the nature of cuisine and the indiosyncracies of chefs, it is entirely possible that ingredients the traveler actually finds when ordering from menus in French restaurants may not be precisely as described in this dictionary. Moreover, the definitions contained herein are not to be construed as being the only possible definitions. Therefore, the author cannot accept any liability for any adverse consequences arising from the information contained herein.

This dictionary contains some words which have or are asserted to have proprietary status as trademarks or otherwise. Their inclusion does not imply that they have acquired for legal purposes a non-proprietary or general significance nor any other judgement concerning their legal status. In cases where the author has some evidence that a word has proprietary status, this is indicated in the entry for that word but no judgement concerning the legal status of such words is made or implied thereby.

Preface

Whether you are eating in French restaurants or shopping in the markets for food to prepare in your rented apartment, this translation dictionary should come in handy. Even if you are quite fluent in French, you may very well be baffled at some of the terms that you encounter in the markets or see on menus. Every effort has been made to include many of these gems in this tome.

Do not worry about pronunciation. If you do not know how to pronounce French words, you can always resort to pointing at the items on the menu. Most French servers really do want you to have an enjoyable dining experience, so it is most likely that they will accommodate you.

The author of this dictionary travels to France quite frequently and, over the years, has become fairly fluent in the language. Despite his language skills, he is constantly amazed and often baffled by French menus. As a result, he has written this book which he carries with him wherever he goes in French-speaking countries. By publishing this book, he not only shares it with his fellow travelers, but also invites them to inform him of food items they come across which are not listed herein. On that note, please contact the author if you would like to contribute some of your discoveries. They will be included in subsequent editions of this book.

Please email the author at:
frenchfooddictionary@gmail.com

How to Use this Book

Entries
There are 5,200+ alphabetical entries in this dictionary.

Most of the foods and dishes listed herein can be found in restaurants, although some will be found only in grocery stores and specialty shops; more obscure items might be found only in a particular town or village.

Cross references
Many of the food items you will find on menus in French restaurants contain two, three or more words. In most cases, you need only look up one of the words because this translation dictionary lists such items multiple times, once for each term. For example, you might find *agneau de pré-salé* on the menu. In this book, you will find out what that means by looking up either *agneau* or *pré-salé*. Be aware, however, that some chefs add names to their creations that are simply not translatable.

Notes on French cuisine

Food
In many cases, the English translation of the French term is followed in square brackets by additional information about the item. This is usually a list of ingredients. French food terms are, in some cases, influenced by regional dialects.

A Strategy for Using this Dictionary
Most French restaurants post a menu outside so that passersby may find out what is on offer. Take advantage of this by pulling out this little dictionary to look up unfamiliar words before you are seated inside. In the larger cities, you may often find waiters who speak some English, so do not be afraid to ask more questions as you make up your mind on what to order.

About the author

Mr. Walker is a writer and traveler who frequently explores the wonderfully varied regions of France, Belgium and Switzerland and other French-speaking regions and enjoys finding ever so many culinary delights.

Because the author is also his own editor and proofreader, and also because the author is a mere mortal, the reader may expect to find a typo or two in this dictionary. Please do not hesitate to contact the author, whether to point out a typographical error or to inform him of inaccurate content or even to contribute items that he may have missed.

> Please email the author at:
> frenchfooddictionary@gmail.com

Also by T. Willliam Walker:

French Menu Companion
Dictionary of French Food, Wine and Cheese

A more encyclopedic dictionary, it has 7000+ entries including over 700 cheeses, 350 wines and 200 sauces along with regional specialties and notes on ingredients.

Bon appétit!

AB/Agriculture Biologique non-GMO; must be at least 95% organic
aiglefin haddock [marine fish]
à la with; in the style of [*au* and *aux* are the other grammatical forms and mean the same thing]
à ma façon my way
à point medium; medium rare
à teneur lipidique réduite reduced-fat spread
à votre gout to your liking
AB/Agriculture Biologique non-GMO, 95% organic
abatis/abattis head, neck, wings, feet, gizzard, heart, liver and kidneys of fowl and poultry
abatis à la bourguignonne poulty giblets (minus the liver) with chopped onions, red wine, garlic, diced bacon and pearl onions added to raw sliced livers
abatis aux navets poulty giblets (minus the liver) with chopped turnips
abatis chipolata poulty giblets (minus the liver) with chopped onions, white wine, garlic, diced pork belly and chestnuts added to raw sliced livers
abats printanier poulty giblets (minus the liver) with chopped onions, red wine, garlic and spring herbs added to raw sliced livers
abats offal; giblets; variety meat
abats de veau veal offal
Abondance AOC cheese [raw cow's milk; matured for 90 days on spruce boards; smooth amber rind; best during the months of July to November; Savoie and Haute-Savoie]
abricot apricot
    aromatisé à l'abricot apricot-flavored
    nectar d'abricot apricot nectar
    sauce à l'abricot apricot sauce [made with apricots, butter and lemon juice]
abricots Bourdaloue poached apricot halves with frangipane cream and crushed macaroons
abricots Colbert poached apricots filled with sweet rice, breaded and deep fried
abricots Cussy lightly baked soft macaroon with diced fruit, apricot purée and poached apricot and meringue
abricots gratinés poached apricots with sweet apple purée, praline icing, lightly browned in the oven
abricots meringués poached apricot on sweet rice with meringue and sugar, lightly browned in the oven and garnished with jam
abricots mireille frozen apricots with skinned apricot kernels and a sprinkling of sugar, served with kirsch and *Chantilly* whipped cream and decorated with flowers
abricots à la parisienne poached apricots with vanilla ice cream on a large macaroon and topped with *Chantilly* whipped cream and hazelnut praline
abricots à la royale poached apricots in a ring of sponge cake with redcurrant jelly
abricots sultane a ring of sponge cake on a layer of apricot jam, filled with dessert rice, frangipane cream and chopped

pistachios, and coated with meringue, poached apricots and chopped pistachios
acidulé tangy; tart; slightly acidic
acra small savory fritters [puréed or whole vegetables or fish mixed into a batter and deep fried; eaten very hot as an appetizer]
addition check (must be requested: Just say "*l'addition, s'il vous plaît.*" "The check, please.")
affiné aged; matured [said of cheese]
agaric champêtre country agaric mushroom; common meadow mushroom [has firm, white flesh and pink blades]
agaric des prés meadow agaric; considered to be superior to the *champignon de Paris* (a cultivated agaric)
agneau lamb [female (ewe) lamb is *agnelle*]
    brochette d'agneau lamb kebab
    carré d'agneau rack of lamb
    cervelle d'agneau lamb's brains
    côte d'agneau lamb chop
    côtelette d'agneau lamb chop
    couscous agneau lamb couscous
    cuisse d'agneau leg of lamb
    curry d'agneau lamb curry
    épaule d'agneau shoulder of lamb
    gigot d'agneau leg of lamb
    langue d'agneau lamb tongue
    navarin d'agneau lamb stew
    noisette d'agneau lamb *noisette* (a small round piece of lamb)
    parures d'agneau lamb trimmings
    ris d'agneau lamb sweetbreads [various glands go by the name of sweetbreads: thymus, pancreas, etc.]
    rognons d'agneau lamb kidneys
    selle d'agneau saddle of lamb
    souris d'agneau knuckle of lamb
agneau à la Hongroise Hungarian breast of lamb with paprika
agneau au cari lamb curry
agneau (en) chilindrón lamb with potatoes, *choricero* peppers and garlic, with or without tomato sauce
agneau de lait suckling lamb; unweaned milk-fed lamb
agneau de pré-salé salt-marsh lamb [lamb raised in the lush meadows of salt marshes, so the meat develops a very special taste]
agneau laiton suckling lamb
agneau pascal spring lamb
agneau rôti roast lamb
agnelet young lamb
agnelle ewe (female) lamb less than one year old
agriade saint-gilloise a specialty casserole of the Saint-Gilles and Lower Rhône made with layers of slices of chuck steak alternating with layers of onions, olive oil, capers, gherkins, anchovies, garlic and parsley
Agriculture Biologique/AB non-GMO, 95% organic
agrumes citrus fruits

aïado roast shoulder of lamb with garlic sauce
aiglefin haddock [fresh, not smoked]
aïgo bouïdo garlic soup
aïgo bouïdo à la ménagère garlic soup with onions, leeks, potatoes, fennel and herbs in saffron water
aïgo saou garlic soup with fish, onion and potatoes
aigo boulido garlic soup
aigrette cheese fritter
aïgrossade cooked vegetables with a mayonnaise and garlic sauce
aiguillat rock salmon
aiguille needle fish; garfish [Mediterrannean fish]
aiguillette fillet; long thin slice
ail garlic
    beurre à l'ail garlic butter
    pain à l'ail garlic bread
    point d'ail touch of garlic
ail des ours wild garlic
ail doux mild garlic; sweet garlic
ail en chemise unpeeled garlic
ail frais fresh garlic
ail sauvage wild garlic
aile wing
aile de poulet chicken wings
aileron wing tip; shark's fin
ailerons de poulet carmelite poached chicken breast and wing bones in aspic with a crayfish mousse, layered with crayfish tails, chilled in a mold and served cold
ailerons de volaille dorée large turkey or chicken wings [typically: wing browned in butter and served with carrots and onions in a white sauce]
ailerons de volaille farcis chipolata grilled stuffed wings [typically: chicken or turkey; stuffed with chipolate sausage]
ailerons de volaille farcis grillés grilled stuffed chicken or turkey wings [typically: stuffed with sausage, breaded and grilled]
aillade southern French preparations made with garlic [such as garlic vinaigrette or garlic bread]
aillé made with garlic
ailloli aioli; garlic mayonnaise
ailloli garni salt cod and vegetables with a garnish of snails
aïoli aioli; garlic mayonnaise
aïoli plat aioli plate [a plate of cold snails or fish (cod or other) and vegetables such as potatoes, beets, green beans served with *aioli*]
aïoli sauce crushed garlic and olive oil [a kind of mayonnaise]
airelle rouge cranberry
albacore albacore tuna; yellow fin tuna
albert tangy sauce [made with cream, egg yolks, horseradish and mustard]
albuféra/sauce albuféra Albuféra sauce [based on a velvety sauce (*velouté*) to which is added a meat glaze, giving it an ivory-white coloring; served with poultry and sweetbreads]
alcool alcohol [an alcoholic beverage is called *boisson alcoolisée*]

alcoolisé with alcohol
Alexandra/sauce Alexandra Alexandra sauce [the classic version is made with a velvety cream sauce (*velouté*) to which is added a stock made from truffles]
algérienne/à la algérienne Algerian style
algue seaweed
    enveloppement d'algues seaweed wrap
algue rouge dulse
Ali Baba small yeast cake saturated with rum and sometimes filled or topped with whipped cream
aligot fluffy mashed potatoes and cheese [the cheese is usually *Laguiole;* typically made with garlic and *crème fraiche* or butter; it should be a very light, creamy puree]
aligot de marinette puréed potatoes with garlic, bacon fat and *Laguiole* cheese
aligotée ordinary white wine made from the *aligotée* grape; fresh and light
    Bourgogne Aligotée a light white wine from Bourgogne
alise service berry [the bitter fruit of a wild shrub; used in the making of brandy (*eau de vie*) and cider]
allache large sardine
alla puttanesca hot, spicy, savory Italian sauce [usually with anchovies, garlic and peppers]
allégé low-fat
    yaourt allégé low-fat yoghurt
allumette match stick [refers to a way of cutting food items]
    pommes allumettes French fries cut very thin
allumettes aux anchois puff pastry rectangles with minced fish and anchovy sauce
allumettes aux crevettes puff pastry rectangles with minced whiting and shrimp and a shrimp-butter sauce
allumettes aux fromage cheese sticks
allumettes caprice puff pastry rectangles with minced chicken and cream, chopped ox tongue and truffles
allumettes feuilletées thin strips of puff pastry with savory or sweet coating
almondon almond nut without the skin; the nut of fruits such as apricots, peaches, olives, plums, etc.
alose shad [a small, fine white fish related to the herring]
alose à la provençale shad layered with sorrel and chopped onions [slowly cooked with garlic, herbs and brandy]
alose à la tomate et au vin shad baked with tomatoes, onions, mushrooms and wine
alose à l'étouffée stuffed shad [a dish made with shad and sorrel]
alose de Loire farcie à l'angevine stuffed shad in the style of Ander [typically: shad stuffed with shad caviar, sorrel, shallots, butter, nutmeg]
alose grillée grilled shad
alouette lark [called *mauviette* when served as a meal]
allouette farcie au foie gras roasted lark stuffed with goose liver

alouette sans tête a beef dish [minced meat rolled in a thin slice of meat and cooked in a tomato sauce with wine, mushrooms and herbs [Provence]
aloyau sirloin steak
Alsacienne/à l'Alsacienne in the style of Alsace [where white wine, sauerkraut, ham, bacon, sausage and *foie gras* are common ingredients]
amandine/tartelette amandine small almond "pie" pastry [made with sweet pie crust and stuffed with a creamy almond custard and topped with sliced almonds]
amanite des césars edible Caesar's mushroom [has an orange cap and yellow gills]
ambassadrice/sauce ambassadrice ambassadress sauce [made with a velvety cream sauce (*velouté*) to which are added chicken puree and heavy cream; good with egg, poultry or vegetable dishes]
ambroisie ambrosia-like
ambroisie ambrosia [apéritif liqueur made with brandy (*eau de vie*), white wine, cloves, coriander and aniseed]
americaine/garni à l'americaine fried slices of lobster tail simmered in white wine, fish stock, brandy, meat glaze, chopped shallots, tomatoes, parsley and cayenne pepper
amiral admiral [refers to a variety of seafood garnishes]
amourettes spinal marrow [prepared in the same manner as veal brains; usually diced and served as a garnish]
amuse-bouche hors d'oeuvre, appetizer
amuse-gueule hors d'oeuvre, appetizer; nibbles
anaheim mild green chili pepper
ananas pineapple
ananas à la créole a mold lined with pineapple slices and filled with sweet dessert rice and fruit
ananas à la royale whole cored pineapple filled with fresh fruit flavored with kirsch
ananas Condé poached pineapple on dessert rice
ananas frais fresh pineapple
ananas georgette whole cored pineapple filled with fruit mousse, pineapple purée and *Chantilly* whipped cream
ananas Ninon vanilla ice cream with a filling of pineapple, strawberries, raspberries and pistachios
ananas Virginie whole cored pineapple filled with strawberry mousse and diced pineapple
anchoïade/anchoyade anchovy sauce [anchovies, black olives, olive oil and garlic]
anchoïade/anchoyade raw vegetables served with anchovy sauce
anchois anchovy
    beurre d'anchois anchovy butter [made with anchovies and butter; may have lemon or pepper; to be put on bread]
    pâte d'anchois anchovy paste
anchois à la parisienne fillets of de-salted anchovies with soy sauce and hard-boiled egg yolks and whites arranged in a diamond pattern
anchois au beurre anchovies with butter; to be put on bread

anchois au povrons anchovy hors d'oeuvres with sweet peppers and chopped hard boiled eggs
anchois aux tamarins anchovy hors d'oeuvres with potato and black olives
anchois de Norvège Norwegian anchovies preserved in brine
anchois frais marinés fresh anchovies fried and marinated in lemon juice
anchouiada anchovy fillets mashed with garlic and shallots
ancienne/à la ancienne a style of making various stews [literally "in the old way"]
Andalouse a garnish consisting of peppers, tomatoes, rice and eggplant/aubergine
andouille pork tripe sausage [barnyard aroma; made with pork intestines and stomach; cold or grilled; white, brown or black; dried or smoked]
andouille chaude à la Bovary hot pork tripe sausage [barnyard aroma]
andouille de Guémené black smoked pork tripe sausage [made with pork chitterlings cut into strips, stuffed into casings and smoked over a wood fire (beech or oak); when cured, it is simmered in broth; served hot or cold]
andouille de Vire black smoked pork tripe sausage [made with pork stomach and intestines with no extra fat added; smoked over beech wood for one month, then cured and simmered in broth]
andouille du Val-d'Ajol smoked pork tripe sausage [made with 60% lean and fat pork and 40% pork stomach; smoked over beech wood]
andouille du Coglaise/la Coglaise traditional pork tripe sausage from Bretagne [strong barnyard aroma]
andouille pur porc sausage made with pork shoulder and pork fat
andouille vigneronne bean and sausage stew with bacon, pork rind, carrots, onions and wine
andouillette small pork tripe sausage [strong barnyard aroma; made with coarsely chopped pig chitterlings (small intestine), tripe (stomach), onions, wine and seasonings; may be smoked]
andouillette à la lyonnaise sautéed sausages with onion, parsley and vinegar
andouillette à la strasbourgeoise sausages with sauerkraut and boiled potatoes
andouillette bourguignonne sautéed cut-up sausage with snail butter
andouillette d'Alençon white sausage from Alençon in Normandie [due to Mad Cow Disease, some ingredients in this sausage are forbidden in Europe]
andouillette de Cambrai small sausage made with veal rather than pork
andouillette de Savoie sausage flavored with cumin
andouillette de Troyes pork tripe sausage [strong barnyard aroma; made from the large intestines and stomach, seasoned with onions, salt, pepper and spices, and slowly cooked in an aromatic broth]

andouillette de Troyes au gratin de chaource pork tripe sausage of Troyes in a gratin made with Chaource cheese
aneth dill
angélique angelica [herb related to parsley, carrot and anise]
angelot angel fish; angel shark [large fleshy fins and tail]
angélys pear [ripens in winter]
anglaise/à l'anglais English style [boiled, breaded or with eggs]
    assiette anglaise assorted cold meats
    crème anglaise custard; English cream sauce
angostura angostura bitters [made of spices, citrus, quinine and rum; used in gin or champagne cocktails]
anguille eel
    matelote d'anguille eel stew with red wine, onions and mushrooms
anguille à l'escabèche fried pickled eel, cooled in aspic
anguille à la Beaucaire braised eel stuffed with whiting and mushrooms
anguille à la meunière fried eel with *beurre noisette* (nut-brown butter)
anguille à la romaine eel stewed with peas, lettuce and white wine
anguille à la rouennaise poached eel with poached oysters, poached soft roe and fried smelts
anguille à la tartare eel poached in white wine, then breaded and fried
anguille au vert eel cooked with spinach, white wine sauce and garden herbs
anguille au vert à la flammande eel cooked in beer, with seasonings and garden herbs
anguille au vin blanc et paprika eel with onion, garlic, white wine and paprika
anguille de mer conger eel
anguille en matelote eel stew with onions and crayfish
anguille fumée smoked eel
anguille pompadour eel dipped in egg infused with ham and truffles, then breaded and fried
anguillette small eel
animelles organ meat [especially testicles of rams]
anise anise
anise étoilé star anise
anisette aniseed liqueur
anise vert anise; aniseed
anjou pear [medium size pear with no neck]
anone custard apple; annona fruit [looks like a bumpy, round pear; sweet white flesh with a flavor like cloves or cinnamon]
Antillaise Antilles (Caribbean) style
anversoise/à l'anversoise Antwerp-style [with hop shoots and cream]
AOC/Appellation d'Origin Contrôlée controlled designation of origin [the prestigious French certification granted to specific French butters, cheeses, wines, and other agricultural products according to their geographical origins; guarantees the

authenticity of the location of the production or vintage; the products are held to a rigorous set of clearly defined standards]
AOP/Appellation d'Origine Protégée protected designation of origin [prestigious European certification granted to agricultural products such as butter, cheese and wine governing the production, processing and preparation of the named product within a defined geographical area, thus guaranteeing that the products meet stringent standards; may someday replace the AOC designation]
apéritif aperitif; a pre-dinner drink to stimulate the appetite
apéritive appetizer
appellation contrôlée controlled designation
appellation d'origin designation of origin
apron a perch-like fish from the Rhône River
aquavit grain-based clear brandy (*eau de vie*)
arachide ground nut; peanut
araignée tender rump steak
araignée de mer spider crab
archiduc/à l'archiduc Archduke style [white sauce with paprika]
ardéchois à la crème de marrons cake made with sweet chestnut puree and rum; specialty of Ardèche in Southern France
ardennaise prepared in the Ardenne style [with juniper berries]
ardoise slate, list [found outside the door of a restaurant or just inside; contains the featured menu items]
aréna almond cake
argenteuil gourmet asparagus
argus pheasant from Malaysia and Sumatra
arlésien chocolate cake
arlésienne/à l'arlésienne in the Arles style [with slices of eggplant/aubergine, onions and tomatoes]
arlette fine, crispy puff pastry with sugar icing
armotte fritter [made with cornstarch batter and pork cracklings fried or grilled and served cold or hot]
aromate spice; aromatic plant
aromatisé/aromatique flavored; spicy; seasoned
arrivage arrival
   selon arrivage according to availability
arroche orach [mountain spinach]
artichaut artichoke/sunchoke/globe artichoke
   coeur d'artichaut artichoke heart
   foin d'artichaut choke
   fond d'artichaut artichoke heart
artichaut à la barigoule stuffed artichokes [typical of Provence; the stuffing may be mushrooms, ham or bacon, or vegetables]
artichaut à la grecque Greek-style artichoke hors d'oeuvres
artichaut à la provençale fried artichokes with peas and lettuce
artichaut Cavour small artichokes baked with Parmesan and Gruyère cheese, served with hard boiled eggs and anchovy essence
artichaut Clamart artichokes baked with diced carrots and peas and served with a butter sauce
artichaut de Jerusalem Jerusalem artichoke; sun choke

artichaut Grand Duc boiled artichokes with a Parmesan cheese and butter sauce, with asparagus tips and warm truffles
artichaut poivrade small purple artichoke
asperge asparagus
   pointes d'asperges asparagus tips
asperge à l'italienne asparagus with brown butter and Parmesan cheese
asperge à la flamande asparagus with a sauce of hard boiled egg yolk and butter
asperge à la millanaise asparagus with brown butter and Parmesan cheese
asperge à la polonaise asparagus with chopped hard boiled egg, parsley, browned bread crumbs and brown butter
asperge au gratin asparagus glazed with mornay sauce and Parmesan cheese
asperge blanche de Champagne white (blanched) asparagus
asperge d'Argenteuil white (blanched) asparagus
asperge des sables des Landes an early harvested, high-quality asparagus from southern France
asperge mornay asparagus glazed with mornay sauce and Parmesan cheese
asperge sauce Argenteuil a *mousseline* sauce for asparagus [made with egg yolks, butter, wine vinegar and fresh cream]
asperge verte de Lauris an early harvested asparagus
aspic aspic; gelatin
aspic de bécasses woodcock breast set in an aspic of woodcock leg meat and offal served with a chaud-froid sauce
aspic de volaille gauloise an aspic mold consisting of layers of truffles, chicken, cockscombs, chicken kidneys and slices of ox tongue
aspic de volaille à l'italienne an aspic mold consisting of layers of truffles, chicken breast, ox tongue
assaisonné seasoned; dressed (salad)
assaisonnement seasoning, condiment, salad dressing
assiette plate; a plate of
assiette anglaise assorted cold meats
assiette comtoise a plate consisting of cold cuts of meat, smoked ham, slices of sausage, potatoes and Cancoillotte cheese with some green salad leaves and a vinaigrette sauce
assiette creuse dish, soup dish
assiette de charcuterie plate of sliced sausages
assiette de crudités plate of raw vegetables
assiette de viandes froides plate of cold meats
assiette du pêcheur seafood plate [fish or shellfish, hot or cold]
assiette landaise a plate of hot items such as gizzards, meat fillets and duck combined with with cold items such as lettuce, tomatoes, cucumber, apples and asparagus
assiette scandinave plate of assorted seafood typical of Scandinavia
assortis assorted
athénienne/à l'athénienne Athenian style [with onion, eggplant/augergine, tomato and sweet red pepper]

attereaux meat, seafood or vegetables skewered, marinated and coated in breadcrumbs and deep fried
attereaux à la florentine a skewer of cooked semolina-Parmesan wafers alternating with slices of Gruyère cheese
attereaux à la genevoise breaded and deep fried skewer of mushrooms, truffles, artichoke hearts, chicken livers, lamb brains and sweetbreads
attereaux à la princesse breaded and deep fried skewer of cooked semolina-Parmesan wafers alternating with slices of Gruyère cheese
attereaux à la royale breaded and deep fried skewer of cooked semolina-Parmesan wafers alternating with slices of Gruyère cheese
attereaux d'huitres à la Villeroy breaded and deep fried skewer of oysters and mushrooms
attereaux Villeroy breaded and deep fried skewer of cooked semolina-Parmesan wafers alternating with slices of Gruyère cheese
au with; in the style of
au gratin baked until golden on top (sometimes with cheese and possibly breadcrumbs)
    macaroni au gratin macaroni and cheese
aubepine hawthorn [leaves are used to make tea]
aubergine eggplant/aubergine
aubergine à l'égyptienne deep fried eggplant/aubergine baked with onions and served with chopped tomatoes and parsley
aubergine à l'orientale baked eggplant/aubergine layered with chopped fried eggplant/aubergine, tomatoes and breadcrumbs
aubergine à la bordelaise eggplant/aubergine sautéed with shallots and breadcrumbs and coated with a *bordelaise* sauce (a reduction of red wine and shallots)
aubergine à la napolitaine baked eggplant/aubergine with tomato sauce and Parmesan cheese
aubergine à la parisienne deep fried eggplant/aubergine baked with white meat, bacon fat or marrow, egg yolks and breadcrumbs
aubergine à la provençale deep fried eggplant/aubergine baked with onions, garlic and tomatoes and served with tomato sauce and parsley
aubergine à la turque deep fried eggplant/aubergine baked with mutton, tomatoes, onions and rice and served with tomato sauce
aumônière "purse" pastry [a thin crêpe with sweet or savory filling, formed into a bundle and tied at the top]
aumônières de pommes au calvados "purse" pastry filled with apples and *Calvados* (apple brandy)
aurore with the addition of tomato sauce or tomato purée
autrichienne/à l'autrichienne Austrian style [typically: with sour cream, onions, paprika and fennel]
aux with; in the style of [plural form of *à la*]
aveline hazelnut; filbert
avocat avocado

avocat épicure diced avocado with diced gherkins, walnuts, mayonnaise and paprika
avoine oats
   gruau d'avoine oatmeal; gruel
axoa minced beef or veal flavored with spices, onions and peppers
azerole Mediterranean medlar [the orange or yellow sweet-sour fruit of a species of hawthorn tree]
aziminu seafood bouillabaisse [made with several varieties of rock fish (scorpion fish, conger eel, sea bream, sea bass, whiting, and sometimes lobster and/or crab]
azyme unleavened bread
baba au kirsch a small ring cake saturated with kirsch syrup
baba au rhum a small ring cake saturated with rum and sometimes filled or topped with whipped cream
babeurre buttermilk
bacon bacon [lean, usually smoked]
   couenne de bacon bacon rind
   oeufs au bacon bacon and eggs
   tranche de bacon thin slice of bacon
bacon croustillant crispy fried bacon
bacon en tranches slices of bacon
badasco rascasse [marine fish found in soups and bouillabaisse]
badèche sea bas; bar
badine a thin, flexible baguette [literally "cane" or "switch"]
badiane star anise
bagna small *Niçoise* salad served in a hollowed-out bun
baguette long skinny loaf of bread with a crunchy crust
baie berry
baie de genièvre juniper berry [partially dried, slightly pungent]
baie de ronce blackberry
baie de sureau elderberry
baie rose pink peppercorn [related to cashews; may cause allergic reaction]
baie sauvage wild berry
baiser literally: a kiss [a dessert made with a pair of meringue shells filled with whipped cream]
baiser de Chaumont chocolate pastry
bajana chestnut soup [sometimes made with prunes and nutmeg]
bajoue pig's cheek
ballon drinking glass
ballotine boned thigh meat of poultry stuffed with minced meat, and possibly truffles and/or *foie gras* [cooked by roasting, braising, or poaching; usually shaped like a sausage or the leg, sometimes with a cleaned piece of bone protruding]
bamboche a method of frying
   morue en bamboche fried cod with fried eggs or diced vegetables in a cream sauce
   oeufs frites en bamboche fried eggs with fried cod and diced vegetables
bamboo bamboo
   pousse de bamboo bamboo shoots
banane banana

banane flambée banana flambé
banane plantain plantain
bananier banana palm
   feuille de bananier banana palm leaf
bar sea bass
bar de ligne sea bass
bar de ligne au beurre blanc sea bass with white butter
barbarée winter cress
   figue de barbarie prickly pear
barbeau barbel [river fish with whiskers]
barbecue barbecue
barberon salsify
barbillon young barbel [river fish with whiskers]
barbotine tansy
barbouillade a dish of fava beans and artichokes
barbouillade stuffed eggplant stew
barbue bearded clam
barbue brill [a type of flat fish in the turbot family]
barbue au cidre brill in cider [baked with shrimp, bacon, mushrooms, potatoes, and cabbage in a cider sauce]
bardatte cabbage stuffed with rabbit
barde streaky bacon
bardé wrapped with streaky bacon or fat [usually a roast beef]
barigoule a way to cook artichokes [may be stuffed with wild barigoule mushrooms, spinach, carrots, or cheese; or may be braised with onions, garlic and carrots in a wine broth]
barigoule wild mushroom [saffron milk cap mushroom]
baron d'agneau baron of lamb [the saddle plus the two hind legs]
barquette small pastry [shaped like a boat (*barquette* means "small boat") with savory or sweet filling; appetizer or dessert]
bartavelle Greek partridge; rock partridge
bas de carré top shoulder of veal
baselle baselle; Indian spinach
basse low
   cuit à basse température cooked a low temperature
basse venaison meat from small game animals
basilic basil
basquaise Basque-style garnish [usually tomatoes, peppers, garlic and Bayonne ham]
basse-côte literally: lower side [cut of beef from the middle rib and chuck area]
bastella meat or vegetables in a folded pastry
bâtarde mongrel
   pain bâtard mongrel bread [wheat bread with a long oval shape and a crunchy brown crust]
   sauce bâtarde mongrel sauce [a white sauce with added egg yolks, lemon and butter]
batavia lettuce [has frilly, crunchy leaves]
batelière ferryman style; boatman style
bâton long baguette-type of bread
bâton long, thin cut of root vegetable
bâton de Jacob an *éclair* with caramel icing

bâtonnet small stick [vegetables cut into small sticks]
bâtons royaux small patty of minced game or chicken
baudroie monkfish; angler fish; frog fish
bavarois Bavarian cream [a dessert made with vanilla-flavored egg custard (or a fruit syrup with gelatin) to which whipped cream and sugar are added]
bavarois au marasqium cherry-flavored Bavarian cream
bavaroise hot milk and tea with eggs and sugar, flavored with vanilla or liqueur
bavette a type of flank steak [considered to be one of the most flavorful cuts of steak]
bavette/bavette de flanchet flank steak; skirt steak
bavettes long thin strips of pasta noodles
bayaldi de légumes gratin of vegetables [sliced eggplant/aubergine, tomatoes, onions, and zucchini/ courgettes arranged alternately and baked until golden brown on top]
bayenne potato and onion casserole
bayonnaise/à la bayonnaise Bayonne-style [with Bayonne ham]
Beaufort AOC cheese [raw cow's milk; similar to a Gruyère; distinct pungent aroma and a smooth, creamy texture]
Beaufort d'alpage cheese [raw cow's milk; the cows graze on high alpine meadows which give the cheese its distinctive flavor]
Beaufort d'été summer Beaufort cheese [raw cow's milk; creamy, supple; hints of hazelnuts]
bec de Flers apple-rhubarb tart
bécasse woodcock [a small grouse-like woodland bird]
bécasse comtesse dubarry [woodcock prepared in the Countess DuBarry style; the bird is surrounded with slices of bacon, browned, then served on triangles of toasted bread and covered with a sauce]
bécasseau young woodcock
bécasse de mer trumpet fish [prepared like tuna fish]
bécassine snipe
béchamel/sauce béchamel white sauce [made from a white roux (butter and flour) and milk and can be flavored with bay leaves, nutmeg and sometimes onion]
bedeu tripe
beigne fritter; doughnut [often with icing or a dusting of fine sugar]
beignet fritter; doughnut [often made with a light puff pastry dough]
beignet breton apple fritter
beignet de crevettes prawn cracker
beignet de fleurs de courgette zucchini/courgette flower fritters [flowers are dipped in batter and deep fried]
beignet de pommes de terre râpée potato pancake
beignet de poulet chicken nugget
beignet en forme de coeur heart-shaped doughnut
beignet normand aux pommes de terre potato pancake
beignet soufflé light, deep fried sweet fritter

belle Hélène beautiful Helen [a cold dessert consisting of a pear boiled in syrup, chilled and served with vanilla ice cream and hot chocolate sauce]
bellevue cold fish or poultry in a layer of gelatin
belon oyster [a flat oyster of very high quality]
béluga Beluga caviar [true caviar; the rarest and most expensive caviar; the large eggs vary in color from dark to light gray]
Bénédictine herbal liqueur [ingredients are kept secret]
benoiton/à la benoiton fish in a reduced red wine and shallot sauce
berdelle crêpe stuffed with mushrooms and ham
bergamot sour orange [zest is used in cooking; oil from the bark of the bergamot tree is used in Earl Grey tea]
bergamote bergamot [refers to either the edible flowers of monarda (beebalm) or to the bark of the bergamot tree; used to flavor pastries, cookies and candies]
　citron bergamote bergamot lemon [a cross between lime and bitter orange]
　poire bergamote bergamot pear
　thé à la bergamote bergamot tea
bergère/à la bergère shepherdess style [with fried mushrooms and potatoes]
berlingot de mer slipper limpet [an edible salt-water gastropod; eaten raw or cooked, boiled or fricassee; said to have a nutty flavor]
berlinguette a delicacy based on boiled eggs [may be hard-boiled eggs stuffed with anchovies, bread and egg yolks, or made with vegetables, leeks and spinach incorporated into a white sauce and served with hard-boiled eggs and slices of grilled bread]
berlinoise Berlin style [there seems to be no set definition of "Berlin style"; it could refer to a style of bread or sausage or types of ingredients in sauces]
bernard l'ermite/bernard l'hermite hermit crab
bernicle barnacle [can be baked with a sauce to make tender]
bernique barnacle
berrichone a garnish made with cabbage, onion, chestnuts and bacon
Bethmale semi-firm goat or cow cheese [made with goat's milk or raw cow's milk; the goat-milk version has a nutty aroma and a sweet, mellow flavor while the cow's milk version has an aroma of mushrooms and earth]
bêtise de Cambrai a candy flavored with mint and veined with caramelized sugar
bette swiss chard; white beet
　côtes de bettes chard ribs
bettelmann (**aux cerises**) cherry bread pudding
betterave beetroot
　sucre de betterave beet sugar
　salade de betterave beetroot salad
betterave potagère rosé beetroot
betterave sucrière sugar beet
betteuse buttermilk

beurre butter [must contain a minimum of 82% milk fat]
  coquille de beurre butter curl
  crème au beurre butter cream
  galette pur beurre shortbread cookie/biscuit
  haricot beurre yellow French bean
  petit-beurre sweet butter biscuit/cookie
  pur beurre all butter
  sauce au beurre butter sauce
  tartine beurrée a piece of bread and butter
beurre à la polonaise Polish butter [dark brown butter with breadcrumbs]
beurre Bercy Bercy butter [made with unsalted butter, white wine, shallots, marrow, lemon, parsley, salt and pepper]
beurre blanc white butter [a rich butter with shallots and a reduction of wine and either lemon or vinegar; herbs may be added]
beurre bordier churned gourmet salted butter
beurre Café de Paris Café of Paris butter [made with butter, anchovy fillets and mustard (sometimes shallots and garlic, Cognac, white wine and lemon juice) and seasoned with herbs and spices]
beurre chivry Ravigote butter [compound butter with herbs; herbs may be parsley, tarragon, chervil, chives or shallots]
beurre colbert colbert butter [made with veal stock, unsalted butter, shallots, tarragon, parsley, lemon, salt and pepper]
beurre d'ail garlic butter [basically, butter with finely chopped garlic, although other ingredients may be added]
beurre d'anchois anchovy paste [made with butter, anchovies, shallots and lemon]
beurre d'arachide peanut butter
beurre d'aveline hazelnut butter/filbert butter
beurre d'Echiré AOC delicate butter with a nutty flavor
beurre d'érable maple butter
beurre d'eschalotes shallot butter [equal parts shallots and butter]
beurre d'Isigny AOC Isigny butter [a regional butter of high quality]
beurre d'amande almond butter [a paste with the consistency of peanut butter]
beurre de baratte butter made from tangy, sour cream and flakes of sea salt [slight taste of hazelnuts]
beurre de cacahuète peanut butter
beurre de cacao cocoa butter
beurre de caviar caviar butter
beurre de Charentes/beurre Charentes-Poitou AOC Charentes butter [made from pasteurized cream; characterized by a creamy aroma; consisting of 82% fat, it is easy to spread]
beurre de citron [butter flavored with lemon or lemon and lime]
beurre de corail coral butter [a compound butter made by adding a paste of very finely ground up shells of lobster, crab, shrimp, crayfish or scallops]

beurre de crabe crab butter [made with butter and crab chopped and ground into a fine paste]
beurre de cresson watercress butter
beurre de crevette shrimp butter [made with butter and shrimp chopped and ground into a fine paste]
beurre de hareng herring butter
beurre de homard lobster butter [butter to which is added a paste made of lobster shell]
beurre de laitance roe butter [made with butter mixed with roe of red herring]
beurre de langouste prawn butter [butter to which is added a paste made of prawn shells]
beurre de mangue mango butter
beurre de Montpellier a savory herbed butter [butter with watercress, parsley, chervil, tarragon, chives, spinach, pickles, garlic, anchovy, egg yolks and olive oil; used with cold fish]
beurre de moutarde mustard butter
beurre de noisettes hazelnut butter
beurre de paprika a savory butter [compound butter with copped onions and paprika]
beurre de piments sweet pepper butter [a compound butter with sweet red pepper]
beurre de Provence garlic mayonnaise [another name for *aioli*]
beurre de raifort horseradish butter
beurre de saumon fumé smoked salmon butter
beurre de truffes truffle butter
beurre des Deux-Sèvres AOC Deux-Sèvres butter [a regional butter of high quality]
beurre d'escargot butter for snails [usually made with just butter and garlic, although herbs or spices may be added]
beurre doux unsalted butter
beurre fondu melted butter [butter with a bit of water or wine, boiled and sieved, then served hot with fish or vegetables]
beurre Giffard pear [ripens in summer; fine, fragrant juicy flesh]
beurré Hardy pear [ripens in autumn]
beurre maître d'hôtel parsley butter [a mixture of unsalted butter, finely chopped parsley and a dash of lemon]
beurre marchand de vin "wine merchant" butter [made with butter, shallots, red wine, and possibly parsley and lemon]
beurre meunière browned butter
beurre Nantais Nantais butter [a variation of *beurre blanc* to which cream is added to make a kind of white cream sauce]
beurre noir black butter [a butter sauce in which the butter is cooked until it turns very dark brown; often flavored]
beurre noisette browned butter [has a nutty flavor and is used in the making of pastry]
beurre printanier equal parts butter and spring vegetables pounded together
beurre ravigote Ravigote butter [compound butter with herbs such as parsley, tarragon, chervil and chives along with shallots]
beurre rouge red butter [a rich butter in a reduction of red wine with shallots and either lemon or vinegar; herbs may be added]

beurre roux butter roux [made with flour cooked in butter]
beurre salé salted butter fudge
beurre vert green butter [butter with shallots and green herbs such as parsley, chervil, tarragon, chives and salad burnet]
bézuque sea bass; bar [marine fish]
biche doe/venison
    carré de biche rack of doe
    rôti de biche au four oven roasted doe/venison
bicornes de l'Amiral puff pastry filled with cream, grated coconut, onion, garlic and chives
bien cuit well done
bière beer
    demi de bière half pint of beer
bière allégée light/lite beer [low in sugar but normal alcohol levels]
bière blonde lager
bière brune dark beer [ranging from brown to mahogany to black in color; made with roasted malt]
bière de spécialité special beer [seasonal beer or an administrative category or type of beer coming from a particular region]
bière en bouteille bottled beer
bière en fût beer on tap
bière panachée shandy; beer mixed with lemonade
bière pression draft/draught beer
bière rouge red ale [could refer to a type of Belgian beer aged in oak barrels for 18 months; caramel malt gives it its color; low in alcohol; has a sweet and sour taste]
bière sans alcool non-alcohol beer
bifteck steak
bifteck aux pommes frites steak and chips/French fries
bifteck bleu seared and almost rare steak
bifteck d'alouyau sirloin steak
bifteck de cheval horsemeat steak
bifteck à point medium/medium rare steak
bifteck haché beef burger
bifteck saignant rare steak (literally "bloody")
bigarde rich brown sauce [made with deglazed duck meat, oranges and wine, Grand Marnier or Cointreau]
bigarde Seville orange [bitter; used for jams, alcoholic drinks and sauces for game, especially duck]
bigarreau sweet cherry [large, heart-shaped with firm flesh]
bigorneau periwinkle; winkle [sea mollusk with a spiral shell; boiled or raw]
bigoli Italian pasta [like large spaghetti, served with a variety of sauces]
bigoudine/à la bigoudine Bigouden style [with baked slices of potatoes, skins on]
billy by/bilibi mussel soup [mussels cooked in white wine; typically with onions, parsley, celery and fish stock; served hot or cold with fresh cream and a sprinkling of Parmesan]
bimbo tropical fruit cocktail

bio/biologique organic
    aliments bio organic foods
    alimentation bio organic food
Biscotin d'Aix small round pastry scented with orange blossom
Biscotin de Bédarieux elongated soft biscuit scented with orange blossom
biscotte re-baked bread; rusk; zwieback
biscuit cookie; biscuit; sponge cake
biscuit à la cuiller sponge finger
biscuit à la cuillère sponge finger
biscuit à la farine complète graham cracker
biscuit apéritif appetizer cracker
biscuit au fromage cheese biscuit
biscuit d'avoine oatcake
biscuit de Savoie sponge cake
biscuit fourré custard cream
biscuit rose de Reims pink biscuit made with fresh eggs, flour, sugar and natural dye
biscuit sablé shortbread cookie
biscuit salé savory biscuit; appetizer
biscuit scandinave crispbread
biscuit sec cookie [biscuit without icing]
bisque a thick, delicate shellfish soup [fine, creamy smooth, sometimes highly seasoned soup made from a broth of lobster, crab, shrimp, scallops or crayfish]
bisteu potato pie [typically: made with potatoes, cream, smoked bacon and onion]
bitok/bitoke meat cakes; meat balls [typically: made with onion and seasonings and fried in butter; served with sour cream]
bitter any bitter aperitif (Campari, Cinzano, etc.)
blanc/blanche white
    au blanc cooked in a white sauce
    boudin blanc white pudding
    brut blanc de blanc dry champagne made from white grapes only
    champagne blanc de blanc champagne made from white grapes only
    chocolat blanc white chocolate
    fromage blanc soft white cheese
    raisin blanc white grape
    vin blanc white wine
blanc cassis kir
blanc d'oeuf egg white
blanc de blanc white wine made from white grapes only, as opposed to white wines that can be made from red or black grapes
blanc de dinde turkey breast
blanc de noir white wine made from dark grapes
blanc de poireau white portion of the leek
blanc de poulet chicken breast
blanc de seiche cuttlefish fillet
blanchaille whitebait [young herring]

blanche de Provence summer truffle [resembles the black truffle; has clear white or beige flesh]
blanchette corn salad; mâche
blanc-manger blancmange [dessert made with milk or cream, sugar and gelatin and flavored with almonds; usually set in a mold]
blanquette white; white grape
blanquette white-meat stew [usually veal that has not been browned]
Blanquette de Limoux French sparkling white wine
blanquette de poulet chicken in a white cream sauce; ragout of chicken
blanquette de veau veal in a white cream sauce; ragout of veal
blanquette rouge red wine grape
blé wheat
    germe de blé wheat germ
blé noir buckwheat
blennie blenny [small, freshwater fish without scales]
blesson pear [a cooking pear]
blette Swiss chard
    tourte des blettes Swiss chard pie
bleu blue
    au bleu/cuisson au bleu cooking very fresh fish (usually trout) quickly in boiling water and vinegar so that they turn blue
    cordon-blue cordon-blue [literally "blue ribbon"; consists of boneless chicken, veal or ham flattened and then rolled with cheese (usually Swiss) and ham, sometimes with bacon]
bleu blue cheese [a generic term for cheeses from cow's, goat's or sheep's milk which have cultures of penicillium mold occurring naturally or induced artificially]
bleu literally: blue [very rare (steak); hot seared on the outside and still cool in the center]
bock small beer glass
boeuf beef
    bavette de boeuf flank steak
    bouilli de boeuf beef stew
    bouillon de boeuf beef broth
    carré de boeuf rack of beef
    coeur de boeuf beef heart
    côte de boeuf beef rib
    daube de boeuf beef pot roast
    émincé de boeuf shredded beef; thin slices of beef
    entrecot de boeuf steak
    filet de boeuf beef tenderloin
    hachis de boeuf beef hash
    hampe de boeuf beef flank
    langue de boeuf ox tongue
    médaillon de boeuf medallion of beef
    onglet de boeuf beef back steak
    paleron de boeuf beef chuck
    pièce de boeuf piece of beef
    queue de boeuf ox tail

ragoût de boeuf beef stew
rôti de boeuf a joint of beef/roast beef
tranche de boeuf beefsteak
boeuf à la ficelle beef on a string [beef such as tenderloin roast tied with twine (*ficelle*) and poached in a broth; the tail of the string is used to lower the beef into the pot and retrieve it when it has cooked]
boeuf arlésien a beef stew [with white wine and green olives]
boeuf bouilli boiled beef
boeuf bourguignon beef stew [made with a rich reduced red wine sauce, onions, bacon and mushrooms]
boeuf braisé à la normande braised beef [with onion, garlic, carrots along with bacon marinated in Calvados and cider]
boeuf d'Aubrac Aubrac breed of beef [raised primarily on pasturage; yields tender, naturally marbled meat]
boeuf de Bazas Bazas breed of beef [raised on pasturage, then fattened on grain]
boeuf de Chalosse IGP, **Label Rouge** Chalosse breed of beef [raised entirely on vegetable matter (grass, corn and wheat)]
boeuf de Charolles AOC Charolais beef [the cattle must graze on pasture grass from March to November; slaughtered at six years of age rather than the usual five]
boeuf en croûte beef in a crust of puff pastry
boeuf en daube beef casserole/braised beef
boeuf gros sel stewed beef [beef cooked in bouillon with carrots, turnips, leeks, celery, onions and bone marrow or oxtail with coarse sea salt (*gros sel*); served as a piece of beef with the other ingredients on the side (rather than as a stew)]
boeuf miroton boiled beef with onion and mustard sauce
boeuf mode pot roast [cooked with vegetables, red wine, and bouillon; a way to cook the less tender cuts of beef]
boeuf salé corned beef; smoked brisket of beef
boeuf strogonoff beef stroganoff [beef cooked in red wine and beef broth with onions and mushrooms; usually served with pasta and either yoghurt or sour cream]
bogue sea bream
bohémienne an eggplant-tomato dish [sometimes with zucchini/courgette, peppers, garlic and onions]
boisson drink; beverage
boisson alcoolisée alcoholic drink
boisson allégée diet drink
boisson frappee iced drink
boisson gazeuse fizzy drink/carbonated drink
boisson light diet drink
boisson non-alcoolisée soft drink
bol de céréalés a bowl of cereal
bolée Loraine an aperitif [made with clear brandy (*eau de vie*), lemon syrup, sugar and Perrier]
bolognaise Bologna style
   sauce bolognaise bolognaise sauce [an Italian tomato sauce with ground beef, tomatoes, carrots, onions and beef broth]

bombe/bombe glacée ice cream frozen in the shape of a half-cannon ball; may consist of layers of ice cream and sherbet
bombine a dish usually consisting of small cubes of potatoes simmered with carrots, onions, black olives and pieces of bacon or lamb's or calf's foot
bonbon candy; sweet
bonbon à la violette candy made of violets crystalized in sugar
bonbon acidulés lemon drop candy
bonbon fondant taffy
bonbon gélifié jelly bean
bon-chrétien Williams pear [yellow skin, sweet, juicv]
bondelle whitefish; houting [found in the lakes in Switzerland]
bonite bonito; Boston mackerel
boniton little tunny [common tuna fish]
bonne bouchée literally: good mouthful [savory canapé]
bonne femme/à la bonne femme literally: good woman [a generic name attached mostly simple, rustic dishes; sometimes refers to soup or other dishes made with slowly simmered vegetables such as potatoes, carrots, and leeks or onions]
bonnotte de Noirmoutier heirloom potato [early to harvest]
boonesupp à l'Est bean soup with regional variations [might include coarsely chopped vegetables and chunks of sausage]
borlotti/borlotto red-veined dry bean
bortsch/bortch borsch [soup made with beef broth, beets, tomatoes, cabbage, potatoes (and sometimes turnips and leeks) and garnished with sour cream]
boucaud shrimp
bouchée small puff pastry shell [literally "mouth-shaped"; may contain either a sweet or savory filling]
bouchée à la reine small puff pastry shell filled with mushrooms and veal or chicken in a creamy wine sauce
bouchée de fruits de mer small puff pastry shell filled with chopped mushrooms and shellfish bound in a white wine sauce
bouchère with bone marrow [a way of preparing certain foods]
boucherie butcher's shop
boucherie chevaline horse meat butcher's shop
bouchon cork
bouchons d'Alençon a crunchy cookie filled with sweet toasted almond praline
bouchot shrimp
boudin sausage/pudding
boudin à la crème black sausage/pudding [blood, cream, butter, onions and seasonings]
boudin à la crème et au calvados de Saint-Romain black sausage/pudding with cream and Saint-Roman calvados
boudin à la Flamande black sausage/pudding [blood, onion, raisins and parsley]
boudin à la viande meat sausage [composed of 30% to 50% pig's blood, pork rinds and pig tongue or heart; sold fresh or dried; served hot or cold]
boudin Asturien Spanish-style black pudding/sausage [made with pig blood, pork and pork fat]

boudin blanc white sausage/pudding [often made with milk and a starchy binder such as bread and eggs; a fat such as butter, cream or pork fat; white meat such as veal or chicken or pork (or all three); sometimes with onion or shallots, chestnuts, mushrooms, carrots; and with flavorings such as Port or Madeira, tarragon, basil, parsley, allspice, mace, salt, pepper and possibly cinnamon, orange blossom water, vanilla or kirsch; popular around Christmas time]

boudin blanc à l'ancienne white sausage/pudding [made with raw fish, chicken breast, sweetbreads, carp roe, rice, onion, bindings and seasonings]

boudin blanc à la Richelieu white sausage/pudding [made with raw poultry livers, lean veal and raw foie gras (no pork); presented in small rectangles wrapped in netted casing and studded with truffles]

boudin blanc catalan white sausage/pudding [rich with eggs and herbs, but no starchy bindings]

boudin blanc d'Avranches white sausage/pudding [made with white chicken meat. fat, onions, bindings and seasonings]

boudin blanc d'Ourville white sausage/pudding [pork fat, onions, butter, bindings and seasonings]

boudin blanc de Liège very famous white sausage/pudding from Belgium [handcrafted with prime pork; subtle flavor of marjoram]

boudin blanc de Paris white sausage/pudding [finely chopped poultry breast, pork, pork fat, onions, bindings and seasonings; boiled and then fried]

boudin blanc de Toulouse white sausage/pudding [made with white chicken meat, pork and at least 20% foie gras of duck or goose; may be flavored with truffle or cognac]

boudin blanc de Rethel white sausage/pudding [fresh pork meat, pork fat. milk and eggs]

boudin blanc du Mans white sausage/pudding [made with pork and pork fat, similar to *boudin blanc de Rethel*, but seasoned with parsley and onion]

boudin blanc havrais white sausage/pudding [made with pork fat (no meat), whole eggs, bread crumbs and flour]

boudin blanc rennais white sausage/pudding [chopped poultry breast, pork and pork fat, onions, bindings and seasonings; boiled, then fried]

boudin blanc truffé white sausage with truffles

boudin blanc d'Essay white sausage/pudding [fine texture; made of ham, pork, eggs and spices]

boudin Breton black sausage/pudding [pig's and calf's blood]

boudin de Brest black sausage/pudding [blood, fat, cream and puréed onions]

boudin de Lyon black sausage/pudding [blood, fat, paprika, chives, thyme, parsley and brandy]

boudin du Poitou aux épinards black sausage/pudding with spinach [flavored with gin, orange flower water and thyme]

boudin noir black/blood pudding/sausage [made with pig blood, pork and pork fat]

boudin noir à l'ail black sausage/pudding [blood, fat, garlic]
boudin noir à l'anglais black sausage/pudding [blood, fat, boiled rice or barley]
boudin noir à la normande black sausage/pudding [blood pudding/sausage sliced and served with peeled apples sautéed in butter]
boudin noir alsacien black sausage/pudding [blood, fat and chopped apples]
boudin noir de Paris black sausage/pudding [made with 1/3 fresh pig's blood, 1/3 pork fat and 1/3 cooked onions]
boudin noir de Coutances black sausage/pudding [made with pig's blood, raw onion, fat and pork rinds]
boudin noir aux châtaignes black sausage/pudding with chestnuts
boudin noir de Mortagne black sausage/pudding [made with pig's blood, pork fat, chopped onions and cream]
boudins entre ciel et terre literally: sausage/pudding between heaven and earth [grilled sausage on top of potatoes mashed with butter and apple sauce]
boudoir little biscuit sprinkled with sugar icing [basis for *charlottes* and *tiramisu*]
bouffi lightly salted herring
bougnette potato doughnut
bougnette thin, flat, light and crispy fried fritter (doughnut) the size of a small plate and sprinkled with sugar
bougnette de Castres a big ball of pork belly hash mixed with a binder of bread and egg and wrapped in a membrane
bougras a stew-like vegetable soup [prepared with sausage, cabbage, kale, carrots, turnip, onion, leek, celery, potatoes and bouquet garni; traditionally served during carnival time]
bouillabaisse fish stew [traditionally made from red rascasse, sea robin and European conger, but other fish may be used along with shellfish; simmered with vegetables such as leeks, onions, celery, potatoes and tomatoes]
bouilleture a dish made with eel, mushrooms, onions, butter, red or white wine and bouquet garni; sometimes with prunes
bouilli boiled
bouilli buckwheat porridge or gruel
bouillie d'avoine porridge
bouilli de boeuf beef stew
bouillie de flocons d'avoine oatmeal
bouillie de sarrasin buckwheat porridge
bouillinada/bouillinade a type of fish stew similar to a *bouillabaise*, but made with scorpion fish and rock fish, potatoes, onion, garlic and sweet peppers
bouillon broth [usually made by simmering beef, veal, poultry or shrimp with diced carrots, onions, celery and herbs]
boulanger baker
boulangère/à la boulangère literally: baker's wife [refers to dishes (usually potatoes) cooked with sliced onions in a casserole]
boulangerie bakery
boule ball, sphere
   pan boule round loaf of bread with a dusting of flour

boule de glace scoop of ice cream
boule de neige snowball cake [small round cakes covered with white butter frosting, whipped cream, or coconut]
boule de Picoulat meatball made of beef and pork
boule d'or a kind of golden-yellow turnip
   navet boule d'or golden turnip
boulet de Metz chocolate pastry the size and shape of a cannon ball [a large biscuit filled with ganache, coated with chocolate almond paste and caramel, and covered with roasted hazelnut chips and a thin layer of dark chocolate]
boulette cheese dumpling
boulette meatball [ball of minced meat bound with egg; may be breaded and deep fried]
boulette small puff pastry filled with meat or poultry, then breaded and deep fried
boulette de crevette frite fried shrimp dumpling
boulette de pate dumpling
boulette de viande meatball
boulgour bulgur
bouligou donut or pancake made from a thick batter
bouquet red shrimp; common prawn
bouquet garni literally: garnished bouquet [a combination of pungent herbs tied together and cooked in soup stock or various stews to add flavor, then removed before serving; the herbs vary according to the recipe, but the classic combination includes thyme, bay leaf and parsley (and sometimes leeks)]
bouquetière a garnish of mixed fresh vegetables in the form of a bouquet
bouquette buckwheat and raisin pancake
bourdaine apple dumpling with jam
bourdaloue/tarte bourdaloue pear and almond paste pie
bourdelots aux pommes apple pastry [a whole apple cored and filled with calvados and a dab of butter and surrounded by a pastry shell]
bouri mullet
bouri buttermilk
bourgeons de cassis blackcurrant buds
bourgeoise/à la bourgeoise cooked by braising with carrots and small onions (and sometimes bacon or celery)
   gâteau la bourgeoise cake made with almonds, pistachios and hazelnuts
   langue de boeuf bourgeoise bourgeoise style beef tongue
   poulet à la bourgeoise bourgeoise style chicken
bourgoule cooked sweet rice milk with cinnamon [served warm with a bun and cider]
bourguignonne Burgundy style [with red wine, shallots or onions, mushrooms and bacon]
   boeuf bourguignonne beef stew [made with a rich reduced red wine sauce, onions, bacon and mushrooms]
   fondue bourguignonne a way of serving beef by dipping small cubes of meat into a hot oil then into a sauce

sauce bourguignonne Bourguignonne sauce [made with red wine, shallots, mushrooms, onion, butter, flour, seasonings]
bourrache borage
bourride fish soup thickened with egg yolks and/or *aïoli* (garlic mayonnaise)
bourride à la sétoise fish soup [typically: made with carrots, leeks, celery, onion, garlic, and parsley]
bourriol buckwheat pancake
bourriquette sorrel soup with poached eggs
boursotto anchovy, vegetable, cheese and rice pastry
boutargue/poutargue mullet roe (caviar) [a luxury dish from Martigues, France, but found all around the Mediterranean; the roe pouch is dried and salt-cured and sometimes coated in beeswax for preservation; served in thin slices or grated into a pasta dish, or on buttered toast]
bouteille bottle
   demi-bouteille half-bottle
   eau en bouteille bottled water
   bière en bouteille bottled beer
   vin en bouteille bottled wine
   mise en bouteille au château château-bottled
bouteille d'eau bottle of water
bouteille de bière beer bottle; bottle of beer
bouteille millésimée bottle of vintage wine
brabançonne Brabant style [a dish made with chicory and/or Brussels sprouts]
   faisan à la brabançonne pheasant prepared with chicory
bragardise de Saint-Dizier biscuit made with cane sugar, flour, butter, cinnamon and coconut
brageole beef roll [beef cutlets seasoned with garlic, parsley, salt and pepper, then rolled and held together with a toothpick]
braisé braised
branche/en branche whole vegetables
   céleri branche celery
brandade fish purée [usually salt cod; may also be smoked trout]
brandade de morue salt cod purée [a purée of salt cod, olive oil, lemon juice and garlic often served with bread or potatoes]
brandade de thon tuna and beans
brandon a dessert consisting of a pastry filled with custard and almonds and flavored with Calvados, then baked and topped with apple slices cooked in butter and flambéed in Calvados
brasillé pancake puff pastry [made with flaky *brioche* dough and lard; sprinkled with sugar and eaten warm]
brassado a pretzel-like *brioche* in the shape of a large bracelet
brasserie brewery
brasserie informal restaurant with a simple menu and a place to drink beer; often open outside of regular restaurant hours
bar brasserie brewery-bar
   restaurant brasserie informal restaurant with a selection of beer which may or may not be brewed on site
brebis ewe
   fromage de brebis sheep's milk cheese

bréjaude vegetable soup [typically: made with vegetables such as turnips, potatoes, and carrots crushed to make a porridge; contains bacon]
brème bream [a flat freshwater fish related to carp]
brème de mer pomfret: butterfish [large, flat marine fish]
bresaola air-dried, salted beef [aged for two or three months; very dark red]
brési salted smoked beef [has a dark red color; consumed in very thin slices covered by a *raclette* (melted Swiss cheese) or in a plate of cold meats]
bressane/galette Bressane a fluffy, cake-like pastry filled with vanilla crème fraîche (fresh cream) and topped with a sprinkling of sugar "rocks"
breton/gâteau Breton Breton cake typically: [a one-layer cake with a crumbly texture; sometimes filled with prune, raspberry or caramel cream and may be flavored with rum or orange blossom]
bretonne/sauce bretonne Breton sauce for fish [typically: made from a velvety sauce and julienned onion, leeks, celery heart, mushrooms, butter and cream]
bretonne/sauce bretonne Breton sauce for beans [typically: made with fried onions, white wine, tomato sauce and garlic]
brettoneau turbot [marine flat fish]
bretzel pretzel
Brie soft cheese [cow's milk; bloomy white rind; a family of creamy soft cheeses; the two main types are *Brie de Meaux AOC* (milder) and *Brie de Melun AOC* (more pungent); blue Brie was invented by the Germans and then copied by the French]
Brie de Meaux AOC soft cheese [raw cow's milk; thin, bloomy white rind with red dots; mild and creamy but not runny straw-yellow cheese]
Brie de Melun AOC cheese [raw cow's milk; has a strong flavor and can be somewhat salty; the *Vieux-Brie* or *Brie noir* varieties are aged longer and are dry and brown with a stronger, straw-like taste]
brimbelle blueberry
brioché *brioche*-like
brioche sweet bun [richer than normal bread, but not like a pastry; contains a high amount of egg and butter]
brioche à tête a pair of sweet buns, with the smaller sitting on top of the larger
brioche de Nanterre a loaf of brioche [made with two parallel pieces of dough baked together]
brioche du Vast brioche of Vast [baked in a V-shaped fluted pan]
brioche mousseline sweet bun [same ingredients as a regular brioche, but with sugar added]
brioche tressée de Metz woven brioche of Metz [made by interlacing three balls of brioche dough and baking them together]
brioche vendéenne braided brioche loaf [flavored with orange flowers]
briochette small *brioche*/bun

brissaouda/bressauda/bressaudo a great slice of toasted country bread rubbed with garlic and drizzled with fresh olive oil
brisure literally: break, fragment
brisure de chocolat flakes of chocolate
brisure de riz broken rice
broche skewer; spit
  à la broche cooked on a skewer/spit
brochet pike
brochet de mer barracuda
brocheton pickerel; small pike
brochette skewer; kebab
brocoli broccoli
brou de noix a liqueur made from walnuts, cinnamon and nutmeg
brouet gruel or broth
brosme cusk; tusk; brismak; brosmius; torsk; moonfish [cod-like fish in the ling family]
broufada/broufade/broufado beef stew [typically: slowly cooked for hours with garlic, anchovies, onions, capers and olive oil; served with potatoes, carrots, tomatoes and rice]
brouillade scrambled eggs
brouillade stew made with oil
brouillé scrambled
  oeufs brouillés scrambled eggs
broyé du Poitou cake [with sugar, flour, salted butter, eggs]
brugnon nectarine
brûlé literally: burnt [caramelized; browned]
  crème brûlée custard topped with caramel
brun brown
bruni browned
brunoise/brunoise de légumes diced; diced vegetables
brut raw, crude, unrefined
  champagne brut extra-dry champagne
Bruxelloise/à la Bruxelloise Brussels style [with chicory/endive, brussels sprouts and potatoes]
  garniture Bruxelloise a garnish made with Brussels sprouts and chicory (and/or potatoes)
  sauce Bruxelloise a sauce made with butter, salt, pepper, lemon juice and chopped hard-boiled egg; served on asparagus
bûche de Noël yule-log cake [many variations: all are based on a rectangular layer of cake and a layer of flavored cream rolled into a log, then frosted with icing to look like a log and often decorated with Christmas ornaments]
bûche glacée ice cream log [scores of variations exist; may be made with ice cream and/or sorbet (and maybe meringue), in layers rolled into a log or put into a mold]
buchette individual log cake
buckling smoked herring
buereka savory pastry [made with flaky dough filled with cheese, minced meat or vegetables]
buffet buffet
buffet campagnard country buffet [a generic name; can include salads and cold cuts, breads, cheeses and possibly desserts]

buffet champêtre country buffet [a generic name; can include salads and cold cuts, breads, cheeses and possibly desserts]
buffet chaud warm buffet
buffet de desserts dessert buffet
buffet froid cold buffet
buffle buffalo [similar to beef, but leaner]
bugne sweet fritter [flour, butter, eggs, sugar, orange flower; fried and dusted with powdered sugar]
buisson a method of displaying certain foods such as shellfish, vegetables, sweet fritters or fries in a pyramid on a plate
bulbe de fenouil fennel bulb
bulot whelk [large sea mollusk with a robust taste; lightly boiled and served with garlic mayonnaise or cooked in a spicy bouillon]
bun bun
burgou chestnuts cake with honey and almonds
cabache de Châlons chocolate praline with pistachio-sugar icing
cabassol sheep's head stew; a dish prepared with veal shank, ham, vegetables and vinaigrette
cabécou a generic name for raw goat's milk cheese
Cabécou Rocamadour AOC goat cheese [raw goat's milk; natural rind, soft, creamy cheese eaten fresh, but can age and take on a stronger flavor; 45% fat]
cabliaud cod
cabillaud cod
   filet de cabillaud scrod [cod that is spit and boned for cooking
cabillaud à la boulangère baked cod with potatoes and parsley
cabillaud à la flamande poached cod with shallots
cabosse the fruit-pod of the cacao/cocoa tree containing the cocoa beans which are used for making chocolate
cabot chub [fish]
cabus/chou cabus white cabbage
cacahuète/cacahouète peanut
   beurre de cacahuète peanut butter
   beurre de cacahuète croquant crunchy peanut butter
   cacahuète grillée roasted peanut
   cacahuètes salées salted peanuts
   sandwich au beurre de cacahuète peanut butter sandwich
   tarte au beurre de cacahuète peanut butter tart
cacao cocoa [the powder or the drink]
   beurre de cacao cocoa butter
cacasse à cul nu a ragout of potatoes rubbed with bacon and onions
cacasse à cul nu culotée a ragout of potatoes rubbed with bacon and onions and served with sausage and bacon
caccavellu Easter bread-like cake [the dough is formed into a circle and has an egg held in place by two braids; marks the end of Lent]
cacolac a milk chocolate drink
cacou fruit baked in batter [a cake-like dessert usually made with cherries (especially Montmorency), sugar, flour, milk and eggs]
café coffee (typically espresso)
   pousse-café after-dinner liqueur

café allongé slightly diluted espresso
café americain filtered coffee
café arabica Arabica coffee
café brûlot black coffee, sometimes with cardamom, flamed with brandy
café crème coffee/espresso with cream; cappuccino
café décaféiné decaffeinated coffee
café flltre filter/drip coffee
café glacé iced coffee
café instané instant coffee
café irelandais Irish coffee
café liégeoise iced coffee with ice cream or whipped cream
café noir black coffee
café noisette strong espresso with milk
café turc Turkish coffee
cagouille edible snail
caillé curd cheese [like cottage cheese; this is the first stage of most cheese]
caille quail
caille à la clefmontaise quail roasted with grapes
caille en sarcophage quail in puff pastry with *fois gras* and truffle sauce
Caille flambées au calvados roasted quail flambéed with Calvados
cailleteau young quail
caillette flattened meatball [sometimes elaborately prepared]
caillette pork meat pâté [a dish consisting of pork, Swiss chard, spinach or other greens, and spices; may include egg, walnuts, chestnuts, alcohol]
caillettes de foie de porc pig liver strips with bacon and chopped pig's sweetbreads
caillettes provençales chopped pork, pork belly and liver with shallots, garlic and seasonings, fried and formed into balls and then baked
Caisse de Wassy almond meringue dessert [small bar-shaped dessert made with sugar, almonds, egg whites and vanilla]
cajou cashew
  noix de cajou cashew nut
cake cake; bread ["cake" if made with fruit; "bread" if made with vegetables or meat]
cake à la noix de coco coconut cake
cake au citron lemon cake
calmar/calamar squid; calamari
calisson lozenge-shaped almond candy or biscuit
calisson d'Aix confectionary made with crystalized melon (melon *confit*) and almonds (and sometimes crystalized orange)
calmar small squid
Calvados brandy made from the distillation of cider or sometimes pear nectar
Calvados du Domfrontais AOC brandy made from the distillation of *poiré* pears and cider apples; floral and fruity with mineral characteristics
camélia camellia

Camembert generic name for cheese [raw or pasteurized cow's, sheep's or goat's milk; among the most consumed cheeses in France and one of its stereotypical symbols (along with the baguette and the beret); soft, bloomy rind and soft, creamy yellowish cheese with a strong savory, umami flavor; unlike a Brie, it has no extra cream added and is aged longer]
camomille camomile [the flower is used for tea]
campagne countryside; farm-style
canapé small piece of bread, pastry or cracker with a savory topping; served as an appetizer, often with drinks
canard duck
    aiguillette de canard duck fillet [long thin slice of duck meat]
    cuisse de canard duck leg
    filet de canard duck tenderloin
    gigolette de canard duck stew
    magret de canard duck breast
    manchon de canard duck wing
    pilon de canard duck drumstick
    viande de canard duck meat
canard à la presse lightly roasted duck breast in a sauce of brandy, duck blood and duck juices
canard au cidre duck thigh cooked with a creamy cider sauce
canard au sang duck "with blood" [a sauce is made by pressing the blood out of the carcass, crushing the liver and adding them to a reduction of red wine; roasted for 20 minutes then grilled to finish]
canard aux griottes duck breast with cherries
canard confit duck confit [duck meat surrounded by its own fat to preserve it]
canard de Challans Label Rouge Challans duck [free-range, grass-fed; high-quality meat]
canard Duchambais Duchambais duck [duck fillets typically cooked with shallots, garlic, vinegar, chicken stock, cream and *Charroux* mustard]
canard laqué lacquered duck [traditional Chinese duck, cooked on a rotisserie and "lacquered" with a mixture of honey, spices and soy sauce]
canard mandarin Mandarin duck [slices of lacquered duck served on a crêpe, sometimes with cucumber, spring onion and hoisin sauce]
canard rouennais à la presse duck breasts in a sauce of brandy and duck blood and juices
canard rouennais en terrine a terrine of Rouen duck [chopped duck meat loaf]
canardeau duckling
cancalaise oysters prepared with shrimp or beef in a wine sauce
candi candied
Candiss/fraises Candiss high-quality strawberry
cane female duck
canelé bordelais cupcake [flavored with rum and vanilla and covered with a thick caramelized crust]
caneton duckling

canette duckling
canette rôti roasted duckling
caneton à la rouennaise roast duckling with blood sauce [the carcass is pressed to recover the blood, then the liver is puréed then added to a sauce made of chopped shallots reduction of Bordeaux wine; the fillets, cut into thin strips and the grilled thighs are then served hot topped with the sauce]
caneton rôti à la Duclair roast Duclair duckling [a highly-prized breed of duck known for the high quality of its meat; prepared in the same manner as *canard au sang*]
canneberge cranberry
cannelier cinnamon tree
    feuille de cannelier cinnamon leaf spice; milder than cinnamon from the bark
cannelle cinnamon
    beignet à la cannelle cinnamon doughnut
    café à la cannelle cinnamon coffee
    pomme cannelle custard apple; cinnamon apple [a kind of spiny soursop; used in fruit salads]
    roulé à la cannelle cinnamon swirl bread
cannelle moulue ground cinnamon
cannelloni cannelloni [large tube pasta that can be stuffed with meats and cheeses]
canotière/à la canotière boatman style [typically: fish with shallots, mushrooms and white wine]
Cantal (latier) AOC cheese [cow's milk; the crust starts out gray-white; matures to golden brown and can be dotted with ocher-colored buttons; the cheese is supple when young, with a sweet, nutty flavor; becomes firmer and more crumbly with age, with a more tangy flavor]
cantaloup cantaloupe
capelan small, smelt-like fish; capelin [used in soups]
capitaine large ocean fish with white, tender flesh
capitolade left-over chicken or game bird in an Italian sauce with mushrooms, parsley and croutons
câpre caper
capron fruit of the caper bush [firm and crunchy as opposed to capers which are the tender un-opened flower buds]
capucin small tart filled with Gruyère cheese
capucine nasturtium [the flowers and leaves are edible; the seeds are pickled to make imitation "capers"]
caquelon fondue pot
caracole snail; escargot
carafe carafe
caraïbes Caribbean
carambar caramel candy
caramel caramel
    crème caramel caramel cream
caramels d'Isigny caramel candy from Isigny [made with fresh milk, butter, cream and sugar]
caramote Mediterranean king prawn
carbonnade/carbonade meat grilled over charcoal

carbonnade de boeuf beef stew [typically: beef stewed with onions, shallots, garlic, spice bread (gingerbread) or mustard, veal stock, brown sugar and a Belgian beer]
carbonnade flamande Flemish beef and dark beer stew [typically: beef stewed with onions, shallots, garlic, spice bread or mustard, veal stock, brown sugar and a Belgian beer]
carbonnisée charred; burned to a crisp
cardamone cardamom [large green, sweet aromatic seed pod used to flavor Arabian coffee and north African dishes]
carde Swiss chard
cardine megrim [marine fish, similar to, but larger than, sole]
cardon cardoon [related to the artichoke]
cargolade snails grilled in their shells filled with lard, salt, pepper and herbs
cari curry
carmaguaise/à la carmaguaise Carmargue style [typically: with tomatoes, olives, garlic, orange peel, and brandy or wine]
carmélite/ à la carmélite cold chicken breasts topped with a cold-hot sauce (*sauce chaud-froid*) and decorated with slivers of truffles and a *mousseline* of crayfish and crayfish tails
   oeufs à la carmélite soft-boiled or poached eggs in a custard crust, garnished with mussles and a white wine cream sauce
caroline small puff-pastry éclair with a savory stuffing
caroline chicken soup with rice and chervil
carotte carrot
carottes râpées grated carrots
carottes vichy tender young carrots cooked in Vichy water and butter and glazed with sugar
caroube carob
carpaccio slices of raw meat [very thinly sliced [raw, marinated or smoked; beef, pork, veal, venison, duck or other meat or fish such as salmon or tuna; usually served as an appetizer]
carpaccio de boeuf beef carpaccio [slices of raw beef]
carpaccio de canard fumé smoked duck carpaccio [slices of smoked duck breast]
carpe carp
carpe chambord whole carp carefully stuffed and braised in red wine
carpe frite du Sundgau fried carp of Sundgau, Alsace
carpeau small carp
carpillon very small carp
carré square
carré rack or loin
Carré de Salers biscuit [a crispy square biscuit rich in butter]
carrelet plaice [flat fish; type of flounder; wild or farmed; mild tender white flesh]
carrelet au cidre plaice with cider
carry curry
carte menu; list
   à la carte à la carte
carte des desserts dessert list
carte des mets list of the dishes/food

carte des vins wine list
carthame safflower
carvi caraway
cascabel mildly hot pepper [yellowish green when young, then red when ripe; sometimes used in place of Poblano peppers]
casher/cacher kosher
cassate cassata [Neapolitan ice cream]
casse-croûte snack [slang]
casserole casserole dish or pan
    cuisson à la casserole cooked in a casserole dish or pan
    en casserole cooked in a sauce pan on top of the stove
casseron cuttlefish [similar to squid]
cassis blackcurrant
    boule de glace cassis scoop of blackcurrant ice cream
    confiture de cassis blackcurrant jam
    couilis de cassis thick blackcurrant sauce
    glace cassis blackcurrant ice cream
cassolade cornbread cake [made with corn flour and honey and flavored with bergamot]
cassonade brown sugar
cassoulet sausage and bean hotpot [a rich, slow-cooked stew or casserole containing tender white beans, tomato sauce, sausages and bacon; could include duck, partridge or mutton]
castagnou aperitif [a type of kir; one part chestnut liqueur and two parts white wine]
cata dogfish [shark]
catalane/à la catalane Catalan-style [typically: with tomatoes and rice and maybe olives and eggplant/aubergine]
catigot eel and/or carp grilled with onion and bacon and simmered with tomato sauce or boiled with potatoes, leeks and tomatoes
catigot d'anguilles eel stew [eel of the Rhône River typically cooked with garlic, dried orange peel, red pepper, olive oil and bouquet garni soaked in red wine]
cauchoise/à la cauchoise Caux-style [with apples, cream and calvados]
caudière/caudrée a pot of vegetables and fish [the cooking liquid is served as a soup and the fish and vegetables are served as a separate dish]
cavaillon melon [small Charantais-type melon with golden orange, sweet, ambrosia fragrant flesh; highly prized]
caviar caviar [true caviar refers only to roe (eggs) of the sturgeon; other fish roe are forbidden to be called *caviar* in France]
caviar dip [made of vegetables such as peppers, tomatoes, beets, eggplant/aubergine or mushrooms]
caviar blanc mullet roe [not true *caviar*]
caviar d'aubergines eggplant/aubergine dip
caviar de saumon salmon roe [not true *caviar*]
caviar rouge salmon roe [not true *caviar*]
cawcher kosher
cayenne cayenne
    poivre de cayenne cayenne pepper
cébette small white onion; spring onion; scallion

cecina cured, air-dried or smoke-dried beef
cédrat/cédrat de Corse a kind of large lemon from Corsica
cédratine lemon liqueur from Corsica (flavored with the *cédrat* lemon)
céleri celery
    branche de céleri celery stick
    coeur de céleri celery heart
    pied de céleri head of celery
    purée de céleri celery purée
céleri rave celery root; celeriac [has a woodsy, celery-like flavor; can be cooked]
céleri rémoulade celeriac rémoulade [salad made with grated or julienned celery root and a mayonnaise-mustard sauce]
célestine a garnish for *consommé celestine*
    consommé célestine typically: veal, carrots, leeks and onions on a plate garnished with strips of crêpes made with chives and parsley
cendre cinders; ashes
cendré gray/with ashes [fine wood ashes are used to coat cheese while it ages to protect it from insects and mold]
cèpe porcini mushroom; penny bun mushroom [rich earthy flavor with a smooth, meaty texture]
céréale cereal
    barre de céréales cereal bar
    grain de céréale corn
    pain aux céréales cereal bread
    pain aux cinq céréales multigrain bread
céréale complète whole grain cereal
cerf venison; deer
cerfeuil chervil [one of the *fines herbes* along with tarragon, chives and parsley]
cerfeuil bulbeux turnip-rooted chervil [sweet vegetable root; flavor hints of potatoes and chestnuts]
cerfeuil tubéreux turnip-rooted chervil chervil [sweet vegetable root; flavor hints of potatoes and chestnuts]
cerise cherry
    tomate cerise cherry tomato
cerise à eau de vie brandied cherry
cerise de Montmorency Montmorency cherry [small, tart, bright red cherry]
cerise de Duclair Duclair cherry [frequently baked in pies]
cerisette alcoholic drink based on cherry juice
cerisette small prune resembling a cherry
cerisette Belgian chocolate-covered cherry (the cherry is first soaked in *kirsch*)
cerisier cherry tree
    feuille de cerisier cherry leaf
cerneau unripe walnut; half-shelled walnut
cervelas saveloy sausage [short fat sausage; made with 50% pork, 20% beef plus beef brains, veal, lard and sugar]
    salade de cervelas salad with saveloy sausage, onions and vinaigrette

cervelas obernois/cervelas à l'alsacienne sausage garnished with cheese and wrapped with bacon and then fried
cervelas de Paris beef and pork sausage of Paris
cervelas de L'Aigle beef and pork sausage of Aigle [dried sausage, smoked over beech wood; with a fragrance of Calvados]
cervelas maigre à la bénédictine eel and carp sausage [smoked for three days, then poached in white wine]
cervelle brains [there may be restrictions in Europe and elsewhere due to the danger of mad cow disease]
Cervelle de canut cheese spread [cottage cheese or cream cheese beaten with herbs, shallots, salt, pepper, olive oil and vinegar; spread on toast or served with baked potatoes]
céteau wedge sole [flat marine fish]
cévenole/à la cévenole a dish (sweet or savory) made with chestnuts [mashed in stews, whole or poached accompanying roasted meats, or candied and added to desserts]
ceviche ceviche [raw seafood "cooked" in lemon or lime juice]
Chabichou du Poitou AOC goat cheese [goat's milk; natural crust, soft, white cheese]
chablisienne chablis-style
  à la chablisienne/au chablis dishes characterized by the use chablis wine
chaboisseau sculpin [from the Atlantic and Arctic oceans and from freshwater rivers in France; used in soups and stews]
chabot sculpin [from the Atlantic and Arctic oceans and from freshwater rivers in France; used in soups and stews]
chabrol/chabrot red wine mixed into soup [an ancient custom of Occitan (southern France); the wine dilutes the broth, then the bowl is brought to the mouth so that the soup can be swallowed in large gulps]
chachlik shashlik [chunks of meat grilled on skewers or grilled minced meat, sometimes with onions, peppers, mushrooms]
chair meat; flesh
chair blanche white meat [chicken breast]
chair noir dark meat [chicken thigh, leg]
chambord chambord [the name given to whole, large fish such as carp, salmon and sole carefully stuffed and braised in red wine]
chamoure pumpkin flan [made with pumpkin, brown sugar, eggs, milk, and butter, and may have ginger and cinnamon]
champêtre rustic; farm-style
champignon mushroom
champignon de couche cultivated mushroom
champignon de Paris cultivated mushroom; button mushroom
champignon noir Judas' ear mushroom [purplish-pink mushroom, wrinkled with veins]
champignon à la normande Normandy style mushrooms [typically: mushrooms cooked in butter, fresh cream, smoked bacon, and Calvados]
champigon de bois wood mushroom
champigon pleurote oyster mushroom
champigny flaky, layered pastry filled with apricot marmalade
champoiré pear champagne

champvallon rustic dish of mutton or lamb chops cooked with potatoes and onions

chanteclair cake [made with meringue and whipped cream and flavored with praline and mocha; decorated with a "rooster"]

chanterelle chanterelle mushroom [a culinary delicacy; generally not eaten raw as its rich woody, earthy, fruity or even spicy flavor comes out when it is cooked]

chantilly whipped cream [heavy cream with granulated sugar and vanilla added

   crème chantilly sweet whipped cream [sweetened with vanilla, sugar, or brandy]

   sauce chantilly thick mayonnaise made with lemon juice and whipped cream

chapelure dried bread crumbs

chapan garlic crouton

chapon a piece of the end of a loaf of bread flavored with garlic vinaigrette [accompanies a salad]

chapon capon [rooster that has been castrated at six weeks of age, then fattened; larger than a chicken, well marbled and more flavorful; well suited to roasting]

chapon aux morilles capon stuffed with morille mushrooms

chapon de mer red scorpion fish

chapon de pintade male guinea fowl

chapon du Lauragais capon stuffed with chestnuts

charbon barbecue

charcuterie deli meats

charcutière pork delicatessen

chardon wild thistle [edible juice can be extracted from leaves and tender stems]

charentais/melon charentais melon [smaller, sweeter and more succulent than a cantaloupe]

Charlotte/fraises Charlotte high-quality strawberry

charlotte a dessert made by lining a deep mold with soft biscuits side-by-side around the mold and filling it with any sort of sweet concoction, such as strawberries in cream, chocolate sauce, spicy apples, creamy cheeses, or savories such as carrots or zucchini/courgette

charlotte salad potato

charolais knuckle of beef [tender, choice cut]

Chartreuse green liqueur [sweet, spicy and pungent; the recipe involving perhaps 130 medicinal and aromatic plants and flowers remains a secret and is still made by monks]

chartreuse de pommes chartreuse apple dessert [a sweet concoction made with sliced apples sweetened with honey, whipped cream and caramel and set into a mold and baked then cooled, removed from the mold and drizzled with a sweet sauce or candied fruit]

chasselas de Thomery white table grape [has a smooth and sweet freshness; must be hand-harvested; immersing the end of the cluster in water treated with powdered carbon helps to preserve the clusters for up to three months after they have been harvested]

chasseur/à la chasseur hunter-style
chasseur salami sausage [beef and lean pork finely minced, dried and smoked]
chat de mer spiny dogfish; spurdog; mud shark; piked dogfish
châtaigne chestnut [edible fruit of the chestnut tree]
   flan à la châtaigne chestnut flan [a dessert made with chestnut flour, milk, eggs, sugar, vanilla and brandy]
   farine de châtaigne chestnut flour
châtaignes grillées grilled chestnuts
châtaignons des marrons d'Olargues chestnuts dried over a wood fire
château castle
   pommes chateaux potatoes cut into thick "fingers" and cooked in butter
châteaubriand a meat dish made with *châteaubriand steak*
châteaubriand châteaubriand steak [a cut of tenderloin beef]
châtelaine any sort of fancy garnish used to dress up a dish
châtelaine/à la châtelaine typically: with chestnuts, artichoke hearts, puréed onions and a cream sauce
chaudeau sweet pudding sauce
chadeu orange pie
chaud-froid hot-cold [refers to a dish that has been cooked and then chilled covered with a gelatin or sauce and served cold]
   sauce chaud-froid jellied white sauce [literally, "hot-cold sauce"; made from a hot creamy white sauce and veal, chicken or fish stock thickened with cream and meat jelly (clear natural gelatin made from meat and bones); allowed to cool, then spooned over cooked chicken, game or fish which is then refrigerated and served cold; several named variations exist]
chaudrée (à la) vendéenne fish chowder [thick fish soup; the *fouirasine* version is typically made with eels, cuttlefish, potatoes and local white wine]
chausson pastry turnover, usually filled
chausson aux pommes apple turnover
chausson aux queues de langoustines lobster turnover
chayote chayote [a tropical squash used like summer squash; mild flavored, though some people find it unpalatable; shaped like a large pear; the skin is furrowed, rough or smooth, and light green or white according to the variety]
chemise shirt
   en chemise with the skin on
   pommes de terre en chemise jacket potatoes; potatoes served in their skins
chérimole cherimoya; custard apple [has a sweet vanilla or strawberry aroma]
chevaine chub [freshwater fish, very boney]
cheval horse; horse meat
chevesne chub [freshwater fish, very boney]
cheveu d'ange angel's hair
chevreau kid [young male goat]
chèvre goat; goat cheese
   crottin de chèvre goat cheese

chèvre crab; velvet swimming crab [small crab with thin meat, but quite delicious]
chèvre frais fresh goat cheese
chevrette kid [young female goat]
chevreuil venison
  carrée de chevreuil rack of venison
  en chevreuil a way of preparing non-game meat as though it were game meat
  gigot de chevreuil haunch of venison; rack of venison
  gigue de chevreuil haunch of venison; rack of venison
  rôti de chevreuil roast venison
chevrier thin, flat, pale green dry bean [subtle flavor]
chiche-kebab shish-kebab grilled skewers of mutton or lamb typically with onion, peppers and tomatoes
chichi frégi chickpea donut/fritter [long oval pastry, made with wheat and chickpea flour, powdered sugar and orange blossom water; fried in oil and rolled in granulated sugar]
chicon endive
chicons au gratin endive au gratin [endive baked with cheeses]
chicorée endive; chicory
chicorée roots of the chicory plant used to make "coffee"
chicorée à café chicory coffee [generally taken at breakfast as a coffee substitute or mixed with coffee]
chicorée frisée chicory; Louviers endive
chiffonade a soup of finely cut herbs
chiffonade finely cut ribbons of herbs, lettuces or leafy greens
chilaca pepper [mild to medium hot with a rich flavor]
chimayo chimayó pepper [tastes sweet, then becomes medium hot]
chinois candied kumquat
chilboust/crème chilboust a pastry cream lightened with stiffly-beaten egg whites and sometimes flavored with vanilla, orange zest or liqueurs
chili type of chili pepper
  poudre de chili chili pepper [powder]
chiltepin hot pepper [pea-sized pepper; hotter than habanero]
chinchard Atlantic horse mackerel
chioggia beet [has rings of red and white]
chipeau gadwall [type of wild duck]
chipiron cuttlefish; calamari
chipirons à la luzienne baby squid [with onions, tomatoes, peppers and rice]
chipolata small, thin sausage, similar to Italian sausage, breakfast sausage or bangers
chips potato chips
  pommes chips potato chips
chips aux crevettes prawn crackers
chique/chique blanc white cheese
chocart large puff pastry filled with thick apple marmalade flavored with cinnamon and lemon zest; eaten hot
chocolat chocolate
chocolat au lait milk chocolate

chocolat aux noisettes hazelnut chocolate
chocolat blanc white chocolate
chocolat chaud hot chocolate
chocolat mi-amer semi-sweet chocolate
choiseul/sauce choiseul white wine sauce with truffles
choix choice; of very good quality
   au choix your choice
   desserts au choix your choice of dessert
chomphu rose apple [tropical fruit; red, bell-shaped; crisp, not sweet]
choquart/chocart large puff pastry filled with thick apple marmalade flavored with cinnamon and lemon zest; eaten hot
chorba spicy North African vegetable soup
choricero type of red pimento pepper, usually dried
chorizo basquais mild chorizo sausage
chou cabbage
chou à la crème choux bun; cream puff
chou blanc white cabbage
chou cabus white cabbage
chou chinois pak-choi
chou de Bruxelles Brussels sprout
chou de mer sea kale
chou de Milan Savoy cabbage
chou farci stuffed cabbage [beef or pork stuffing, with onions, tomatoes, rice and sometimes mushrooms; boiled or steamed]
chou frisé kale; borecole
chou marin sea kale
chou palmiste palm heart
chou pomme white cabbage
chou pommé cabbage with apples
chou précoce spring greens
chou rouge à la flamande Flemish red cabbage [typically: red cabbage cooked with apples]
chou vert green cabbage
chouchen mead [alcoholic beverage made by fermenting honey in apple juice; dark color, strong taste]
chouchou chayote [a tropical squash used like summer squash; mild flavored, though some people find it unpalatable; shaped like a large pear; the skin is furrowed, rough or smooth, and light green or white according to the variety]
choucroute sauerkraut
choucroute aux poissons sauerkraut with poached fish and a white wine cream sauce
choucroute d'Alsace sauerkraut of Alsace [finely chopped cabbage fermented in brine; must be cooked before eating (usually in white wine or beer along with some meat); traditionally served with sausages, cured/smoked meats, and potatoes]
choucroute de Brienne sauerkraut of Brienne [cooked in Champagne]
choucroute garni sauerkraut with meat [sausage, salt pork, smoked bacon and *knack* (hot dog)]
chou-fleur cauliflower

chou-fleur cauliflower mushroom [sweet-smelling; edible when young; brown, deeply crinkled, resembling cauliflower or coral]
chou-navet rutabaga
chou-pomme apple-cabbage
chouquette sugar-topped pastry puff [sometimes filled with custard or mouse, or dipped in chocolate]
choux cabbages
choux puff pastry
    pâte à choux a light pastry dough; creampuff pastry
    petits choux small puff pastries
christollen Christmas bread [small fruit cake with colorful bits of candied fruits and almonds]
christophone chayote [a tropical squash used like summer squash; mild flavored, though some people find it unpalatable]
chutney aux algues sea weed chutney
ciboule scallion; spring onion; chive
ciboulette small chive
    terrine de coquille saint-jacques à la ciboulette scallop terrine with chives
cicerelle sand eel
circuma turmeric
cidre cider
cidre bouché sparkling cider [in champagne-style bottle; has a slight amount of alcohol]
cidre Briard organic cider [unpasteurized, without sulfites]
cidre brut dry cider
cidre de pommes apple cider
cidre doux sweet cider
cidre fermier farm cider
cidre du Pays d'Auge, AOC hard cider [naturally fermented, unpasteurized, not carbonated; golden color with orange highlights; intense nose with aromas of ripe apples; mouth is round with generous structure; sweetness balanced by some tartness; continues to ferment in the bottle; can be kept for one or two years]
Ciflorette/fraises Ciflorette high-quality strawberry
cigale de mer slipper lobster; spiny lobster
cigarette/biscuit cigarette cigarette-shaped biscuit [typically served with a *pot de crème* (cream pot) or ice cream]
cinq-épices Chinese five-spice [star anise, cloves, fennel, cinnamon, pepper]
cinq-parfumes Chinese five-spice [star anise, cloves, fennel, cinnamon, pepper]
Cirafine/fraises Cirafine high-quality strawberry
ciselé diced; shredded
ciboulette ciselée uniformly chopped chives
citrange bitter-tasting hybrid between the sweet orange and the bitter Chinese orange
citron lemon
    berlingot saveur citron lemon flavor candy
    écorce de citron lemon peel
    essence de citron lemon oil

glace citron vert lime ice cream
jus de citron lemon juice
zeste de citron lemon peel
citron bergamote bergamot lemon [a cross between lime and bitter orange]
citron combava kafir lime; makrut lime
citron givré lemon sorbet
citron jaune lemon
citron pressé fresh lemon juice
citron vert lime
citronelle citronella; lemon verbena
citronné flavored with lemon
citrouille pumpkin
    tarte à la citrouille pumpkin pie
    tourte à la citrouille pumpkin pie
cive chive
civelle baby eel; elver [the fry of European eel when it enters rivers from the sea]
civet stew
civet de chevreuil venison stew
civet de lapin rabbit stew
civet de sanglier wild boar stew [typically: meat cooked for up to two days with diced vegetables, blood and marinade]
civet de homard au cidre lobster stew with cider [made with lobster, cider, butter, cream, eggs, carrots and onions]
civette chive
clafoutis baked dessert [a pancake-like dessert filled with fruits, especially cherries]
claire clear
claire fattened oyster
    fin de claire IGP oyster [high quality oyster cultured in clear (*claire*) ponds in the Marennes Olèron basin]
    fin de claire verte Label Rouge oyster [high quality cultured oyster with green gills (from the algae that it filters)]
clairet a pale red or dark pink wine; full-bodied rosé wine
clairette white wine grape with aromas of peaches and apricots
clam clam
clapotons sheep's trotters
claret dark red wine from Bordeaux
clamart market garden
    à la clamart accompanied by green peas
    potage clamart pea soup
clarifié clarified
    beurre clarifié clarified butter
clavaire edible mushroom [generally looks like coral]
clavaire en chou-fleur cauliflower clavaire mushroom [looks a bit like pink cauliflower; slightly bitter]
clavaire dorée golden clavaire mushroom [yellow to yellow-orange; sweet flavored]
clavaire en pilon pestle clavaire mushroom [yellow to reddish; pestle-shaped; bitter taste]

clavaire tronquée truncated clavaire mushroom [stubby pestle-shaped; orange to reddish; sweet tasting]
clavelado skate [marine fish]
clémentine clementine orange
Clery/fraises Clery high-quality strawberry
clitocybe edible mushroom
clitocybe en entonnoir funnel clltocybe mushroom [beige, funnel-shaped; tastes of anise and bitter almond]
clitocybe géant giant clitocybe mushroom [large funnel-shaped; white to creamy yellow; sweet tasting]
clitocybe géotrope monk's head clitocybe mushroom [yellow-ochre to creamy white; tastes of lavender, mint and fragrant herbs]
clitocybe laqué lacquered clitocybe mushroom [brownish-pink to violet-lavender; sweet]
clitocybe odorant fragrant clitocyte mushroom [blue-green to gray-green; strong aroma of anise]
clitocybe orangé chanterelle mushroom [yellow-orange; fruity aroma, peppery, slightly bitter taste]
clitocybe à pied en massue pine clitocybe mushroom [yellowish or brownish gray; slight aroma of cinnamon and orange flower; sweet taste]
clitocybe retourné inverted clitocybe mushroom [yellow-brown to beige-brown; slightly acidic, but agreeable]
clitopile petite-prune small plum clitopile mushroom [edible mushroom; grayish white cap with pink gills; strong aroma of fresh flour]
clou de girofle clove [the spice]
clouté studded; pressed into
    bar clouté sea bass prepared for cooking by pressing coarse sea salt into the skin]
    oignon clouté an onion cut in half with a bay leaf attached with two cloves
clovis/clovisse carpet shell clam
    pates aux clovis pasta with clams
cochelin Parisian flan [flan baked on a crust made of flour, sugar, butter, milk and eggs]
cochon pig
cochon de lait suckling piglet
cochon en pain d'épices de Vesoul chocolate covered gingerbread in the shape of a pig
cochonaille pork products
coco large white dry bean
    noix de coco coconut
coco blanc white bean
coco de Paimpol AOC white dry bean [rich in fiber, vitamin B5, B1 and iron; low in carbohydrates and high in protein; thin skinned and said to not cause flatulence]
coco rouge red bean
coco rose red-veined bean
cococha cooked ripe banana plantains made into a dough and baked with crushed almond-like nut called *akpis*

cocotte casserole; casserole dish; stew pot
   en cocotte a way to cook eggs in a ramekin placed in boiling water
   oeufs en cocotte shirred eggs/baked eggs
cocotte de moules buckets of mussels
coeur heart
   cuit à coeur cooked to the core
   fait à coeur cheese that is ripe all the way through
coeur à la crème cream cheese or cheese curd in a mold with summer fruits
coeur de filet (de boeuf) the best cut of the fillet (of beef)
coeur de laitue lettuce heart
coeur de palmier heart of palm
Cognac brandy
cognasse small wild quince
coing quince
   pain coing quince bread
Cointreau orange liqueur [from sweet and bitter oranges]
colbert fried fish [fillet of fish cooked in compound butter]
colerave apple-cabbage; also known as *chou-pomme*
colère fried fish [whole fish with tail tied to its mouth; *colère* means "angry"]
colin hake; pollock; pollack [a member of the cod family; more subtle flavor than cod; firm, sweet white meat]
colin lieu saithe; pollock or pollack
colin noir saithe; pollock or pollack
colineau young hake
colombe dove
colombine a breaded and fried *croquette* coated with semolina or Parmesan cheese; served as a warm appetizer]
colvert mallard duck
combava/combawa kaffir lime; makrut lime
comice pear [big, plump, juicy and sweet]
communard aperitif made with red wine and blackcurrant liqueur
compote compote [a dessert made by cooking fruit in sugar syrup to which sweet seasonings, almonds, coconut or raisins are added]
compote de lapereau au cidre et au calvados rabbit roasted with cider, bacon, shallots, and Calvados
compote de pomme apple sauce
compris included
   service compris service included [you need not leave a tip]
Comté AOC cheese [raw cow's milk; grainy golden yellow to brown rind in summer, ivory color in winter; summer cheese is yellow because the cows feed on natural pasture grasses; winter cheese is paler because the cows are fed hay inside barns; great variety in aromas and taste according to time of year and aging processes, but in general the cheese may have aromas of milk, fruit or nuts, green vegetation, mushrooms and spices and may taste a bit salty, sweet and sometimes with a bitter aftertaste]
comtesse small cakes (or cookies) somewhat like shortbread [made with flour, butter and lard, eggs, sugar]

concassé chopped; peeled, seeded and diced (tomatoes)
concombre cucumber
concorde pear [ripens in autumn]
condé pastry or dessert rice with poached fruit, jam glaze and whipped cream
condé au fromage puff pastry with a white sauce and cheese
condiment condiment
confiserie sweets, candies, confectionary
confit meat preserved in fat or fruit preserved in sugar [meat *confit* are usually duck or goose, sometimes turkey or pork cooked and then covered and stored in their own fat]
confit de canard duck preserved in fat
confit de pétales de rose de Provins rose petals preserved in sugar
confiture jam; marmalade
  tartine de confiture slice of bread and jam
confiture de lait milk jam [mixture of milk and sugar which is boiled then baked until thickened and caramel in color]
congolais coconut macaroon
congre conger eel
congre à la bretonne Brittany style conger eel [eel cooked with potatoes, onions and muscadet wine]
conseillé recommended
conserve canned food
consommé consommé; stock
consommé aux profiteroles hot consommé with baked "peas" of puff pastry
consommé du volaille chicken consommé
consommé en tasse cold jellied consommé in a cup
consommé julienne hot consommé with julienne of carrot, turnip and leek
consommé madrilène hot consommé with tomato and celery
consommé vermicelle hot consommé with vermicelli
conti lentil purée
  à la conti garnished with lentils and bacon
contre-filet ribeye steak; boneless sirloin
conversation/tarte conversation almond tart with sugar icing
copeau pastry twist
copeaux shavings
copeaux de chocolat chocolate flakes for decoration
coppa di Corsica raw cured ham [boneless pork loin, salted, dried and cured for six months or longer; when sliced, it is red with pinkish white veins]
coq à la bière rooster/chicken in beer [typically: with smoked bacon, onions, garlic, carrots and beer in a cream sauce]
coq au Chambertin rooster in red wine [young rooster cooked with bacon, shallots, garlic, mushrooms and *Chambertin* wine]
coq au riesling rooster in white wine [rooster cooked with butter, shallots, mushrooms, cognac, fresh cream and riesling wine]
coq au vin de chanturgue rooster in red wine [rooster cooked with onions, bacon, butter, red wine, garlic, onions and blood]

coq au vin jaune chicken with yellow wine [a fattened chicken and morel mushrooms cooked with butter, flour, fresh cream and a strong yellow wine]
coq de bruyère black grouse
coq en pâte chicken pie
coque generic name for cockles (edible mollusks)
   oeuf à la coque soft-boiled egg
coque blanche white cockle
coque commune common cockle
coque Saint-Aphrodise a pastry in the form of a brioche scented with orange flower
coquelet young rooster
coquillage shellfish
coquillages de Bouzigues farmed oysters and mussels
coquille shell
coquille Saint-Jacques scallop
   terrine de coquille saint-jacques à la ciboulette scallop terrine with chives
corail coral
   beurre de corail coral butter [a compound butter made by adding shells of lobster, crab, shrimp, crayfish or scallops ground into a fine paste]
corbeille basket
cordifole salad purslane [thick, succulent leaves used fresh in salads or sautéed; light citrus flavor]
cordial liqueur [as an apéritif or a digestive in the evening]
cordon-blue cordon-blue [literally "blue ribbon;" consists of boneless meat flattened and then rolled with cheese (usually Swiss) and ham, sometimes with bacon; the boneless meat is usually chicken, but may be veal or ham; *halal* versions substitute beef or lamb for ham/bacon]
corégon lake whitefish [freshwater salmonid fish in Alpine lakes]
coriandre coriander
corne greque okra
cornet horn; horn shaped
cornet de jambon curved rolled ham slice
cornet de Murat hand-rolled pastry shaped like a horn (*cornet*), filled with cream and topped with whipped cream
cornette curly endive
cornichon tiny pickle/gherkin
cornichon à l'aneth dill pickle
cornichon de câprier caper
corniottes cheese pastry [eaten for breakfast or as a snack]
cornouille cornelian cherry [fruit of the *Cornus mas* tree; a red fruit is the size of an olive; rather tart, but becomes sweet when very ripe and taste a bit like cherries; eaten fresh or made into marmalade]
corossol épineux spiny soursop; custard apple
correlet dab [marine fish]
Corse AOP Corsican ham [known as *prisuttu* in Corsica; the only French ham to have the AOP designation; pigs feed on acorns and chestnuts]

cortinaire mushroom [edible when young; becomes bitter as it ages]
côte beef rib; cutlet or chop (mutton or pork)
côte de porc bruxelloise pork chop with endive
côte de porc fumée smoked pork chop
côte première loin chop
côte de veau à la normande veal chop, Normandy style [typically: cooked with mushrooms, Calvados liqueur, butter and cream]
côtes de veau au pommeau veal chop casserole with *pommeau* (a blend of apple juice and Calvados)
côtelette chop
côtelettes de saumon à l'andouille de Vire salmon and sausages cooked in red wine
côtelettes premières lamb rib cutlets
côtes couvertes rolled beef rib
côtes premières side of lamb or veal, used for roasting; best cut
côtes secondes side of lamb or veal, used for roasting
côtes de porc à la normande Normandy-style pork chops [usually cooked with cider and fresh cream]
côtes de porc grillées au camembert grilled pork chops with melted Camembert cheese; typically served with apple slices cooked in butter
côtes de veau à la crème veal chops cooked with mushrooms, white wine and fresh cream
côtes de veau vallée d'Auge veal chops cooked with mushrooms, onions, fresh cream and Calvados
côtière coastal
cotignac quince jelly
cotriade fish stew [a northern type of bouillabaisse considered to be more refined if more varieties of fish are included, and more civilized if crustaceans and vegetables are added; served with potatoes, the broth is drunk first, then the fish are eaten]
cottage cottage cheese
cou neck
coucou de Rennes black and white speckled hen from Rennes
coucoulelli diamond-shaped pastry from Corsica made with white wine, olive oil, sugar and flour
coucougnettes delicate sweets made with almonds, almond butter and chocolate, made by hand and dipped in raspberry juice
coucoune Caesar's mushroom [rare and highly valued; firm white flesh; has a pleasant aroma and a sweet, nutty flavor]
coudenac pork sausage
coudenou/coudenou de Mazamet white pork sausage [the skin is crispy when cooked; used in cabbage stew and *cassoulets*]
couenne rind; pork skin
couenne de bacon bacon rind
    saucisse de couenne pork rind sausage [used in cabbage stew and *cassoulets*]
cougnou Christmas brioche [bun in the form of the infant Jesus eaten during the period of Saint Nicolas at Christmas]
couille du pape fig jam
coulant runny (cheese)

coulemelle edible parasol mushroom; wild or cultivated
coulibiac Russian pie [usually made with fish such as salmon or sturgeon baked with rice or buckwheat in a puff pastry]
coulis thick sauce (veggie or fruit)
coulis d'écrevisse crawfish bisque
coulis de cassis blackcurrant sauce
coulis de framboise raspberry sauce
coulis de tomate tomato sauce
Coulommiers cheese [cow's milk; bloomy white rind dotted with red, soft straw-yellow cheese; un-cooked, un-pressed, 45% to 50% fat]
coupe dish of ice cream with fruit, fruit sauce, whipped cream and other decorations
coupe St-Jacques fruit salad with ice cream
couque biscuit or pastry [in Belgium: gingerbread cake]
couque de Dinant honey and spice biscuit
couque de Rins soft honey and spice pastry
couque suisse spiral-shaped brioche with raisins and pastry cream (and sometimes cinnamon, like a cinnamon bun)
couquebaques crêpes made with beer for leavening
courbine croaker fish; meager fish; shade-fish; corvina; salmon-basse or stone basse [similar to sea bass, but not as delicate]
courge vegetable marrow; winter squash
courge à la moelle vegetable marrow
courge butternut butternut squash
courge cireuse Chinese squash [a type of summer squash]
courge d'été summer squash; zucchini/courgette
courge d'hiver winter squash
courge de Chine Chinese squash [a type of summer squash]
courge de Hubbard winter squash [hard shelled squash with thick flesh; sweet flavor, very aromatic and of high quality]
courge gland acorn squash
courge longue de Nice long squash of Nice [firm flesh with a musky, sweet taste; clear green skin turning ochre at maturity]
courge musquée butternut squash
courge musquée de Provence musk squash of Provence [clear orange-red flesh, tender and juicy, fruity and not fibrous]
courge patidou sweet dumpling [a type of squash, tasting like fresh chestnuts; eaten raw (grated) or cooked]
courge spaghetti spaghetti squash
courgette zucchini/courgette
couronne nattée braided sweet brioche-type bread
courquinois seafood soup [made with chopped leeks, conger, crab, mullet and mussels]
court bouillon a lightly flavored broth used to poach fish and shellfish
couscous couscous [semolina]
cousinette green soup [typically: made with green leaves such as spinach, chard, lettuce, and sorrel with aromatics such as leeks and garlic; the broth may be flavored with ham]
cousteille lamb cutlet with *aioli* (garlic mayonnaise)
couteau knife

au couteau knife-cut (by hand)
  tartare de boeuf au couteau knife-cut raw beef (as opposed to minced raw beef)
couteau razor clam
crabe crab
crabe cerise crab; velvet swimming crab [small crab with thin meat, but quite delicious]
crabe laineux crab; velvet swimming crab [small crab with thin meat, but quite delicious]
crabe nageur crab; velvet swimming crab [small crab with thin meat, but quite delicious]
crabe vert shore crab
cracker water biscuit; dry English biscuit
cramique cream puff with a crackly topping [in Belgium, it is a brioche with sugar]
cranson horseradish
crapaudine butterflied and then trussed to look like a toad
  sauce crapaudine butterflied style sauce [made with butter, flour, broth, chopped shallots, vinegar]
crâpiau thick buckwheat pancake flavored with bacon, parsley and garlic
craquelin cracker; crispy biscuit [North American cracker]
craquelin cream puff with a crackly topping [in Belgium, it is a brioche with sugar]
craquelins de Châlus very dry, sweet, red cake
craquelot lightly salted smoked herring
crécy prepared with carrots
  crème crécy creamed carrot soup garnished with boiled rice
crème cream
  café crème espresso coffee with milk
  chou à la crème choux bun
  sauce à la crème cream sauce [usually made with *crème fraîche* (fresh cream); other possible ingredients (wine, vinegar, lemon juice, herbs, etc.) depend on what the sauce will accompany]
crème (à l') anglaise custard [a thick egg custard made with egg yolks, sugar, milk and vanilla or lemon; served hot or cold]
crème (au) beurre butter cream [for cake filling or icing; made with hot sugar syrup, egg yolks and flavoring such as chocolate, coffee, vanilla or fruit puree]
crème à vanille vanilla custard
crème aigre sour cream
crème au café coffee cream
crème au caramel caramel custard
crème au chocolat chocolate cream
crème au citron lemon custard
crème bachique a custard flavored with cinnamon and Sauternes, a sweet white wine from the Bordeaux region
crème brulée a rich egg custard with a caramel crust usually baked in a ramekin, but sometimes in a large dish
crème caramel crème caramel
crème Chantilly sweet whipped cream

crème chiboust a pastry cream lightened with stiffly-beaten egg whites and sometimes flavored with vanilla, orange zest or liqueurs
crème crécy creamed carrot soup garnished with boiled rice
crème d'amandes almond cream
crème d'asperges cream of asparagus soup
crème de marrons cream of chestnut [made with chestnuts, syrup, sugar and vanilla]
crème d'orges barley soup
crème d'oseille cream of sorrel soup
Crème de Brie de Meaux melted cheese (fondue) [commercial trademark; made with Brie cheese]
crème de cassis blackcurrant liqueur [essential ingredient in *kir* or as an after dinner liqueur]
crème de chou-fleur aux moules creamy mussels and cauliflower soup made with white wine
crème de fruits de mer à la marinière marinara-style seafood in a creamy white sauce
crème de riz creamy rice soup
crème épaisse double cream
crème fouettée whipped cream
crème fraîche soured cream [contains a lactobacillus culture which gives it a slightly sour taste; does not separate when boiled]
crème fraîche épaisse thick soured cream [literally "thick fresh cream"]
crème frite thick custard [made with egg yolks, flour, a sweetener and flavoring; it is cooked and then cooled, then sliced, breaded and deep fried]
crème glacée ice cream; ice cream sundae
crème moulée baked egg custard [baked in a mold then served cold in the mold or demolded]
crème patissière/crème patisserie pastry cream; confectioner's custard [a kind of light custard made with cream, eggs, sugar, vanilla and flour]
crème plombières light custard cream
crème pralinée pastry cream (*crème patissière*) with praline powder for flavoring
crème renversée demolded caramel custard (*crème caramel*)
crème St. Germain rich, creamy, velvety pea soup garnished with chopped mint
crèmeux/crèmeuse creamy
    riz au lait crémeux rice in creamy milk
crémet cottage cheese; cream cheese
crèmeux/crèmeuse creamy
créole/à la créole Creole style [usually with rice and possibly with tomatoes and sweet peppers]
crêpe very thin pancake
    mille crêpes [a cake made of many crêpe layers]
    petite crêpe épaisse crumpet; small thick pancake
crêpe à la Bénédictine crêpe with Bénédictine liqueur, often flambéed

crêpe au caramel au beurre salée salted butter caramel crêpe
crêpe au gros lait crêpe with thick, tangy, creamy milk, somewhat like yoghurt
crêpe bretonne traditional crêpe served plain or garnished with sweets or savories; sweet crêpes are made with wheat flour and savory crêpes are made with buckwheat flower
crêpe complete crêpe with ham, cheese and egg
crêpe cauchoises flambées aux pommes Cauchois-style crêpe with slices of apples, flambéed in rum
crêpe dentelle crispy biscuit [made with a very thin layer of crêpe rolled into a cigar shape and baked]
crêpe épaisse flapjack; pancake (literally: thick crêpe)
crêpe graisse salée crêpe with highly seasoned pork fat
crêpe Parmentier potato pancake
crêpe Saint-Pierre au pommeau sweet crêpe garnished with a sauce made with *pommel* (Calvados with apple juice added)
crêpe salée salted crêpe [made with buckwheat flour and not sweetened]
crêpe sucrée sweet crêpe [made with wheat flour and lightly sweetened]
crêpe suzette crêpe suzette [made with a sauce containing orange zest, butter, sugar, orange juice, cognac and Grand Marnier]
crêpe taminoise beer pancake [thick pancake sprinkled with sugar]
crépiâ thick buckwheat pancake flavored with bacon, parsley and garlic
crépinette minced meatball [ground meat such as pork, poultry, organ meats or fish stuffed into pig's caul
crépinette *croquette* wrapped with bacon and then grilled or fried
crépinette d'agneau à la liégeoise minced lamb meatball with onions and juniper berries
crépinette de foie de porc à la vauclusienne baked pig's liver meatball with bacon, spinach, onion and black olives
crépinette Reine Jeanne sheep's or calf's brains meatballs with chopped shallots, mushrooms and truffles, breaded and fried
crépinette de volaille chicken meatballs with mushrooms or truffles
crèque bullace [plum-like fruit]
crespeou herb omelets stacked in layers, eaten cold with or without tomato sauce
cresson watercress
cresson alénois land cress
cresson de fontaine watercress
cresson d'Inde nasturtium
cresson de ruisseau watercress
cressonade watercress sauce
cressonière potato and onion and watercress purée
cretons crackling
cretons bacon rind and pork simmered with onion and spices, then pounded into a smooth texture, thickened with breadcrumbs and set in a mold
crevette shrimp

crevette au cidre shrimp with cider
crevette grise gray shrimp
crevette grise fried shrimp [as a specialty of Dunkerque, often prepared combined with a white sauce, breaded and deep fried (as is done in Belgium), though sometimes fried plain and served with buttered bread]
crevette obsiblue blue shrimp from New Caledonia [said to be harvested in an eco-friendly way; may be eaten raw]
crevette rose pink shrimp
crevette rose du large pink king prawn
crevette rouge prawn [reddish jumbo shrimp]
crevette royale king prawn
crique potato pancake
criste-marine samphire; rock samphire; sea fennel [edible coastal plant with fleshy aromatic spicy leaves]
croissant croissant
cromesqui savory fritter [small deep-fried sphere of dough which can be filled with cheese, chicken, lentils, seafood or vegetables]
croquant crisp, crunchy
croquant dry biscuit from southern France [plain, or with almonds and honey or almonds and olives]
croque-a-cheval grilled ham and cheese sandwich with a fried or poached egg on top
croque au sel raw vegetables seasoned only with salt
  à la croque au sel with just a sprinkling of salt
croque auvergnat grilled ham and cheese sandwich with *Bleu d'Auvergne* cheese
croque bolognese grilled ham and cheese sandwich with Bolognese sauce
croque Boum-Boum grilled ham and cheese sandwich with Bolognese sauce
croque gagnet grilled ham and cheese sandwich with Gouda cheese and Andouille sausage
croque galois cheddar cheese melted in a pot of beer and flavored with mustard; typically served on toasted bread with a slice of ham
croque Hawaiian grilled ham and cheese sandwich with a slice of pineapple
croque madame grilled ham and cheese sandwich with a fried or poached egg on top (sometimes the ham is omitted)
croque mademoiselle grilled sandwich [for cheese, tomatoes, a slice of chicken and a fried egg; or cheese, cucumber, chives and ham; or low-fat cheese, cucumber, chives and ham]
croque monsieur grilled ham and cheese sandwich [made with *jambon de Paris* (Paris ham) and either Emmental or Gruyère cheese
croque
croque norvégien grilled cheese sandwich with smoked salmon
croque provençal grilled ham and cheese sandwich with tomato
croque señor grilled ham and cheese sandwich with tomato salsa
croquembouche crockenbush [a tall tower or pyramid made of profiteroles (hollow pastry balls) filled with crème patissière (vanilla-scented pastry cream) and dipped in caramel to make

them stick together; sometimes used as a substitute for a wedding cake]
croquer to be crisp; to munch; to be crunchy
   chocolat à croquer dark chocolate
   comprimé à croquer chewable tablet
croquet tartiflette grilled ham and cheese sandwich with sliced potatoes and Reblochon cheese
croquet almond biscuit
croquette minced food bound with egg, formed and coated with breadcrumbs and fried; fried roll containing mashed potatoes, fish, cheese, ground meat or vegetables; may contain a white or brown sauce
croquette de camembert breaded and fried Camembert cheese
croquette de poisson fishcake
croquette de pomme de terre potato croquette
croquette de viande meatball croquette
croquette de volaille chicken croquette
croquignole dry biscuit [very dry, crunchy biscuit, pink or white, served with frozen desserts, creams or fruits or with coffee]
crosgne Chinese artichoke [an edible white tuber]
crosgne du Japon Japanese artichoke
crosse de boeuf beef knuckle; calf's foot
crotte drop (as in chocolate drop)
crotte de chocolat/croquette de chocolat small round chocolate; chocolate drop
crottin avesnois small walnut brioche [filled with cream of *Maroilles* cheese]
crottins du haras sweets from Normandie [literally: horse droppings]
crouis fresh ear-shaped pasta
croupion Parson's nose [delicate morsel of poultry meat; the extreme posterior part that supports the tail feathers]
croustade dessert made of two extremely thin sheets of puff pasty stuffed with apples (*aux pommes)* or raisins (*aux raisins secs*)
croustade d'oeufs de caille Maintenon pastry boat filled with poached quail eggs, diced shallots, mushrooms and Hollandaise sauce
crousti-fondant golden-crisp
croustillant crispy; crusty
   bacon croustillant crispy fried bacon
croûte crust; crouton
casse-croûte snack
   en croûte in pastry [refers to foods such as Brie, salmon, beef or vegetables surrounded by pastry dough and then baked]
croûte au fromage cheeses on toast
croûte aux champignons mushrooms in a cream sauce served with croutons (croûtes) or toasted bread
croûte aux morilles morel mushrooms on toast
croûte au pot vegetable and beef soup topped with toasted bread and cheese
croûte forestière mushrooms in a cream sauce served with croutons (croûtes) or toasted bread

croûte normande a dessert made of *brioche* slices stuffed with sweet apple compote, soaked in beaten eggs, Calvados and butter, then sprinkled with sugar and caramelized on the grill
croûtons fried or toasted cubes of bread
crozet small, plump square buckwheat (or sometimes durum) pasta
croziflette baked *crozet* pasta with onions, cured ham, cream and Reblochon cheese
cru raw
cruchade corn or millet porridge
crudités raw vegetables [sometimes served with a dipping vinaigrette or sauce]
crumble crumble
crumble aux fruits fruit crumble
crustacé shellfish; crustacean
   soupe de crustacés shellfish soup
cubanelle mildly hot pepper ["Cuban pepper"; yellowish green when young, then red when ripe; sometimes used in place of Poblano peppers]
cuchaule saffron bun [a type of brioche eaten with *moutarde de Bénichon*, a sweet, spicy jam-like mustard]
cuisse thigh; leg; dark meat
cuisse de grenouille frogs leg [usually sautéed in butter with garlic and parsley, or prepared with a cream sauce]
cuissot haunch
cuit cooked
   assez cuit well enough done
   bien cuit well done
   jambon cuit boiled ham
   mi cuit half cooked
   mi cuit au torchon wrapped in cloth and cooked by boiling or simmering
   pas assez cuit underdone
   trop cuit overdone
   vin cuit fortified wine
cuit à coeur lightly cooked
cuit à point medium; well-cooked
cuit au four baked
cuit au sel salt baked
cul haunch
culatello ham [a refined type of prosciutto, made from heavier pigs, cut smaller; may be cured with wine]
culotte rump steak
culotte de boeuf beef rump steak
culotte de veau veal rump steak
cultivateur/à la cultivateur farmer's style [with mixed vegetables]
   soupe à la cultivateur farmer's style soup [clear fresh vegetable soup]
cumbava kaffir lime; makrut lime
cumin cumin [powder or seeds]
cumin des prés caraway
cumin noir nigella spice; black cumin

cuniu brioche with dried fruits
Curaçao orange liqueur
curcurma turmeric
currie curry
curry curry
curry très épicé very spicy curry
cygne swan-shaped pastry with whipped cream
dacquoise dessert cake [two or three layers of meringue altnernating with layers of almond, hazelnut, or pistachios, and sometimes coconut, or sugar icing or butter cream]
daim deer; buck
daiquiri rum cocktail
dalle thin slice of fish
dame blanche pastry filled with preserved fruit and cream and topped with meringue
dame blanche vanilla ice cream with whipped cream and chocolate sauce
dame blanche du Poitou a molded island of fluffy creamy vanilla soufflé floating in a bowl of cream
damier a checkerboard arrangement of vegetables
damier checkerboard-patterned cake
dariole a mold shaped like a truncated cone used for baking a variety of foods such as *flans*, *soufflés*, *mousses*, or *terrines* of meat or fish
dariole cheese flan; cheese tartlet
dariole small frangipane (almond custard) pastry
darne fish steak
darne de saumon salmon steak
darne de saumon au miel toutes fleurs salmon steaks with wildflower honey
darphin/pommes de terre darphin potato pancake
Darselect/fraises Darselect high-quality strawberry
dartois flaky pastry filled with sweets or savories
datte date
daube braised beef casserole [typically: beef which is braised and slow cooked in red wine with vegetables, garlic and *herbs de Provence*; often served with potatoes or pasta]
   boeuf en daube/daube de boeuf braised beef stew
daube avignonnaise mutton/lamb casserole [made with shoulder of mutton or lamb which is marinated and then cooked in white or red wine with garlic, onions and carrots]
daube comtadine mutton/lamb casserole
daube de biche venison casserole
daube de cèpes mushroom casserole [porcini mushrooms in red or white wine with shallots, pork belly, flour and salt]
daube niçoise beef casserole with tomatoes [braised beef, tomatoes, onions, carrots, garlic, red wine and spices; optional porcini mushrooms]
daube provençale beef casserole with black olives [typically: beef, onion, carrot, garlic, tomato sauce, red wine, optional black olives or bacon]

dauphine: **pommes de terre dauphine** puréed potatoes in a savory puff pastry shell
dauphinoise/gratin dauphinoise potato-cheese casserole [very thinly sliced potatoes in a buttery cream sauce topped with grated cheese]
daurade/dorade sea bream; gilt-head bream [delicate but flavorful flesh; often served whole]
daurade/dorade au cidre bream in cider
daurade/dorade au four baked sea bream
daurade/dorade grise black sea bream
daurade/dorade rose pink sea bream
daurade/dorade royale gilthead sea bream [small fish with tender white flesh with a rich, succulent taste; usually grilled or braised; mostly farmed because wild stock has diminished]
daurade/dorade royale en papillote sea bream baked or grilled in foil, often with vegetables such as onions, carrots and tomatoes plus herbs
de Árbol chili pepper [small and potent; subtle smoky flavor]
de campagne country; farmhouse
de l'Ardèche from Ardèche area in the Rhône-Alpes
    jambon de l'Ardèche IGP Ardèche ham
déca decaf coffee
décaffiné decaffeinated
déclinaison decoration
    déclinaison autour du saumon decorations around salmon
décliné decorated
décoction concentrated liquid stock
décortiqué shelled; pealed; hulled
découpé cut up; sliced
déglacé deglazed [browned food residue removed by pouring a liquid, usually wine, into the pan to pick up the bits that have caramelized]
dégraissé with the fat removed or skimmed
dégustation tasting; tasting menu (for wine or oysters)
    verre de dégustation wine tasting glass
dégustation d'huîtres oyster tasting
dégustation de vin wine tasting
dégustation privée de vin private wine tasting
délice literally: delight [a generic term for various pastries or other delicacies]
demi half
demi-bouteille half-bottle
demi-deuil literally: semi-mourning [any dish with black and white components]
    sauce demi-deuil white sauce with black truffles
demidoff surname of a once wealthy philanthropic Russian family (Деми́довы)
    blinis demidoff buckwheat cakes with sour cream and caviar [a dish featured in the film, *Babette's Feast*]
    suprême de volaille demidoff chicken breast with truffles and mushrooms

demi-glace demi-glace sauce [a "mother sauce" used as the base for many other sauces; in its purest form, it should start with a concentrated (reduced) brown roux to which is added a mixture of finely diced celery, onions and carrots; often cooked with ham or bacon and a few herbs]
demi-panaché a small glass of shandy [a blend of beer and a carbonated soft drink such as lemonade or ginger ale; maximum 1.2% alcohol by volume]
demi-sec semi-dry [when describing a wine, except for champagne, in which case it means "sweet"]
demi-sec semi-firm [when describing goat cheese]
demi-sel lightly salted [can refer to foods that have been preserved in salt, then rinsed or soaked to remove some of the salt]
demoiselle de canard roasted duck [to be eaten with the fingers and a knife for removing the meat from the bones, along with a rustic bread and local wine]
demoiselles de Cherbourg small lobsters cooked in a flavored broth and served in their cooking juices
demoiselles de Cherbourg à la nage small lobsters cooked in a light broth of white wine, onion, carrots, and *bouquet garni*; served with a dash of cognac and a sprinkling of parsley
dent-de-lion dandelion
dent-de-loup literally: wolf's tooth [small cakes shaped like "wolf's teeth"; can be vanilla, caramel, cinnamon, pistachio, etc.]
denté common dentex [Mediterranean fish, similar to sea bream]
dentelle lace [said of finely sliced meat or fish]
    crêpe dentelle very thin crêpe which is rolled around a flat knife and dried; can be used crumbled to add crunchiness to pastries; good with ice cream or a cup of coffee]
denti common dentex [Mediterranean fish, similar to sea bream]
dés dice [usually: diced vegetables, such as carrots, onions and celery]
désossé de-boned
    jambon fumé désossé daisy ham [boned and smoked pork shoulder]
desossé with bones removed
dessert dessert
diable kidneys served with *sauce diable* [veal or beef stock, tomato paste, shallots, white wine, vinegar, and may be flavored with parsley, thyme, cayenne pepper]
diable devil [an earthenware pan for slow cooking to allow for preservation of flavors]
    sauce à la diable devil sauce [made with veal or beef stock, tomato paste, shallots, white wine, vinegar, and may be flavored with parsley, thyme, cayenne pepper]
diablo menthe green mint syrup in soda water
diablotins cheese-flavored croutons
dieppoise Dieppe-style
diète diet
digestif alcohol taken at the end of a meal
Dijon/moutarde de Dijon Dijon mustard

dijonnaise Dijon style
Dimanche Sunday
dinde turkey hen
   blanc de dinde turkey breast
   gigolette de dinde turkey stew
   paupiette de dinde turkey olive
dinde rouge des Ardennes red turkey of Ardennes; raised on protein-supplemented grains and finished on milk
dindon male turkey
dindonneau young turkey
dîner dinner
diot pork sausage
diplomate dessert cake or pudding
dit called; known as
docteur Jules Guyot pear [ripens in summer]
dodine boned duck or game bird [usually stuffed and poached or braised; the bird may skinned and boned and the meat ground and stuffed back into the skin and then served in thin slices]
dodine de canard aux pistaches duck pâté with pistachio
dolic/dolique cow pea; black-eye pea, crowder-pea
dorade/daurade sea bream [delicate but flavorful flesh]
dorade/daurade au cidre bream in cider
dorade/daurade au four baked sea bream
dorade grise black sea bream
dorade rose pink sea bream
dorade/daurade royale gilthead sea bream [small fish with tender white flesh with a rich, succulent taste]
dorade/daurade royale en papillote sea bream baked or grilled in foil, often with vegetables such as onions, carrots and tomatoes plus herbs
doré browned
doré glazed; iced (cake)
doré golden; sun-kissed
dorée John Dory fish
dormeur/crabe dormeur sleeper crab [delicate flesh]
dos back; saddle
dos de lapin saddle of rabbit
dos de saumon salmon fillet
double crème double cream
douce sweet
   aigre-douce bittersweet; sweet and sour
   amande douce sweet almond
   eau douce fresh water
   moutarde douce sweet mustard
   orange douce sweet orange
   patate douce sweet potato
douce-amère sweet-sour
doucette corn salad; lamb's lettuce
douceur sweetness; mildness; softness
douceur argentanaise cake [has a carefully guarded recipe]
douillon baked fruit [apple or pear]

douillon aux poires baked pears [hollowed out and filled with any of a variety of sweet concoctions]
douillon aux pommes baked apples [hollowed out and filled with any of a variety of sweet concoctions]
doux sweet; soft
   aigre-doux bittersweet; sweet and sour
doux d'Espagne mild/sweet pepper [long, green pepper with a good flavor]
doux de Valence mild/sweet pepper [long, green pepper with a good flavor]
doux long des Landes small sweet, fragrant pepper
doyenné du comice pear [big, plump, with smooth thick skin, fine white flesh, juicy and sweet; ripens in autumn]
dressé garnished
du Barry cauliflower garnish [cauliflower in *mornay* sauce]
   chou fleur Du Barry/Dubarry creamed cauliflower or cauliflower soup
du jour of the day
   soupe du jour soup of the day
du moment of the moment; current
duchesse/sauce duchesse duchess sauce [usually made with white wine, mustard, and cream]
dugléré poached fish in fish broth and white wine and served on a bed of chopped tomatoes, onions, shallots and parsley
dur hard
   oeuf dur hard-boiled egg
duxelles finely minced cooked mushrooms cooked in butter or olive oil and seasoned with herbs and shallots
eau water
   melon d'eau watermelon
eau de Seltz soda water
eau de source spring water
eau de vie brandy [clear unsweetened brandy made by distilling fruits such as plums, pears, cherries and raspberries]
eau distillée distilled water
eau du robinet tap water
eau en bouteille bottled water
eau gazeuse sparkling water; carbonated water
eau minérale mineral water
eau non potable non-drinking water [for washing]
eau pétillante sparkling water
eau plate non-carbonated water; still water
eau potable drinking water
eau salé salty water
ébarbé with beard removed [from shellfish]
ébouillanté scalded
écaillé with scales removed
échalote shallot
échalote brun rougeâtre reddish brown shallot
échalote grise gray shallot
échalote rose pink shallot
échalote cuisse de poulet onion [literally: chicken leg shallot]

échaudé literally: parboiled or scalded [refers to a firm cookie or biscuit that is first poached in hot water before being baked]

échaudés aveyronnais ring-shaped par-boiled orange-water biscuit

échaudés tarnais parboiled anise biscuit

échine pork cuts including the neck region and first five ribs; pork shoulder

éclade mussels cooked with pine needles [the mussels are packed closely together vertically so that the shells do not open (usually on a wet board placed on the sand of a beach); dry pine needles are placed on top and then burned; successive layers of needles are used until the mussels are cooked

éclair oblong cake [made with pâte à choux (a light pastry dough) and filled (with custard or whipped cream) then topped with chocolate or vanilla icing

éclanche shoulder of mutton

éclat fragment

écorce peel

écorce de citron lemon peel

écorce d'orange orange peel

écossaise/à la écossaise Scottish-style [typically: may include barley and root vegetables]

Écosse Scotland

écrasé crushed

écrasé de pommes de terre mashed potatoes

écrevisse crayfish
   beurre d'écrevisse shrimp paste
   bisque d'écrevisses crayfish bisque
   buisson d'écrevisses buisson (pyramid) of crayfish
   coulis d'écrevisse crawfish bisque

écrevisse à la bordelaise crayfish with white Bordeaux wine [cooked with white wine, butter, olive oil, onions, carrots, shallots, garlic, tomatoes, cognac, thyme, bay leaf, tarragon and parsley]

écrevisse à pattes rouges freshwater crayfish

écume froth; foam [once considered a defect to be removed, but now sometimes included in *nouvelle cuisine* dishes]
   crème de pétoncles et écrume de curcuma cream of scallops with turmeric foam
   soupe de moules en écume de safran mussel soup with saffron foam

écumé skimmed; with froth removed

écume de betterave glacée au marscapone iced beet foam with marscapone cheese

écureuil squirrel

édulcoré sweetened

effilé cut into thin strips; to slice thinly; flaked (almonds); with the string removed (from string beans)

effiloché shredded [for example, cabbage]

éclade/églade mussels cooked with pine needles [mussels cooked with pine needles [the mussels are packed closely together vertically so that the shells do not open (usually on a wet board

placed on the sand of a beach); dry pine needles are placed on top and then burned; successive layers of needles are used until the mussels are cooked]
eglefin small haddock
eglefin fumé smoked haddock
égouté drained
égyptienne/à l'égyptienne Egyptian style
   purée égyptienne yellow pea soup
élan elk; moose
élédone curled octopus; musky octopus
élixir elixir [herbal liqueur]
élixir du révérend Père Gaucher alcoholic elixir [based on honey and extracts of plants gathered in the local mountains such as thyme and rosemary]
elzekaria cabbage and bean soup [typically: white cabbage, onions, white beans; garlic, *espelette* pepper and vinegar]
emballé wrapped
embeurré de chou buttered cabbage
embuscade alcoholic cocktail [a mix of blackberry syrup, white wine, Calvados and beer]
émietté crumbled
émincé thinly sliced
emisole dogfish; smooth hound [small shark]
Emmental AOC Swiss cheese [commercial trademark; cow's milk; supple pale yellow cheese with holes; aged seven weeks but can be aged for eight to twelve months to take on a stronger flavor]
émondé blanched
   amande émondé blanched almond
émoule ground
   piment émoulu ground pepper
empereur emperor [marine fish]
empereur harak blackspot emperor [marine fish]
empereur miniatus trumpet emperor [marine fish]
emporter/à emporter take-away/take out
émulsion emulsion
émulsionné emulsified
en in
en cocotte in covered baking dish
en croûte wrapped in pastry and cooked [usually beef, sometimes pork]
en papillote wrapped in paper or foil
enchaud preserved pork [roast pork, pierced with garlic, preserved in goose or duck fat, sometimes with truffles]
encornet squid
encre squid ink
   à l'encre squid served in its juice
endive au jambon endive with ham [ham and endives with grated cheese and butter, covered with a *béchamel* sauce (white sauce made with butter and flour)]
endive endive; witloof
   chicorée endive chicory
endives caramélisées caramelized endives

endives rôties roasted endives
enlevé removed
enrobé coated [for example, with a sauce]
entame the outside (first) slice of beef or ham
entier/entière entire; whole
   lait entier whole milk
entolome en bouclier buckle agaric mushroom [pleasant aroma of fresh flour]
entrecôte rib steak; rib-eye, Scotch fillet, club, Delmonico [literally: between the ribs; specifically, the traditional entrecôte steak comes from between the 9th and 11th ribs]
entrecôte grillée au coeur de camembert rib-eye steak with cheese [a steak covered with finely chopped turnips and Camembert cheese]
entrecôte marchand de vin rib steak in a sauce of onion, red wine and cream
entrecôte minute minute steak
entrecôte Mère Poulard rib-eye steak with apples and Roquefort cheese sauce
entrée starter [in the US, the entrée is the main dish; however, in France, *entrée* is the "opening" dish (served after the appetizers); this is a smaller dish that precedes the main dish, which is called the *plat*]
   en entrée poultry trussed with a drumstick
entrelardé larded; studded with diced bacon
entremets cream dessert; multi-layered mousse cake
entremets side dish [literally: in-between dish]
enveloppé enveloped, wrapped
épais/épaisse thick
   crème épaisse heavy cream
   crème fraîche épaisse double cream
   crêpe épaisse flapjack; pancake
   soupe épaisse de palourdes clam chowder
   petite crêpe épaisse crumpet
épaule shoulder
épautre spelt
   pain d'épeautre spelt bread
épepiné seeded; cored; with stone removed (peach, cherry, etc.)
éperlan smelt [small marine fish with sweet, delicate flesh; often fried]
épi ear
   maïs en épi corn on the cob
épi de maïs ear of corn
épice spice
épicé spiced
épice moulue ground spice
épicerie grocery store
épices composées spice mix [ground basil, bay leaf, coriander, mace, peppercorns, and thyme]
épicurienne/sauce épicurienne sauce made of mayonnaise, gherkins and chutney

épigramme lamb or mutton cutlet taken from the shoulder and part of the chest [seasoned or marinated; grilled or broiled]
épinard spinach
épine loin of meat
épine-vinette barberry [ripe red berries can be made into preserves; unripe green berries can be pickled and used as capers]
épluché peeled
épluchures peelings
épulché peeled
équille small eel that buries itself in the sand; boney [almost always fried]
erable sugar maple
   sirop d'erable maple syrup
eriphie small furry Mediterrannean crab
ésaü containing lentils
escabèche sauce or marinade for preserving sardines or other seafood
   sauce escabèche sauce [made with garlic, red chili pepper, carrots, onions, vinegar, and possibly tomato purée; poured over grilled sardines, cooked mussels, tuna or served cold on toast, tapas or steamed vegetables]
escalope boneless cutlet
escalope de dinde turkey cutlet
escalope de dinde à la normande turkey cutlet [usually cooked with white wine, butter, tarragon butter, mushrooms, cream; a variation might use onions, cider and Calvados]
escalope de veau veal cutlet
escalope de veau Comtoise veal cutlet [typically: cooked with local veal, Comté cheese, cream, butter and white wine]
escalope de veau vallée d'Auge veal cutlet [typically: sautéed with cream, ham, mushrooms and apples]
escalope panée breaded cutlet
escalopine cutlet
escaoudoun landais pork stew [typically: consists of *porc noir de Gascogne* (pork loin of the black pig of Gasgogne), sweet white wine, onions, leeks, garlic, bouquet garni, Madeira, Armagnac and goose or duck fat]
escargot cooked land snail [Helix pomatia, Helix aspersa (*petit-gris*), Helix lucorum; usually served as an appetizer; the digestive systems of the live snails are purged for several days on a diet of ground cereals before they are cooked, usually in garlic, butter and parsley]
escargot à la bourguignonne snails in garlic-parsley butter
escargot à la provencale cooked snail of Provence [Helix aspers (*petit-gris*); typically: accompanied by garlic mayonnaise or a tomato sauce]
escargot chagriné snail [Helix aspers: *escargot petit-gris*]
escargot de Bourgogne Burgundy snail
escargot de mer periwinkle; winkle [sea mollusk with a spiral shell; boiled or raw]

escargot gros blanc de Champagne large white snail of Champagne [Helix pomatia]
escargot petit-gris little gray snail
escarole chicory
espadon swordfish
espagnole/sauce espagnole brown veal stock thickened with a brown roux [considered to be one of the five "mother" sauces; tomato purée may be added]
espelette AOC chili; pepper
   piment d'espelette chili pepper [dried and used whole or ground into a hot powder; used to flavor Bayonne ham]
espresso Italian coffee [made by forcing boiling water through fine coffee grounds; concentrated coffee with a foam on top; used as the base for caffè latte, cappuccino, caffè macchiato, caffè mocha and caffè Americano]
esquimau au yaourt yoghurt sorbet on a stick
esquinade spider crab
essence essence; extract
essence de café coffee extract
essence de citron lemon extract; lemon oil
estocafic dried cod [traditionally cooked with olive oil, peppers, leeks, onions, garlic, potatoes, tomatoes, brandy and bouquet garni]
estoficado codfish stew [made with tomatoes, onions, garlic, olive oil and seasonings]
estofinade potato and dried fish [dried cod or haddock with potatoes, eggs, cream and walnut oil]
estouffade a rich brown stock [typically: beef shin bones, veal knuckles, raw ham, pork rind, carrots, onions, parsley, thyme, bay leaves and garlic]
estouffade beef or pork pot roast [in stock or wine with vegetables or beans]
estouffade de boeuf beef stew with pigs' trotters
estouffade du trissu potato sausage casserole [with onion, garlic and white wine]
estouffat de marcassin à la bière young wild boar cooked in beer
estragon tarragon
esturgeon sturgeon [sturgeon eggs are called *caviar*]
étouffat beef or pork pot roast
étouffé/à l'étouffée steamed; braised or simmered without browning
étrille crab; velvet swimming crab [small crab with thin meat, but quite delicious]
étuvée/à l'étuvée braised
exocet flying fish [rare; has delicate flesh]
express/café express small black coffee
extra very special
extra fin extra fine (chocolate)
extra fort very strong
extrait extract
façon way
   à ma façon in my way; in my fashion

fagot pork liver pâté [minced pork liver and pork fat cooked in lard]
faine beechnut
faisan pheasant
  coq faisan cock pheasant
  poule faisane hen pheasant
faisandeau young pheasant
fait maison house-made; homemade
falculelle baked *brocciu* (sheep's milk cheese), egg yolk and sugar
falette/fallette breast of mutton or lamb [typically: stuffed with spinach, chard, garlic and onion and cooked with carrots, sausage or ham, tomatoes and white beans]
fallue a desert brioche often served with rice pudding
faluche soft white bread eaten for breakfast with butter and jam or later as a snack with butter, cheese or brown sugar
fane de carotte carrot top
fane de radis radish top
fanchette small puff pastry tart with pastry-cream filling and meringue
fanchonette small cream-filled puff pastry tart topped with meringue
far rum flavored tart or flan
far thick, baked pancake
far à l'oseille sorrel quiche-like pie made with sorrel leaves, spinach, onions, herbs, butter and eggs
far breton a thick baked pancake with prunes or other dried fruits, similar to *clafoutis*; dark rum may be added
far breton prune custard flan
far du Poitou spinach custard quiche
farce forcemeats [a mixture of different raw or cooked foods, often finely minced, usually seasoned and sometimes bound with breading]
farce stuffing
farce dure a kind of potato dumpling the size of a fist [typically: grated raw potatoes are mixed with boiled mashed potatoes, garlic and parsley and formed into a ball which is cooked in a pot of water; may sometimes be stuffed with a piece of sausage or bacon]
farci/farcie stuffed; deviled
  blanc de dinde farci stuffed turkey breast
  blanc de poulet farci stuffed chicken breast
  magret de canard farci stuffed duck breast
  poitrine d'agneau farci stuffed lamb breast
  tomate farcie stuffed tomato
farcidure a kind of potato dumpling the size of a fist [typically: grated raw potatoes are mixed with boiled mashed potatoes, garlic and parsley and formed into a ball which is cooked in a pot of water; may sometimes be stuffed with a piece of sausage or bacon]
farcis stuffed vegetables [vegetables such as tomatoes, zucchini (courgette), onions, artichokes, peppers, cabbage and eggplant

(aubergine) stuffed with meat or sausage, bread crumbs and spices; served hot or cold]

farçons/farcouns mashed potatoes baked with eggs and herbs

farçon au cerfeuil baked grated potatoes with chervil [typically: potatoes, eggs, milk, bacon, onions, shallots, raisins, cheese, seasonings and chervil]

farçous/farçous de l'Aveyron fried hash/pancakes typically made with cooked chopped chard and sausage, seasoned with onion, garlic or chives, and parsley, bound together with egg and bread or flour

farée bacon-stuffed cabbage

farinade a dish made with grated or chopped potatoes and eggs mixed with flour and milk or cream cooked in a pan like a very large thick potato pancake

farinade a kind of baked gruel [rye flour or chestnut flour, potatoes, shallots and cheeses enclosed in foil or floured cloth and baked]

farine flour

farinette pancake [sweet or savory]

farofa toasted cassava flour mixture

faséole kidney bean

faubonne puréed vegetable soup

   crème faubonne cream for white bean soup

   potage crème faubonne white bean soup

fausse/faux false, fake

fausse tortue mock turtle

faux-filet sirloin steak

favorite favorite

   à la favorite garnished with asparagus tips [and sometimes *pâté de foie gras* and truffles]

   à la favorite garnished with artichoke hearts, potatoes and celery

   potage à la favorite asparagus soup

   salade à la favorite asparagus salad with truffles and crayfish

favouille very small dark green crab used in soups and bisques

fayot dry bean [colloquial term]

fechun cabbage rolls stuffed with pork

feijoa small South American fruit used in preserves and sorbets; tastes like strawberries or pineapple

fenouil fennel

fenugrec fenugreek

féra freshwater fish related to salmon [light, delicate flesh; found in Lake Geneva, Switzerland]

ferme literally "farm" [can mean "free range"]

   de ferme farm-made

fermé closed

fermier farm-made

fermière farm-wife style

   potage fermière buttery vegetable soup

feta goat cheese, Greek style

feu fire, flame

   au feu de bois cooked in a wood fire oven

feuille leaf
feuille de bananier banana palm leaf
feuille de chêne curly leaf lettuce; oakleaf lettuce
feuille de vigne farci stuffed grape leaf
feuille de laurier bay leaf
feuille de vigne vine leaf; grape leaf
feuilletage puff pastry; flaky pastry
feuilleté flaky
    pâte feuilletée flaky pastry; puff pastry; savory pastry
feuillete leaf/flake
feuilleté au fromage cheese puff pastry
feuilleté au jambon ham puff pastry
feuilleté au camembert puff pastry with Camembert cheese
feuilleté aux pommes à la normande puff pastry with apples
feuilleté d'andouille de Vire au camembert au lait cru sausage and raw-milk Camembert cheese puff pastry
feuilleté de poularde riviera chicken pie
feuilleton thin, flattened veal cutlet rolls stuffed with ham and mushrooms
fève broad bean; fava bean
fève de cacao cocoa bean
fève de cacaoyer cocoa bean
fèves au lard baked navy beans with bacon
fèves de chantier baked white beans with bacon
fèves germinées bean sprouts
fevette small fava bean
fiadone Corsican cheesecake/tartlet [made with soft *brocciu* cheese]
ficelle string or twine
    boeuf à la ficelle beef such as tenderloin roast tied with twine (*ficelle*) and poached in a broth [the tail of the string is used to lower the beef into the pot and retrieve it when it has cooked]
ficelle du pays de Caux apple omelet flambé [the apple-filled omelet is sprinkled with sugar then flambéed with Calvados]
ficelle picarde ham and mushroom crêpe with melted Gruyère cheese on top
figaro/sauce figaro a hollandaise sauce with tomato purée and minced parsley; goes well with fish or chicken
figatelli smoked lamb's or pig's liver sausage [long and thin; eaten raw or grilled]
figue de barbarie prickly pear
figue fig
figue de Barbarie prickly pear
figue de Solliès Solliès fig [purple-black skin; firm, supple strawberry-red flesh; aromas of watermelon, strawberry and other red fruits; sweet to tangy taste]
filet fillet
    contre-filet sirloin
faux filet sirloin
filet américain raw minced steak; tartar
filet de boeuf beef fillet [fillet mignon]
filet de canard duck tenderloin

filet de dinde turkey tenderloin
filet de lotte monkfish fillet [firm white meat, mild flavor, sometimes compared to lobster]
filet de poisson deboned fish fillet
filet de rougets au Pineau blanc des charentes [fillets of red mullet with potatoes and white wine cream sauce
filet de Saxe smoked pork/bard of bacon fillet
filet de viande meat fillet [beef, veal or pork]
filet de julienne de Saint-Malo fillet of ling [salt water fish with white flesh]
filet de sole à la normande Normandy style fillet of sole [many variations exist, but most of them include white wine and a white sauce and may include cider]
filet mignon (pork) fillet mignon; pork fillet [literally "cute fillet" or "dainty fillet"; on menus in France, *filet mignon* often refers to pork rather than beef; *filet de boeuf* refers to beef fillet mignon]
fin de siècle/pomme de terre fin de siècle a variety of white potato with smooth yellow skin
fin gras du Mézenc AOP fattened beef [the heifers are fattened on natural hay from local mountain meadows]
financier small sponge cake [resembles a gold brick; made with egg whites, flour, powdered sugar, browned butter and ground almonds or almond flavoring]
financière literally: financial
  à la financière financier-style [with kidneys, cockscombs, truffles, mushrooms and olives]
fine champagne quality cognac brandy liqueur [a blend of *Grande Champagne Cognac* (at least 50%) and *Petite Champagne Cognac*]
fine de claire very high quality oyster
fines herbes fine herbs [non-pungent herbs, usually fresh chervil, chives, parsley and tarragon]
fistuline beefsteak mushroom
flageolet thin, flat kidney-type bean; green shell bean
flamande Flemish-style
  salade flamande potato salad with Belgian endive and onions
flamande typically: stuffed cabbage with carrots, turnips and potatoes
flambé flamed; served in flaming brandy or other liquor
flamiche leek tart [one of the most iconic dishes of Picardy; sometimes includes *Maroilles* or other strong local cheese]
flammkuche a pizza-like tart [thin bread dough covered with thick cream or cottage cheese and topped with bacon and raw onion rings and quickly baked in a very hot oven]
flamri semolina flan: Moroccan custard pie with almonds
flamusse apple flan/pie [sliced apples baked with eggs, cream and sugar]
flan flan [open pie which can be sweet or savory]
flan halibut [flat fish with delicate flesh]
flan à la châtaigne chestnut flan [chestnut flour or chestnut jam baked with eggs, cream, sugar baked in a mold]
flan limousin baked pancake-type dessert with fruit or nuts

flan normand/tarte normande Normandy-style apple tart [typically: sliced apples, almonds and sugar and creamy egg custard with a caramelized crust]
flanchet beef flank; veal flank
flaugnarde thick baked pancake, similar to a *clafoutis*, but with apples (or sometimes pears, plums or blueberries)
flaune a type of pastry in the form of a pie [typically: a sweet pie crust filled with mixture of soft creamy cheese, cream and sugar and flavored with orange flower]
flétan halibut; flounder
flétan blanc Atlantic halibut
flétan noir Greenland halibut; Greenland turbot
fleur flower
fleur de courgette zucchini/courgette flower
fleur de lait (raw) cream [cream that forms on the surface of raw milk]
fleur de sel crystalized salt
fleurette/crème fleurette light cream; low-fat cream
fleuron small puff pastry used for decoration
flip a drink made with eggs beaten into alcohol
flip warm alcoholic drink made with equal parts sweet cider and Calvados, sweetened with honey
flondre flounder
florentin biscuit/cookie made with chopped nuts and candied fruit
florentine/à la florentine with a garnish of spinach
flûte thin loaf of bread, smaller than a baguette
foie liver
    pâté de foie liver pâté
    pâté de foie gras fat liver pâté
foie de génisse cow's liver
foie de poulet chicken liver
foie de veau calf's liver
foie de veau à la bordelaise veal liver in white wine
foie de veau moissonnière fried calf's liver with onions, herbs and red wine
foie de volaille chicken liver
foie gras literally: fat liver [foie gras; made from liver of goose or duck fattened by force feeding; may be whole, or as a *mousse* (purée containing a minimum of 55% foie gras; beaten to incorporate air bubbles) *parfait* (very smooth meat paste) or as a *pâté* (meat ground to a spreadable consistency); usually accompanies steak or other food item; the flavor should be rich, delicate and buttery]
foie gras au pineau des charentes duck or goose liver with red or white wine [liver gently cooked with salt, pepper, sugar and wine (and possibly cognac) then refrigerated and served cold]
foie gras en croûte foie gras in a pastry shell
foie haché chopped liver
foie-de-boeuf beefsteak mushroom
foin hay
    jambon au foin ham cooked in hay [a lightly brined cured ham is nested in hay a large vessel to which water, thyme, bay leaves,

cloves and juniper berries are added, then simmered (not boiled) until cooked through; served hot or cold]
foncé dark
fond stock [*fond* literally means foundation or base; made by cooking meats and vegetables for several hours in liquid and then filtering the liquid]
fond blanc stock from white meats and aromatic vegetables, cooked without browning them first and then filtered
fond brun stock of meat bones and vegetables which are browned before liquid is added to the pot
fond brun lié a clear brown stock with arrow-root or other binder
fond de marmite white beef stock
fond de veau veal stock
fond de volaille poultry stock
fondant bittersweet chocolate
fondant melting; slow-cooked
    carottes fondantes tender cooked carrots [slowly cooked on low heat a long time (sometimes with garlic, rosemary, leeks or other aromatics) until they are very soft, or in some cases, almost melted and candied]
    pommes de terre fondantes pan roasted potatoes [peeled potatoes cut into uniform cylinders and browned in oil (or duck or goose fat or butter) until they are crisp on all sides]
fondant au chocolat chocolate dessert similar to brownies [a mixture of chocolate, butter, sugar, flour and eggs baked together]
fondant pâtissier pastry icing [a sugar concoction for coating éclairs, cakes and various other pastries; chocolate or other flavoring or coloring may be added]
fondu creusois melted Camembert cheese sauce [melted cheese with cream, egg yolk and flour; traditionally, fried potatoes are dipped into this fondue; often accompanied by an omelet]
fondu/fondue literally: melted [refers to a dish in which meat, bread or fruit is dipped into a hot sauce or broth]
fromage fondu cheese spread
fondue melted
fondue au chocolat aux fruits a dessert in which pieces of fruit are dipped into warm, melted chocolate
fondue au fromage melted cheese flavored with wine, into which bits of bread are dipped
fondue bourguignonne a meat dish in which pieces of raw meat are dipped into a pot of hot oil; the cooked meat is accompanied by various sauces such as mayonnaise or béarnaise
fondue Bresse small cubes of chicken are dipped into a pot of hot broth, then dipped in egg yolk and covered with breadcrumbs
fondue chinoise thin slices of beef dipped into a pot of hot broth, then dipped in a variety of sauces or relishes
fondue neufchâteloise a fondue of melted Gruyère and Emmental cheeses with white wine, cayenne pepper and kirsch into which cubes of bread are dipped
fondue normande Normandy-style melted cheese sauce [made with local soft cheeses (rather than the usual hard cheeses) and

local milk and cream; the fondue pot is rubbed with shallots rather than with garlic; Calvados may be added to the sauce; the sauce may be sprinkled with dry cider]
fondue savoyarde Savoie fondue [three local cheeses melted with wine and garlic, served with pieces of bread]
fondue vigneronne winemaker fondue [meat, seafood and vegetables are dipped into boiling white wine to which chicken stock and spices have been added; the food items thus cooked are then dipped into various sauces before being eaten; when everything has been consumed, it is customary to place an egg yolk into a ramekin (one for each participant) and pour the boiling wine over it to cook the egg]
forestière wild mushroom, bacon and potato garnish
fortuné tiny cake with icing sugar, topped with half a cherry
fouace Aveyronnaise sweet bread/brioche [ingredients vary by region, but generally include flour, eggs, yeast, milk (or cream) and orange flower water and may have candied fruits; the baked bread is sprinkled with powdered sugar]
fouasse sweet brioche bun
foudjou a dish made with pungent goat cheese, garlic and brandy; served with potatoes
fouetté whipped
   crème fouettée whipped cream
fougasse focaccia [a flat bread cooked on a fireplace or a fire under the ashes; similar to pizza]
fougasse sweet bread flavored with almonds and orange-flower water
fougasse aux grattons de canard focaccia bread with duck cracklings/scratchings
fougasse aux grattons d'oie focaccia bread with goose cracklings/scratchings [goose cracklings are similar to pork cracklings/rinds/scratchings; the rind and fat are are fried to make them edible, often as a snack]
fougasse d'Aigues-Mortes sweet brioche made with brioche dough, sugar and orange flower
fougasettes olive oil bread flavored with orange flower water
fougère des mers sea mustard [seaweed with a sweet, subtle flavor]
four oven
   au four doux in a low temperature oven
   petit four tiny cake; savory pastry; miniature appetizer
fourré filled
fourré à la crème cream filled
foyot/sauce foyot foyot sauce [a variation of *béarnaise* sauce in which concentrated meat glaze is added to give the sauce a rich meaty flavor]
   côte de veau foyot veal cutlet in a batter of Gruyère cheese, breadcrumbs and butter
fraîche/frais fresh
   crème fraîche soured cream cultured with *lactobacillus*
   crème fraîche épaisse thick soured cream
   crème fraiche liquid thin soured cream

frais/fraîche fresh
fraise strawberry
fraise de Beaulieu-sur-Dordogne high quality strawberry
fraise de bois wild strawberry
fraise de Plougastel Plougastel strawberry [early, sweet, fragrant berry]
fraise du Périgord IGP high quality strawberry
fraisier sponge cake filled with butter cream and strawberries
fraisier musquée musk strawberry
fraises Romanoff strawberries soaked in liqueur and orange juice and topped with whipped cream
framboise raspberry
   confiture de framboise raspberry jam
   liqueur de framboise raspberry liqueur
framboise raspberry beer/liqueur [Belgian Lambic beer; fermented using raspberries; usually served in a small goblet or champagne-type glass; quite sweet, though some tart varieties exist; may seem more like a sweet wine than a beer]
framboise raspberry brandy; raspberry *eau de vie*
framboisier sponge cake filled with raspberries
française/à la française French-style [may refer to a garnish of spinach and potatoes or asparagus and lettuce]
francillon/salade francillon a salad of potatoes, mussels and truffles with white wine vinaigrette
frangipane frangipane [creamy almond pastry]
frappe triangular doughnut/fritter [made with flour, sugar, butter, eggs, yeast and orange zest; fried and then dusted with sugar]
frappé chilled or frozen
   boisson frappé chilled/iced drink
   champagne frappé champagne on ice
   café frappé iced coffee
fréchure casserole or stew of pig lungs/organs
fregola/fregula pasta from Sardinia [similar to Israeli couscous]
freneuse/crème freneuse purée of turnips and potatoes thinned with milk or a white sauce
freneuse/potage freneuse creamy turnip and potato soup
frescati sugar crust dessert pastry [a tall cylinder of pastry with a golden brown crust and sugar icing, usually crowned with cherries; consists of a layer of sponge cake topped with candied grapes soaked in rum, then a layer of thick, soft Italian meringue; the whole pastry is coated with a coffee sugar icing]
fressure pig (or lamb) offal [liver, heart, lungs, spleen, brains; literally: the pluck, i.e., the parts that are plucked up after the "more noble" meats have been taken]
fretin small fish (any kind) for frying
friand small puff pastry with pork sausage (and/or cheese)
friandisse sweet; candy
fricadelle a "meatball" in the shape of a sausage
fricandeau coarsely chopped pork loin and pork liver, seasoned and bound with egg, then formed into balls or patties and baked
fricandeau fricandeau [sliced veal, beef or fish that is pounded then braised, often with white wine, until extremely tender]

fricaseé braised
fricassée fricassee [a dish made by sautéing cut-up meat (but not letting it brown) then simmering it in a liquid to make a sauce]
fricassée au tourain traditional soup of pork or goose lard and sorrel with bacon and onions]
fricassée d'anguilles eel fricassee
fricassée de chapon, truffes et cidre capon (male chicken) sautéed with truffles and cider
Fricassée de pintade au calvados et aux deux pommes guinea fowl fricassee with Calvados and two apples
fricaude pig offal stew
fricot slang for fricassée
fricot des barques beef stew [traditionally made with anchovies, garlic, onions, and olive oil; often served with potatoes, carrots and tomatoes]
frisée curly; endive; curly lettuce
frisée aux lardons curly lettuce salad with bacon
frit/frite fried
frites French fries; thin potato chips
friton pork or goose cracklings/fried rind
friton pork pâté spread [canned/potted]
fritot savory fritter [food that is first cooked or marinated, then coated with a batter and fried until crispy]
friture deep fried
friture de goujons fried gudgeon [very small freshwater fish]
friture de la Marne fried gudgeon [very small freshwater fish]
frivolité small savories served at the start of a formal dinner
frivolités testicles
froid/froide cold
fromage cheese
    assiette à fromage cheese plate
    croûte au fromage cheese on toast
fromagé with grated cheese added
fromage à crème cream cheese
fromage à la croûte Welsh rarebit
fromage à pâté semi-hard cheese
fromage à pâte dur hard cheese
fromage à pâte molle soft cheese; un-pressed, unheated; the pulp is then smooth or flowing at full maturation
fromage affiné aged cheese
fromage aux noix cheese with walnuts [a mixture of processed cow's milk cheeses decorated with walnuts]
fromage blanc soft white runny cheese; low fat (although cream may be added for flavor); tangy; similar to yoghurt
fromage bleu blue cheese
fromage d'alpage cheese produced at mountain dairies at the height of summer milking
fromage de chèvre goat cheese
fromage de Laguiole AOC cheese [raw cow's milk; cows must graze on pasturage for at least four months a year to give the cheese its fragrance; dry rind, white to gray to amber brown

with age; firm ivory to yellow cheese, velvety texture, dense, creamy, sharp and tangy with the perfume of wild flowers]
fromage de lait de vache cow's milk cheese
fromage de tête brawn; head cheese [not a dairy cheese, but a terrine (meat preserved in aspic) made with the meat from the head of calf, pig, sheep or cow]
Fromage de Munster AOC cheese [cow's milk; washed light brick-red rind; soft, supple cheese with a characterful flavor of the local *terroir*; matured two to three months; in Alsace, it is typically eaten with hot potatoes or a salad rather than with bread; in Paris, often seasoned with cumin or caraway]
Fromage des Pyrénées sheep cheese [dry rind, sometimes black; strong tasting yellow semi-hard cheese]
Fromage du Pays Basque cheese from Basque country [generally these are artisanal cheeses made from sheep's or goat's milk]
Fromage fermier de Corse artisanal cheese from Corsica [sheep's or goat's milk; hand-made on and sold by the farms where the sheep and goats are raised]
fromage fondu cheese spread
fromage frais fresh cheese [soft, often enriched with cream; similar to cottage cheese; often used as a dessert mixed with fruit, or as a substitute for cream in certain recipes]
fromage glacé ice cream in the shape of cheese
fromage maigre low-fat cheese
fromage râpé grated cheese
froment wheat
fruit fruit
fruit à l'alcool fruit preserved in brandy (*eau-de-vie*)
fruit à pain breadfruit
fruit au sirop fruit preserved in syrup
fruit au vinaigre fruit soaked or softened in vinegar
fruit candi candied fruit
fruit confit fruit preserved in sugar
fruit confit d'Apt candied fruit from Apt [fruit glazed with sugar; used to decorate cakes]
fruit cuit stewed fruit
fruit de la passiflore passion fruit
fruit de la passion passion fruit
fruit déguisé literally: disguised fruit [pieces of fruit coated with caramel, almond paste or sugar icing]
fruit en conserve preserved fruit
fruit givré frosted fruit [fruit such as oranges that can be hollowed out; the pulp is frozen into a sort of sherbet and returned to the hollow shell]
fruit givré fruit frosted with sugar [fruits and berries dipped in beaten egg whites and rolled in crystalized sugar]
fruit glacé candied fruit
fruit Melba ice cream and fruit
fruit rafraichi fruit soaked and chilled in alcohol
fruit sec dried fruit

fruits de mer shellfish such as oysters, shrimp, lobster, crab, prawns, crayfish, mussels, scallops or clams [oysters are not considered by some to be *fruits de mer*]
   pâtes aux fruits de mer pasta with seafood
fruits rafraîchis fruit salad
fueillleté flaky
   pâte fueillletée pastry; flaky pastry
fugu pufferfish [highly toxic internal organs, small amounts of which create a sensation on the tongue that is sought after by connoiseurs]
fumage smoking
fumaison smoking [a way to preserve food and impart flavor [a treatment for raw, dried ham, partially cooked meats, cooked meats such as sausages, and fish]
fumé smoked
   boeuf fumé pastrami
   goût de fumé smoky taste
   hareng fumé kipper; smoked herring
   jambon fumé désossé daisy ham
   jambon fumé smoked ham
   lard fumé smoked bacon
   poisson fumé smoked fish
   saumon fumé smoked salmon
fumet aroma; aromatic liquid
fumet de poisson a concentrated fish stock made by adding extra fish and/or fish bones to a broth along with white wine, shallots, onion, *bouquet garni* and peppercorns and then straining the liquid and reducing it to make it thicker
fumet de champignon a concentrated mushroom stock made by adding extra mushrooms to a broth along with other ingredients such as red wine, shallots, cream, butter, chives or chervil and then straining the liquid and cooking it down to make it thicker
gâche pastry-like pancake
gâche raisin bread
gâche a kind of *brioche*/bun
galabart blood sausage/black pudding [pork organ meat]
galanga galangal [similar to ginger; used in Asian cuisine]
galantine cold appetizer of boned white meat or fish, stuffed, poached and molded in gelatin
galapian d'Apt cake [made with flour milled in Apt, ground almonds, eggs, sugar, lavender honey and candied fruit]
galétous thick buckwheat crêpe [as appetizers, cut up and served warm with savory toppings; as desserts, topped with fresh sweet cheese, preserves or honey]
galette savory buckwheat crêpe
galette wafer; hardtack; biscuit
galette sweet cake or biscuit made from puff pastry, almond paste, potatoes, shortbread or batter
galette en pâte d'amande du Havre almond pastry
galette bretonne savory crêpe in Haute-Bretagne; butter cookie in Basse-Bretagne
galette comtoise flaky pasty/brioche flavored with orange flower

galette de blé noir buckwheat pancake
galette de maïs corn pancake
galette de Normandie Normandy-style buckwheat pancake
galette de pomme de terre potato pancake
galette de pommes de Gacé apple pancake
galette de riz soufflé rice cake
galette pancake [made with buckwheat flour]
galette de sarrasin buckwheat pancake
galette feuilletée à la frangipane pastry made with almond paste between two flaky pastry layers
galette pur beurre shortbread biscuit
galette végétarienne vegetarian cake or bread
galette à la pâte d'amande pastry made with almond paste between two flaky pastry layers
galette briarde sugar crust pastry made with Brie cheese
galette fécampoise savory flaky pastry made with salt cod and potatoes
galette-saucisse hot grilled sausage wrapped in a thin cold buckwheat pancake
galinette tub gurnard [fish related to mullet; very boney]
gamba jumbo shrimp
ganache a rich chocolate mixture [made by pouring heated cream over chopped chocolate, then blended until smooth; used as a filling or icing]
ganga pintailed grouse [said to have delicate flesh]
garbure cabbage or vegetable soup with ham and bacon
garçon boy [in the old days, a waiter was a *garçon*, but it is considered rude to use that term today; instead, it is better to say *monsieur* or *madame* to get the wait person's attention]
gardiane/gardianne Camargue bull meat stew made with red wine
gardon golden shiner minnow; freshwater roach [small fish with fine flesh; pan fried (*poêlé*) or deep fried (*frit*)]
gargouillau thick baked pancake with pears
gargouillou colorful salad of vegetables, leaves, fruits and flowers
Garhiofilatum spicy white wine [an ancient method from the twelfth century; consists of white wine to which is added honey, ginger, cinnamon, cardamom, cloves and valerian root]
Gariguette/fraises Gariguette high-quality strawberry
garni garnished; vegetable side dish or accompaniment
garniture garnish [decorative element]
garniture accompaniment; side dish; filling such as rice or vegetables
   servie avec garniture served with vegetables
garniture à pizza pizza topping
garniture de légumes vegetable accompaniment
garniture de pain sandwich filling
garniture de tarte pie filling
gasconnade roast leg of lamb
gastronomie moléculaire culinary achievements based on a scientific study of the chemical and physical properties and processes involved in cooking [a reliance on non-traditional tools and utensils such as liquid nitrogen, syringes, tabletop

distilleries, as well as food chemicals such as carrageenan and xanthan; often results in unorthodox concoctions such as *faux caviar*, transparent ravioli and liquid pea spheres; also called *gastronomie moléulaire et physique*]
garot a barely-leavened bread made of wheat and oatmeal flour
gaspacho gazpacho [cold soup with tomatoes, cucumbers, onions and sweet peppers]
gastronome/à la gastronome a garnish of truffles and other mushrooms in a champagne sauce
gâteau cake; bun
gâteau au fromage cheesecake
gâteau au vin blanc cake made with white wine
gâteau au vin rouge cake made with red wine
gâteau aux amandes almond cake
gâteau aux mirabelles plum cake
gâteau basque Basque cake made with flour, butter, sugar, almond powder, eggs, and either pastry cream or cherry jam
gâteau battu tall cylindrical yellow cake made with many egg yolks
gâteau breton round, soft, crumbly cake with a golden sugared crust
gâteau creusois hazelnut cake
gâteau de ménage sweet, rich butter bun; may have chocolate chips
gâteau de riz rice pudding dessert
gâteau de semoule semolina pudding
gâteau fouetté de Saint-Lô cake flavored with Calvados
gâteau nantais cake flavored with almonds and rum
gâteau Paris-Brest baked ring of puff pastry filled with whipped cream and topped with sliced almonds
gâteau Pithiviers two layers of puff pastry with a filling of cream, rum and almonds
gâteau sec literally: dry cake [small plain cake; sweet biscuit]
gâteau St. Honoré St. Honoré cake [a classic French dessert: a small round puff pastry topped with a ring of puff pastry filled with crème chiboust (a very light pastry cream) and finished with whipped cream; named after the patron saint of bakers and pastry chefs]
gaudes corn flour porridge [roasted corn flour with milk]
gaufre de Liège sugar-vanilla waffle
gaufre waffle
gaufre à la chantilly waffle with whipped cream
gaufre au chocolat waffle with chocolate topping
gaufre au sucre waffle with sugar
gaufre de Bruxelles rectangular waffle [the batter is made with whipped egg whites and baking powder, flour, butter, sugar and milk; crunchy on the outside and soft in the middle]
gaufre fourrée lilloises vanilla waffle [may also be flavored with rum]
gaufrette thin biscuit used to make ice cream wafers
gaufrette a wafer of fried potato resembling a waffle
gavot fried "ravioli" filled with cooked and mashed potatoes and leeks [variations may include ingredients such as cheese,

spinach, minced meat, or sweet fillings such as prunes, apples or raspberries]
gavotte thin, crisp, lacy crêpe that is folded into prism-like rolls
gayette baked ball of finely diced pig liver, bacon and pork
gayette arlésienne pork liver baked with bacon and pork belly; eaten cold, thickly sliced
gazeuse/gazeux sparkling; carbonated
   boisson gazeuse fizzy drink
   eau gazeuse sparkling water
gelatin jello
gélatine gelatine
gelée jelly; gelatin; aspic
   oeuf en gelée hard-boiled egg in aspic
gelée royale royal bee's jelly
gelifié jellied
gélinotte hazel grouse
gendarme smoked, dried sausage
gendarme red herring [served as an appetizer]
Génépi aromatic liqueur [similar to absinthe; made from Alpine wormwood (*Artemisia*) which is steeped in vodka or clear grain alcohol]
génoise a type of sponge cake
   à la génoise Genoa-style [with tomato sauce]
génoise/spaghetti à la génoise spaghetti with minced beef and tomato sauce
georgette/crêpe georgette pancake with pineapple, apricot jam and powdered sugar [may also have rum or kirsch]
germes de soja bean sprouts
germiny/potage germiny sorrel soup
géssier gizzard
gianduja chocolate-hazelnut spread
gibassié/gibassier focaccia-type bread made with olive oil
gibelotte rabbit fricassée [in wine with potatoes and onions]
gibier game [animals or fowl]
gibier à plume game bird
gibier à poil game animal
gibier d'eau waterfowl
gibelotte game meat stewed in white wine; game meat fricassee
gigolette stew
gigolette de canard leg of duck; duck stew
gigolette de dinde leg of turkey; turkey stew
gigolette de lapin leg of rabbit; rabbit stew
gigot joint; leg of lamb or deer
gigot d'agneau leg of lamb
gigot d'agneau à la couronne d'ail leg of lamb roasted with many cloves of garlic, white wine and brandy
gigot d'Yvetot boiled leg of lamb served with a white caper sauce
gigot de chevreuil haunch of venison; rack of venison; leg of venison
gigot de mer braised or roasted monkfish
gigot de mouton leg of mutton
gigot pascal Easter lamb or kid

gigot pourri leg of lamb roasted with many cloves of garlic
gigue/gigue de chevreuil haunch of venison
gimblette ring-shaped bun [the dough is sweetened with anise, sugar and orange flower, then boiled before it is baked]
gingembre ginger
gingérine watermelon with pale green flesh used for making preserves
girasol sunflower
girelle wrasse [marine fish]
girofle clove [the spice, not "clove of garlic"]
   clou de girofle clove; small button of clove
girolle golden chanterelle [*Cantharellus cibarius*; orange-yellow, meaty, funnel-shaped; has a fruity (apricot-like) and somewhat earthy aroma; mild, peppery or spicy taste; used in sautés, soufflés, cream sauces and soups]
giraumon type of pumpkin from the West Indies [used in salads, in soups or puréed]
gîte lamb shank
gîte-gîte shin beef
gîte à la noix topside of beef; bottom round of beef; thick flank of veal
givré sprinkled with sugar crystals
glaçage icing; frosting; egg glaze
glace ice; ice-cream
glace de poisson fish glaze
glace de viande clear meat glaze or stock
glacé iced; chilled; glossy
glaçon ice cube
   avec des glaçons on the rocks
gloria coffee with alcohol
glutamate de sodium MSG
gluten gluten
   sans gluten gluten-free
glycérie sweet woodruff
gnocchi thick, soft dough dumpling bound with egg; may have cheese, potoato or other ingredients added
gnocchis à la parisienne gnocchi made with Emmental or Gruyère cheese
goberge saithe; pollock or pollack
gobie gobie [small salt-water fish]
godinette aperitif based on white wine, brandy, strawberries and sugar
gogue dried blood sausage [contains bacon, cream, onions, beet leaves and eggs]
gombo okra
gomphide edible mushroom [tart flavor; the outer slimy coating must be washed off before eating]
gonelle blenny; gunnel fish [eel-like fish]
grosette apple turnover
gougère cheese puff [made with pâte à choux (a light pastry dough) and flavored with strong cheese such as Gruyère or Comté, often served as an appetizer]

gougère savory puff pastry filled with a sauce and fish, chicken, mushrooms, kidneys, etc.
gougnette sugar-coated doughnut
goujon gudgeon [freshwater catfish]
goujon strip of fish (usually sole) cut on the diagonal; may also refer to strip of chicken meat
goujonnette small gudgeon [freshwater catfish]
goujonnière ruff fish [freshwater fish similar to pike-perch]
goumeau a thick puff-pastry pie or cake [made with flour and yeast, milk, orange flower, eggs and cream; sprinkled with white or brown sugar after baking]
gourin aux pruneaux tripe cooked with prunes
gousse d'ail clove of garlic
goût taste, liking
  à votre goût to your liking
goûter afternoon snack time
goutte drop
goyave guava fruit
goyère de Valenciennes a thin quiche-like dish consisting of *Maroilles* cheese and cottage cheese, butter and eggs, baked on a flat round yeast bread
graine seed
graine de cassis blackcurrant
graine de groseille redcurrant
graine de moutarde mustard seed
graisse fat; lard
graisse d'oie goose fat
graisse de porc pork fat
graisseron crackling; fried rind
gramolate sorbet made with frozen sugar syrup; served between courses
grand crème double espresso with milk
grand cru superior wine from the best vineyards
grand-duc/au-grand duc garnish made with asparagus, truffles, crayfish and a mornay sauce [especially used for chicken]
Grand Marnier Grand Marnier [orange flavored cognac liqueur, 40% alcohol; the cordon rouge (red ribbon) is the original]
grandmère grandmother [refers to a style of cooking which usually involves onions, bacon, mushrooms and potatoes; may also refer to croûtons in scrambled eggs or pasta in vegetable soup]
grande raie-guitare guitar fish [marine fish; looks like a cross between a shark and a ray]
grande rousette larger spotted dogfish [a kind of shark]
grande tasse mug
grande tétras wood grouse [very large game bird]
grand veneur game meat with black pepper sauce (*poivrade*) made with game stock and blood and red currant jelly
granité granita [partially frozen sugar syrup]
grâpiau thick buckwheat pancake flavored with bacon, parsley and garlic
gras/grasse fat; fatty

au gras cooked with fat; richly cooked
foie gras foie gras
sans matières grasses fat-free
gras de cuisse chicken thigh
grasset cut of beef extending from the posterior of the stomach to the lower and front end of the thigh
gras-double tripe
gratin gratin; baked until golden on top; cheese-topped dish
au gratin baked with cheese
gratin d'huîtres à la Chandivert mussels baked in a cider-cream sauce
gratin Dauphinois thin slices of potato layered with cream and cheese and baked
gratin de chou-fleur cauliflower gratin
gratin de courgette zucchini/courgette gratin
gratin de macaronis macaroni cheese bake
gratin de pommes de terre potatoes au gratin; potato cheese bake
gratiné oven browned [with a topping sauce or glaze]
gratterons fried diced pork
gratton cracklings; fried rinds [of pork, goose or duck; sometimes served warm, but usually cold]
gravenche Lake Geneva whitefish [freshwater lake fish]
gravette oyster
gravlax raw salmon
grecque/à la grecque Greek/Greek style [typically: with olive oil and lemon]
grelot thick, dry cured pork, beef (or other meat) sausage
grémille ruff fish [freshwater fish similar to pike-perch]
gremolata a condiment consisting of equal parts parsley, garlic, lemon zest and orange zest
grenaille pellet
pommes grenailles baby potatoes; new potatoes
grenade pomegranate
grenadier/grenadier de roche rock grenadier; roundnose grenadier; roundhead rat-tail [marine fish]
grenadin larded fillet of veal
grenadin de veau fermier Prince Orloff fillet of veal with chopped mushrooms and *foie gras*
grenadin de veau aux pommes fricassee of veal with cooked apples
grenadine pomegranate syrup
grenobloise/à la grenobloise Grenoble-style [typically: floured fish, fried and garnished with lemon and capers]
grenier médocain pork belly cooked in broth with garlic and African and Asian spices
grenouille frog
cuisses de grenouille frogs' legs
grenouilles comme à Boulay Boulay style frogs' legs [seasoned with parsley, shallots and lemons, breaded and sautéed in butter]
gressin bread stick
griblette pork chop

grignaudes fried shredded pork [a snack food]
grignette a kind of bread stick similar to a baguette; yoghurt is one of the ingredients
grillade grilled meat
grillade à la champagneules toasted fried ham sandwich coated with a cheese and beef fondue
grillé grilled
grillon canned meat/potted meat
gros grillon potted cooked pork belly preserved in fat; eaten cold
grillons de porc a block of pork and bacon with parsley, garlic and herbs; eaten cold on bread or thick crêpes
griotte Morello cherry
griottines cherries soaked in brandy
gris gray
   vin gris pale rosé wine
griset gray shark or black bream
griset du Ventoux gilled Ventoux mushroom [large edible mushroom with a brilliant gray cap and white stem; aroma of oyster and fresh wheat]
grive thrush [a small songbird]
grog grog; rum toddy
grog au cidre cider grog [beverage made with rum, hot milk or hot water, and cider]
grogneur croaker fish; meagre; shade-fish; corvina; salmon-basse or stone basse [similar to sea bass]
grondin/grondin galinette gurnard; sea robin [marine fish]
gros large; thick or coarse
gros lait thick, tangy, creamy milk [halfway between yoghurt and cottage cheese]
gros mollet lumpfish [marine fish; its roe is often harvested]
gros pain large crusty baguette
gros sel cooking salt; coarse salt
groseille currant
   confiture de groseille currant jam
groseille à maquereau gooseberry
groseille blanche white currant
groseille noire blackcurrant
groseille rouge redcurrant
groseille verte gooseberry
grosse large
grosse crevette king prawn [considered to be the best]
grosse palourde venus shell clam
grosses quenelles de pomme de terre large potato dumplings
grosseur/selon grosseur according to size
grouse grouse
gruau gruel
gruau d'avoine oatmeal
Gruyère AOC cheese [raw cow's milk; pressed, cooked cheese; sweet, nutty, slightly salty and creamy when young; with age, it becomes more firm, with a stronger, more complex and earthy flavor; traditionally used in French onion soup]

Gruyère de Beaufort cheese [raw cow's milk; very large, firm cheese, buttery taste with floral and herbal notes]
Gruyère de Comté AOC cheese [raw cow's milk; natural rind; semi-firm, dense, pale yellow cheese with fruity, nutty, salty, savory, smokey sweet flavor]
guai/hareng guai shotten herring
guajillo guajillo chili pepper [the dried *mirasol* chili; said to have a green tea flavor with berry overtones; somewhat spicy, tangy; slightly smoky and sweet; moderately hot]
guanaja an island of Honduras
    chocolat guanaja guanaja chocolate
    mousse guanaja guanaja mousse
guigne dark cherry-like fruit
guignette periwinkle
guignolet wild cherry liqueur
guimauve a kind of marshmallow
guinse buttermilk
guitare guitar fish [marine fish that looks like a cross between a shark and a ray]
Guyot pear [sweet, juicy fragrant flesh]
gyromitre false morel mushroom
habanero habañero chili pepper [very hot; fruity citrus-like]
haché ground (meat); chopped up
    bifteck haché beef burger
    foie haché chopped liver
    porc haché ground pork; shredded pork
    steak haché ground steak [usually served on a plate rather than on a bun]
    veau haché ground veal
    viande hachée ground meat; minced meat
haché de boeuf ground beef
haché fin finely chopped
hachis parmentier baked ground beef and mashed potatoes, usually with cheese
hachua/hachua basque braised veal with diced cured *Bayonne* ham, sweet and hot (*espelette*) peppers and onions
haddock smoked haddock
halbi a drink consisting of pears and fermented apples
hampe breast of venison
hampe de boeuf beef flank
hareng herring
hareng à l'huile herring preserved in oil
hareng bouffi bloater; lightly salted and smoked herring
hareng buckling smoked and salted herring
hareng de la Baltique/Bismark herring marinated in white wine or white wine vinegar with carrots, onions and coriander
hareng franc-saure very dry herring [stays preserved for a very long time]
hareng fumé smoked herring
hareng gendarme smoked, salted herring [the reference to *gendarme* (policeman) is perhaps because some people think that a *gendarme* is as stiff as a smoked herring]

hareng grillé sauce moutarde grilled herring in mustard sauce
hareng kipper kipper; copper-colored herring [due to being lightly smoked and salted]
hareng mariné pickled herring
hareng marinés de Honfleur herring cooked in white wine and vinegar
hareng pec freshly salted herring
hareng rollmops rollmops herring [marinated in vinegar with carrots and onions; rolled around a pickle, cold cut or piece of onion and held in place with toothpicks]
hareng salé bloater [cold-smoked, lightly-salted herring]
hareng sauce Chausey herring in Chausey sauce [a sauce made with shallots, garlic, parsley and butter]
hareng saur kipper; salted herring; red herring
haricot a stew of lamb and vegetables
haricot bean [generally refers to the dry bean unless specified otherwise, e.g., *haricot vert* (green bean, snap bean or string bean)]
haricot azuki azuki bean
haricot beurre butter bean; yellow bean
haricot blanc white bean; haricot
haricot chévrier goatherd bean; green flageolet bean
haricot coco cranberry bean
haricot cornille black-eye bean
haricot d'Espagne Spanish bean
haricot de Lima lima bean
haricot de mouton mutton stew
haricot de Soissons Soissons bean [elongated white bean with thin skin]
haricot lingot similar to a white navy bean, but with more delicate skin
haricot mange-tout string bean; snap bean [may be yellow, green or purple; when immature, the seed pod is edible]
haricot marbré red-veined bean
haricot mungo mungo bean
haricot noir black bean
haricot pinto pinto bean
haricot romain romano bean
haricot rosé pinto bean
haricot rouge kidney bean
haricot sec dried bean
haricot tarbais large white bean with thin, delicate skin, sweet flesh
haricot vert string bean; snap bean [may be yellow, green or purple; when immature, the seed pod is edible]
harira spicy North African tomato-lentil soup [typically: with chickpeas, onions, rice and small amounts of beef, lamb or chicken]
harissa hot chili paste made with a variety of hot peppers, oil (for preservation), garlic and coriander or caraway
helvelle edible mushroom [turban-top or bishop's mitre; light brown fluted cap; thin elastic flesh becomes leathery with age]

herbe herb
  fines herbes a mix of herbs typically including parsley, chives, tarragon and chervil
herbe aromatique aromatic herb
herbes de Provence a mix of aromatic herbs typical to Provence [traditionally, the mix includes thyme, savory and rosemary]
hérison de mer sea urchin [raw or lightly cooked in salt water]
hivernal/hivernale/hivernaux winter
  légumes hivernaux winter vegetables
hochpot hotpot stew [winter vegetables such as carrots, cabbage, leeks, potatoes and meat (traditionally ox tail or mutton shoulder, but now may contain other cuts)]
hollandaise/sauce hollandaise hollandaise sauce [an emulsion of clarified egg yolk, clarified butter and lemon juice; considered to be one of the five "mother" sauces]
homard lobster
  bisque de homard lobster bisque [lobster in a fine and delicate soup; a true bisque must contain *beurre de corail* (a butter flavored with a paste of crushed lobster shell)]
homard à l'américaine American-style lobster [lobster sautéed in butter with shallots, onion, celery, carrot, garlic, chopped tomatoes and white wine, then flambéed with cognac]
homard à l'amoricaine lobster cooked in oil with tomatoes, shallots, brandy and white wine]
homard à la bordelaise lobster sautéed in butter with shallots, onion, celery, carrot, garlic, chopped tomatoes and white wine, then flambéed with cognac and finished with butter, lemon juice, chervil and tarragon
homard cardinal cooked lobster with a pink lobster and truffle sauce, mushrooms, creamy parts from the head, butter and grated cheese
homardine/sauce homardine lobster sauce [typically made with lobster, carrots, onion, shallots, tomato, garlic and cream]
homard thermidor lobster thermador [grilled half lobster on a cream sauce with mustard]
houmous hummus [mashed chickpeas with tahini, olive oil, lemon juice and garlic]
hongroise Hungarian style
  à la hongroise with a sauce made with paprika or onions, tomatoes, paprika and soured cream
hors outside; excluding
hors jours fériés excluding holidays
hors-d'oeuvre appetizer; small dish [literally: apart from the main work or dish; a light dish, sometimes serving as the *entrée* (the starter) not the main dish (*plat*); sometimes served with cocktails when there is no meal]
hot-dog long sausage [usually served in a half baguette]
houblon hops
huile oil
  à l'huile served with oil (usually olive oil) or an oil-based dressing
  filet d'huile dash of oil

huilé oiled
huile blanche poppy seed oil
huile d'amande almond oil
huile d'arachide peanut oil; groundnut oil
huile d'avocat avocado oil
huile d'olive olive oil
   arrosé d'huile d'olive drizzled with olive oil
   filet d'huile d'olive dash of olive oil
   sauce à l'huile d'olive extra vierge extra virgin olive oil dressing
   vinaigrette à l'huile d'olive vinegar and olive oil dressing
huile d'olive extra vierge extra virgin olive oil
huile d'olive vierge virgin olive
huile de colza rapeseed oil
huile de maïs corn oil
huile de noix walnut oil
huile de pépin de raisin grape seed oil
huile de première pression first pressing [of vegetable oil]
huile de sésame sesame oil
huile de table salad oil
huile de tournesol sunflower oil
huile de truffes truffle oil
huile végétale vegetable oil
huile vierge virgin olive oil
huître oyster
huître belon flat oyster
huître creuse a Japanese variety of oyster now farmed in France
huître creuse de Denneville oyster of Denneville
huître de Bélon Bélon oyster [any flat oyster from Brittany]
huître de Bouzigues Bouzigues oyster [a renowned farmed oyster]
huîtres chaudes au champagne warm oysters in champagne sauce [oysters poached in a warm sauce typically made with oyster water, cream, champagne and egg yolk]
huîtres creuses de Denneville grillées roasted Denneville oysters [the oyster is opened, removed from the shell, dried and then roasted in butter on one side so that the other side remains raw; usually served with bacon and chives]
huître portugaise Portuguese oyster
huîtres d'Isigny-sur-Mer oysters from Isigny-sur-Mer in Normandie [said to be sweet and crunchy]
huîtres de Saint-Vaast-la-Hougue oysters from Normandie [said to be plump with a flavor of hazelnuts]
huîtres Dubarry oysters in potato cases
huître Fine de Claire oysters that have spent at least 28 days in clear ponds in order to refine their taste [of highest quality; should be plump and tender with a subtle flavor]
huître gravette flat oyster
huître Spéciale de Claire oysters that have been refined 18 months or longer in special clear ponds [rounder, more fleshy]
huître Fine de Claire Verte green oyster [of highest quality; refined for at least four weeks in special clear ponds where they feed on algae that makes them turn green]
huître plate flat oyster

huître Pousse en Claire oysters that have been refined in special clear ponds for at least two months and given room to grow
hure brawn; head cheese [meat from a pig's or calf's head cooked and then pressed in a jar with jelly]
hure de sanglier wild boar brawn; head cheese
hydromel mead
hysope hyssop
ibérique Iberian
icaque Caribbean fruit of the icaco tree [pink or purple plum-size fruit with white, mealy pulp; sweet or bland]
idéal Mâconnais cake made with meringue, almonds and butter cream
igname yam
IGP abbreviation for *Indication Géographique Protégée* [the Europe-wide label which protects a product and indicates that its characteristics are related to the geographic location with which it is associated; products include fruits and vegetables, seafood, meat and meat products, eggs, flour, honey, salt and pasta]
ile flottante "floating island" dessert [sweet vanilla-flavored cream in a bowl with meringue floating on top; the meringue often has layers of pralines and jam or possibly drizzles of caramel and/or sliced almonds]
imbrucciata savory pastry made with *broccio* cheese filling
indienne/à l'indienne Indian-style, usually with curry; highly spiced
  sauce à l'indienne curry sauce
Indication Géographique Protégée/IGP the Europe-wide label which protects a product and indicates that its characteristics are related to the geographic location with which it is associated
infusion infusion; herbal tea
Irlandais/café Irlandais Irish coffee [coffee with whisky and sugar]
italien Italian
jailles pork stew [pork loin, potatoes and seasonings]
jalapeno jalapeño pepper
jalousie flaky pastry with lattice-like crust [usually filled with apples, or possibly almonds, pears, apricots, or even cheese]
jambon ham
  croissant au jambon ham croissant
  endive au jambon endive with ham
  quiche au jambon quiche with ham
jambon à l'ancienne Label Rouge old-style ham [cooked; cylindrical, without bones, with or without rind]
jambon à l'os ham on the bone
jambon-beurre ham and butter sandwich
jambon blanc cooked and molded cold ham
jambon au bouillon ham cooked in broth [cylindrical, without bones, with or without rind]
jambon au torchon Label Rouge ham cooked in cloth [cylindrical, without bones, but with rind and far, or sometimes skinless; top quality cooked ham]
jambon blanc boiled ham
jambon braisé baked ham

jambon cru raw, cured ham [salted, dried and sometimes smoked]
jambon cru de pays raw, cured country ham
jambon cru des Landes Landes raw cured ham
jambon cru du Morvan Morvan raw cured ham [spicy flavor]
jambon cru salé raw cured brined ham
jambon cuit à l'os Label Rouge ham cooked with its bone [cooked and sold with bone in; sometimes smoked]
jambon cuit braisé braised cooked ham
jambon cuit choix choice cooked ham [boned and molded; contains no gelling]
jambon cuit de porc fermier roasted farm-style ham
jambon cuit standard standard cooked ham [boned and molded; contains additives]
jambon cuit supérieur superior cooked ham [boned and molded; in general, ham of good quality]
jambon cuit supérieur pré-tranché pre-sliced superior cooked ham
jambon d'Ardenne Ardenne ham [a type of prosciutto]
jambon d'Auvergne Auvergne salted and smoked ham
jambon d'York York ham [cooked ham with its bone "salty brine fresh" and slightly smoky]
jambon de Bayonne raw salt-cured ham from Béarn [deep red in color; delicate, mildly salty flavor; very tender]
jambon de Chaves Chaves ham [Portuguese ham; similar to a prosciutto]
jambon de la Forêt-Noire AOP Black Forest ham [raw, deboned and salt-cured; Germany]
jambon de Lacaune IGP Lacaune ham [cured with coarse salt, a little sugar and saltpeter]
jambon de l'Ardèche IGP raw salt- and spice-cured smoked dried ham from Ardèche
jambon de Luxeuil raw smoked dried ham from Luxeuil-les-Bains, Franche Comté
jambon de Paris cooked Paris ham
jambon de Parme Parma ham [must be 100% natural; pigs are fed with grain and Parmesan whey and slaughtered at 9 months; cured with sea salt for 12 to 36 months or more]
jambon de pays cured country ham
jambon de Reims Reims ham [made from pork shoulder or boneless pork, cooked in a special broth and then set into a mold; the "assembled" ham is thus marbled with gelatin]
jambon de Serrano Serrano ham [*sierra* (mountain) ham; less expensive than *jambon ibérique* (but still a delicacy); hams are salted for about two weeks, then dried for about six months, then hung for an additional 6 to 18 months, usually in sheds found at higher elevations (hence: "mountain ham")]
jambon de Vendée IGP Vendée ham [pink in color, tasting of herbs and brandy]
jambon fermier farm-style ham
jambon fumé smoked ham
jambon fumé désossé daisy ham [boned and smoked pork shoulder]

jambon ibérique Iberian ham [Iberian pigs have slender legs and black hooves which stay on the ham as it cures (and distinguish it from serrano ham); high in fat content which allows the ham to be cured much longer; complex, intense flavor with a bit of sweetness]
jambon ibérique de gland Iberian acorn ham [pigs are fed acorns and other natural pasturage; considered to be of superior quality compared to regular Iberian ham]
jambon ibérique de regavage Recebo ham [pigs are fed 50% grain and 50% acorns, preferably grazed from beneath oak trees]
jambon noir de Bigorre Bigorre black ham [intense red color, sweet and succulent]
jambon persillé marbled ham [prepared from ham and pork shoulder cut into cubes, coated with gelatin and seasonings]
jambon salé au sel sec salted ham [literally "salted with dry salt]
jambon sec de Savoie dried Savoie ham [smoky, dark brown with light brown streaks; often strongly salted]
jambon sec des Ardennes IGP dried Ardennes ham [boneless, molded, pear-shaped ham]
jambon sec des Joncquois dried Joncquois ham
jambon sec fumé du Hauts-Doubs smoked dried ham
jambon-beurre ham and butter sandwich
jambonneau ham knuckle; pork hock; small knuckle of ham [smoked or salted, firm, gelatinous, tasty cut of pork covered with a thick rind; used fresh, braised, poached]
jambonnette dry sausage [minced meat (chicken, ham, turkey) formed into a pear shape to resemble a tiny ham; the meat is usually combined with other ingredients]
jambonnette de volaille minced chicken meat sausage formed into a tiny ham; typically: may be prepared with *champignons* (mushrooms), *foie gras* (liver) and *marrons* (chestnuts) or other ingredients]
jaque breadfruit [tropical fruit of the jack tree]
Japonaise/à la Japonaise garnished with Japanese artichokes
jardinière garnished with mixed spring vegetables
jarret knuckle; shank [cut of meat; may be choice and tender, or thin and gelatinous but tasty with rich bone marrow]
jaret d'agneau lamb knuckle/shank [choice, tender cut of meat]
jaret de veau veal knuckle/shank [thin, gelatinous, with tendon, bone and bone marrow]
jasmin jasmine flower [used to scent herbal tea]
jaune yellow
   vin jaune yellow wine [a strong yellow wine from the Jura area of Franche Comté; made from very ripe savagnin grapes; aged a least six years; develops a slight nutty flavor]
jausiereine a thin cake with a filling of raspberries or blueberries
jean doré John dory [marine fish; mild, delicate flesh]
jeanbonhomme/jean bonhomme small brioche in the form of a snowman with small chocolate drops for the eyes, nose and buttons
jésuite flake pastry filled with almond cream (frangipane) and topped with sliced almonds and sugar

Jésus de Morteau smoked pork sausage [flavored with garlic, shallot, coriander, cumin and white wine]
Jeudi Thursday
jindungo chili pepper [very spicy and is used in dishes of African origin]
joue jowl
joue de boeuf beef jowl
joue de lotte monkfish jowl
joue de porc pork jowl
joue de veau veal jowl
jour day
    du jour of the day
    soupe du jour soup of the day
judic/à la judic with potatoes, stuffed tomatoes, braised lettuce (and sometimes truffles and kidney)
judru salami; dry sausage [pure pork; short and stubby; steamed and then dried for two months]
jujube jujube fruit [small red fruit with yellowish white flesh; sweet apple taste]
julienne julienne [cut into long, thin strips; sometimes called "shoe string"]
julienne marine fish with delicate white flesh
julienne de legumes julienne vegetables
juliette des sables potato [small, elongated, yellow potato]
jumeau literally: twin [refers to the cut of beef that comes from the twin muscles of the upper neck]
jus juice
    au jus with its own juices
jus de raisin grape juice
jus de rôti (roast) gravy
jus de viande gravy
jus lié thickened gravy
kabocha Asian winter squash; golden squash
kabu turnip
kaki persimmon
kanouga soft caramel candy with whipped cream; subtly flavored with vanilla, hazelnut, walnut, chocolate or coffee
kari curry
kari Gosse a light curry suitable for shellfish [mixture of ginger, turmeric, cloves, chili pepper, cinnamon and pepper]
kasher/casher kosher
kémia Algerian-style appetizer [could be composed of olives, mussels, peanuts, pistachios, almonds, chickpeas, beans, potatoes, fennel, snails, squid or other]
king/à la king with rich creamy mushroom and green sweet pepper sauce
kipper butterflied and lightly smoked herring
kir aperitif made with *aligoté* (white wine) and *crème de cassis* (blackcurrant liqueur)
kir normand cider and *crème de cassis* (blackcurrant liqueur)
kir royal kir made with blackcurrant liqueur and champagne (instead of white wine)

kiwi kiwi
kiwi de l'Adour IGP kiwi [said to be of very high quality]
kohlrabi kohlrabi
koulibiac/coulibiac meat, fish (especially salmon) or vegetables baked inside a shell of puff pastry
kumquat kumquat [tiny orange-like citrus; edible sour skin with sweet fruit inside]
labre merle brown wrasse [soft, tender, tasty, easy to digest; grilled, fried or stewed]
lactaire délicieux edible mushroom [slightly concave reddish-orange fluted cap; mild aroma and fruity flavor]
lactaire sanguin edible mushroom [slightly concave beige-orange cap; agreeable aroma and mild flavor]
lacté milk
    chocolat lacté milk chocolate
lagopède Pyrenean grouse
Laguiole AOC, AOP cheese [raw cow's milk (from cows whose basic diet is mountain pasturage); thick, natural whitish to light orange rind (becoming amber-brown with age); aged at least four months (and up to twelve months); uncooked, un-pressed, supple, velvety pale yellow hard cheese with warm flavors of dried fruits, toast and butter]
lait milk
    confiture de lait milk jam [a thick brown mixture of milk and sugar simmered together then cooled and put in a jar]
    gâteau aux trois laits three milks cake [Latin-American dessert made from whole milk (or cream) and sweetened and un-sweetened concentrated milk]
    gros lait thick, tangy, creamy milk [halfway between yoghurt and cottage cheese]
    petit-lait whey
    riz au lait rice pudding
lait aigre sour milk
lait battu buttermilk
lait caillé clotted milk; milk curd
lait d'amande almond milk
lait de brebis sheep's milk
lait de chèvre goat's milk
lait de coco coconut milk
lait de pistache pistachio milk
lait de poule eggnog [egg yolk diluted in milk]
lait de riz rice milk
lait de soya soy milk
lait de vache cow's milk
lait demi-écrémé semi-skimmed milk; low-fat milk
lait écrémé skimmed milk
lait fermenté clotted milk
lait pasteurisé pasteurized milk
lait ribot buttermilk
laitance soft roe
laitance d'alose shad roe
laitue lettuce

coeur de laitue lettuce heart
laitue beurrée butter lettuce; round lettuce
laitue croquante iceberg lettuce
laitue pommé cabbage lettuce
laitue romaine romaine lettuce
laitues de Dame Simone stuffed lettuce [hollowed-out head of lettuce stuffed with a mixture of minced chicken, egg, cream, parsley, chives and chervil; simmered in a light broth]
lamballe/crème lamballe rich, creamy, velvety pea soup made garnished with cooked tapioca
lambic Belgian beer [naturally fermented by the local wild yeasts and bacteria; dry, stout, cidery with a sour aftertaste]
lambic fruit fruit-flavored Belgian beer [most notably *framboise* (raspberry), *pêche* (peach), *cassis* (blackcurrant), *druif* (grape) and *aardbei* (strawberry); there is a secondary fermentation in the bottle]
lambic gueuze Belgian beer [a mix of young and old *lambic* that ferments in the bottle; can be kept for 10 to 20 years]
lambic faro Belgian beer sweetened with brown sugar
lambic kriek Belgian beer with sour cherries and a second fermentation in the bottle; dry and sour
lambig cider brandy
lamproie lamprey eel [delicate, fatty flesh]
lamproie à la bordelaise lamprey eel in red wine and blood sauce [simmered for two hours with leeks; served accompanied by garlic croutons]
lançon sand eel [small, long thin marine fish]
landaise/à la landaise Landes-style [typically: cooked in goose fat with garlic and pine nuts]
landjaeier smoked, dried sausage
langouste crawfish; spiny lobster [looks like a small lobster]
langoustine Dublin Bay prawn; scampi, Norway lobster [small lobster-like crustacean]
  timbale de langouste lobster timbale [a creamy mixture baked in a mold]
langue tongue
langue à l'écarlate scarlet beef tongue [typically: marinated in olive oil, garlic, cloves, bay leaves, salt and pepper, then simmered in a pot with carrots, onion, cloves, bay leaves, salt and pepper; served cold with pickles or other condiments]
langue de boeuf beef tongue [very high in fat; cheap and similar in flavor to brisket or corned beef; often cooked and then eaten cold; can be pickled]
langue-de-boeuf beef tongue mushroom; beef liver mushroom [shiny, reddish brown elongated (tongue-like) cap; dense, firm red flesh with whitish veins with the consistency of Bluefin tuna; tart flavor; eaten raw or cooked like a steak; the unusual taste and texture are not to everyone's liking]
langue de mouton fumée smoked sheep's tongue
languedocienne/à la languedocienne Languedoc-style [typically: with eggplant/aubergine, mushrooms, tomatoes and parsley]

langue Lucullus cold smoked beef tongue [encased in a gelatinous mixture of *foie gras*, truffles, butter, cognac and Porto wine; chilled and sliced]
langue d'avocat wedge sole [flat marine fish]
langue-de-chat cat's tongue biscuit [light crunchy cookie/biscuit]
languier smoke-dried pork tongue and throat
laperau young rabbit; bunny
lapin rabbit
   civet de lapin rabbit stew
   cuisse de lapin rabbit leg
   gigolette de lapin rabbit stew
   gibelotte de lapin à la normande rabbit stewed in white wine [typically: with green onions, bacon, mushrooms, carrots, cider, Calvados and herbs]
   terrine de lapin rabbit terrine
lapin à l'ardennaise Ardenne rabbit [typically: with smoked bacon, apples, blond beer, gooseberry jelly and mustard]
lapin à la beaujolaise rabbit in Beaujolais wine [wine, red wine vinegar, onion, bay laurel, thyme, sage]
lapin à la cauchoise rabbit with cream, strong mustard, shallots and white wine
lapin à la havraise rabbit marinated in white wine with cream, strong mustard, butter and shallots
lapin à la moutarde rabbit in Dijon mustard sauce
lapin à la moutarde au Calvados rabbit in mustard and Calvados
lapin à la paimpolaise rabbit with white beans [white *paimpol* beans (soft, thin skinned semi-dry bean with a nutty flavor), bacon, green onion, carrot, garlic, herbs, white wine]
lapin à la Saintongeaise rabbit in rosé wine sauce [typically: rosé wine, bacon, tomato, brandy, shallots, chicken stock and herbs; usually accompanied by potatoes]
lapin au chocolat à la catalane Catalonia-style rabbit in chocolate sauce [typically: smoked bacon, onion, shallot, wine vinegar, dry white wine, chocolate and aromatic herbs]
lapin aux pruneaux d'Agen rabbit with prunes [typically: marinated in red wine, Armagnac, vegetables and aromatic herbs]
lapin avec son saupiquet rabbit with chopped liver sauce [typically: rabbit cooked with mushrooms and served with a thick sauce made from its chopped liver, its blood, wine, vinegar, olive oil, bacon and garlic]
lapin chasseur hunter-style rabbit [typically: slowly cooked in an aromatic bouillon of tomatoes and mushrooms]
lapin de garenne wild rabbit; hare
lapin gibelotte fricassee of rabbit
lard bacon
lard fumé smoked bacon
lard maigre streaky bacon
lardé larded; studded with fat before cooking
lardon larding bacon
lardons diced bacon
   allumette de lardon small bacon dice

petits lardons finely diced bacon
latier edible mushroom [*lactair délicieux* or *lactair sanguin*; pale orange/clear ochre cap, slightly concave; firm]
latier made with milk
latour porbeagle shark [a kind of mackerel shark]
laurie porbeagle shark [a type of mackerel shark]
lavaret de bourget pollan [freshwater salmonid fish; Alpine lakes]
légume vegetable
   crème de légumes cream of vegetable soup
   garniture de légumes vegetable accompaniment; vegetable side dish
   julienne de légumes julienne vegetables
   macédoine de légumes diced mixed vegetables
   pain de légumes bread made with chunks of vegetables mixed into the dough
   pain de légumes terrine of puréed vegetables arranged in layers in a mold
   poêlée de légumes mixed fried vegetables
   purée de légumes vegetable soup
légume cru raw vegetable
légume d'été summer vegetable
légume d'hiver winter vegetable
légume frais fresh vegetable
légume racine root vegetable
légume vert green vegetable
légumes assortis assorted vegetables
légumes des hortillonnages vegetables grown by market gardeners on the "floating gardens" of Amiens (plots of land drained by canals; fertile black soil)
lentille verte du Puy AOC green lentil [a delicacy; sometimes called "poor man's caviar"; less starchy than regular lentils; often cooked and eaten cold in salad]
lentillon de Champagne small pinkish-red lentil with a sweet taste
lépiote wild edible parasol mushroom [the cultured variety is called *coulemele*]
levain leavened bread; sourdough bread
levraut young hare; leveret
levrouté of the color of a young hare [with copper and amber hightlights]
lichette nibble; small quantity
lié bound; thickened [said of sauce or gravy]
Liègeoise iced coffee dessert
lieu jaune green pollock [cod-like marine fish]
lieu noir black cod; pollock
lièvre hare; wild rabbit
lièvre à la royale royal hare [typically: wild rabbit flayed and rolled with stuffing comprised of pork, bacon, bread, goose liver, truffles, and seasonings; gently simmered and served with a blood and red wine sauce]
ligurienne/à la ligurienne Liguria-style [typically: with stuffed tomatoes, saffron-scented risotto and duchesse potatoes]

Lillet aperitif made with Bordeaux wine (85%) and fruit liqueurs (15%) [the fruits are sweet oranges from southern Spain, bitter oranges from Haiti, green oranges from Morocco or Tunisia, and *quinquina* from Peru (aromatized wine from cinchona bark, the same bark that yields quinine)]
limace/limaçon small edible snail
limace/limaçon à la sucarelle snail cooked with sausage, onion, tomatoes and garlic
limande common dab [flat marine fish]
limande sole lemon sole; dab
lime bitter lime
limette sweet lime
limonade lemonade
limousine/à la limsouine Limousin-style [typically: with red cabbage, *cèpe* mushrooms and chestnuts]
lingot white kidney bean [large, thin, oval bean with a delicate flavor]
   haricot lingot white kidney bean
lingue ling cod; long cod; burbot
lingue bleue blue ling [marine fish with delicate white flesh]
liqueur liqueur
liqueur de châtaigne chestnut liqueur
liqueur de gentiane gentian liqueur
liqueur de noix vertes green walnut liqueur
liqueur de noix/liqueur aux noix walnut liqueur
lisette small mackerel
lisettes à la dieppoise/Lisettes de Dieppe mackerel in cider marinade [typically: made with cider, carrots, onions, vinegar and seasonings]
litchi lychee fruit [plum-size tropical fruit]
Livarot AOC cheese [cow's milk; washed orange-colored rind; pungent aroma; soft cheese with hints of nuttiness, salty lemon and spices]
livèche lovage [celery-like herb]
livonienne/sauce livonienne velvety fish soup [typically: with julienne carrots, celery, mushrooms, onions and julienned truffles]
livornaise/à la livornaise Livorno-style [typically: with shallots, tomatoes and truffles]
loche loach fish
logane dragon's eye [tropical fruit similar to lychee]
longe loin; saddle of beef, veal or pork
longeole air-dried, cooked pork sausage
lonzo/lonzu AOP salted Corsican pork [lean and fatty cuts of pork are salted and refrigerated for four or five days, then washed in wine, dried and peppered and put into casings to be smoked and aged in a cellar]
loquette blenny; eelpout [marine fish; common ingredient in Mediterranean soups]
lorgnettes candied fruit
lorgnettes fried onion rings
lorgnettes small dessert biscuits

lotier sweet clover; birdsfoot trefoil [used in marinades or stuffing for rabbit]
Lotte à l'Armoricaine monkfish in crustacean sauce [a tomato-fish stock sauce flavored with prawn shells, onion, carrot and cognac]
lotte de mer monkfish [firm white meat, mild flavor, sometimes compared to lobster]
lotte de rivière burbot; freshwater ling [freshwater cod-like fish]
lotus lotus [roots, young stems and seeds are edible]
lou fassum cabbage stuffed with pork, rice and peas
loubine sea bass [wild populations are in decline; farmed sea bass is now becoming popular]
Louise Bonne d'Arranches pear [quite small fruit, yellow-green skin with red spots]
loup/loup de mer sea bass [wild populations are in decline; farmed sea bass is now becoming popular]
Lundi Monday
   ouvert du Lundi au Vendredi open from Monday to Friday
lusignan/macaron de lusignan almond macaroon
macaron macaroon [made with ground almonds, powdered sugar, sugar and egg whites beaten into a stiff meringue]
macaron d'Amiens honey-almond macaroon
macaron de Nancy said to be the original macaroon
macaron de Paris a macaroon sandwich-cookie with a flavored filling such as buttercream, *ganache* (chocolate icing) or jam
macaronade macaroni with beef and tomato sauce
macaronis tubular macaroni pasta
macédoine diced [cut into small cubes]
macédoine de légumes diced mixed vegetables
macéré soaked in liquid, usually aromatic, in order to make soft or tender
mâche/mâche nantaise mâche; lamb's lettuce
macis mace
mâconnaise/à la mâconnaise a way to poach fish [typically: in white wine and red wine; a garnish of onions, mushrooms, crayfish and croutons and served with fish; a sauce of shallots, mushrooms, white wine and mustard served with *andouillette* sausages]
macre water chestnut
macreuse very lean cut of beef from the anterior part of the shoulder [roasted, grilled, braised or stewed]
macreuse wild duck [has very meager meat]
made burbot; freshwater ling [freshwater cod-like fish]
madeleine small shell-shaped, cake-like pastry [made with eggs, sugar, honey, flour butter, salt, baking powder and lemon or orange zest (or vanilla); may also be made with chocolate chips, walnuts, black olives, various fruits, cinnamon, almonds, or a variety of savories, such as artichoke, chorizo, bacon, or cheese]
madeleine de Commercy/Liverdun the original madeleine created in Commercy and Liverdun, two villages in Lorraine
Madère Madeira [a fortified Portuguese-style red wine which can be dry or sweet]

magret lean fillet of breast meat [usually duck or goose breast]
magret de canard duck breast fillet
magret de canard farci stuffed duck breast
magret séché dried fillet of duck breast [salted and dried like a ham; seasoned with various spices]
magret fumé smoked duck
maguita-tuâ-tuâ hot chili pepper [extremely hot pepper with a distinct flavor enjoyed by many to flavor meat]
maigre lean, low fat; clear (soup)
   au maigre a dish without meat
maigre meagre; croaker fish; shade-fish; corvina; salmon-basse or stone basse [similar to sea bass]
maigret lean fillet of breast meat [usually duck or goose breast]
maigret de canard duck breast fillet
maillot/à la maillot a garnish of green beans, carrots, turnips, lettuce and peas
maïs corn; sweetcorn
   flocon de maïs corn flake
   pan de maïs corn bread; corn pone
maïs en épi corn on the cob
maïs sucré sweet corn
maison/de la maison in the style of the house/restaurant
   fait maison made on the premises
maître d'hôtel head waiter; butler
   beurre maître d'hôtel butter with parsley and lemon
maître queux master chef
   sauce à la maître queux master chef sauce [a white sauce with shallots, parsley and lemon]
makocz/makocz au pavot bleu Polish blue poppy cake
makrilli mackerel
malaga light amber-green grape with thick skin with a musky aroma
malaga sweet Spanish dessert wine
malakoff cheese beignet
   tarte malakoff layers of rum sponge cake alternating with vanilla whipped cream or other rich creamy filling
malard mallard duck
malsat white sausage [rich lean meat (pork, chicken or veal) with herbs]
malt malt
maltaise blood orange
maltaise/à la maltaise Maltese-style [flavored with the juice and zest of blood oranges]
maltaise/sauce maltaise Maltaise sauce [a variation of *hollandaise* sauce in which orange zest and blood orange juice is added]
mancelle/à la mancelle in the style of Le Mans
   omelette à la mancelle omelet with artichoke bottoms and diced potatoes
   rouelles de veau à la mancelle veal prepared with *chipolatas* sausages, mushrooms and chestnuts
manchon a *petit four* of cookie dough or almond paste stuffed with *crème chiboust* or praline butter cream and rolled into a

small cylinder; the ends are dipped in almond powder or chopped pistachios
manchon wing
manchon de canard duck wing
manchon de poulet chicken wing
mandarine mandarin orange; tangerine
mange-tout snow pea
mangoustan tropical Asian purple fruit the size of a golf ball [thick bitter skin; the fruit is tart and sweet]
mangue mango
manioc cassava [tropical starchy root; used for making tapioca]
mannala/männele small brioche formed into the shape of a man
manouls veal tripe stuffed with ham, garlic, parsley and other aromatics
manouls de La Canourgue sheep tripe and paunch (rumen) cooked with salted veal breast and streaky bacon
manqué simple cake made with eggs, sugar, butter and flour; can be flavored with almonds, lemon, chocolate, dried or fresh fruit and topped with jam, custard or chopped almonds
manselle/à la manselle in the style of Mans [typically: roasted or braised chicken, strips of pork or rabbit; an omelet with artichoke hearts and diced potatoes]
manzana apple
maôche stuffed pork belly [belly stuffed with local variations such as cabbage, sausage, carrots, prunes or juniper berries]
maquereau mackerel
　filet de maquereau au poivre fillet of mackerel with pepper
　groseille à maquereau gooseberry
maquereaux au cidre à la rennaise Rennes-style mackerel baked in cider sauce [typically: cider, onions, shallots and cider]
maquereaux marinés au vin blanc mackerel marinated in white wine
Mara des bois/fraises Mara des bois high-quality strawberry
maracuja passion fruit
maraîche porbeagle [marine fish; type of mackerel shark]
maraîcher market-fresh produce
maraîchere/à la maraîchère prepared with fresh vegetables
　couleur maraîchère colorful market vegetables
marasme d'Oréade fairy-ring agaric mushroom [yellowish brown cap; said to have a very good aroma which improves if the mushroom is preserved by drying]
marasque bitter cherry [used for making maraschino liqueur]
marasquin maraschino liqueur
marbrade head cheese [jellied pork head *pâté*]
marbré marbled [can refer to meat, cake or cheese]
marbré striped bream [marine fish]
marc cheap brandy substitute made from the residue (pomace) of pressed grapes
marc residue of grape skins, seeds and stalks after juice has been extracted for wine making

marc de Bourgogne brandy substitute made from distilled grape skins, seeds and stalks after the juice has been extracted for making wine
marc de Champagne brandy substitute made from distilled grape skins, seeds and stalks after the juice has been squeezed out for making wine
marc de pinot noir brandy substitute made from the residue of pinot noir grapes
marc de gewurtztraminer brandy substitute made from the residue of gewürztraminer grapes
marcassin young wild boar
    civet de marcassin stew of young wild boar
    estouffade de marcassin stew of young wild boar
    filet de marcassin roti roast fillet of young wild boar
marcelin a one-layer cake topped with raspberry jam and ground almonds
marchand merchant
marchand de vin wine merchant
    sauce marchand de vin wine merchant sauce [a classic red wine reduction made with red wine, shallots and either a rich brown stock or a *demi-glace*]
marché market
    selon le marché according to market/availability
marcs de café coffee grounds
Mardi Tuesday
    fermé le Mardi closed on Tuesday
maréchal/à la maréchal marshal-style [with asparagus tips, cockscombs, peas and truffles]
marée fresh seafood, both fish and shellfish
marennes small oysters from the largest oyster cultivation area in Europe [estuary of the Charente River, northwest of Bordeaux]
margarine margarine
Marie-Louise/à la Marie-Louise Marie-Louise-style [typically: with artichoke hearts, mushrooms, onion purée and potatoes]
marignan apricot sponge cake with meringue
marinade marinade [a liquid usually consisting of an oil and an acid and flavored with herbs and/or aromatics, in which food is soaked in order to impart flavor and to tenderize; the marinade may also be used as a cooking liquid]
mariné marinated; pickled
marinière/à la marinière boatman-style [with mussels]
marjolaine a dessert cake [rectangular; similar to a *dacquoise*, but consists of layers of almond and hazelnut meringue and chocolate buttercream; may be served with fresh fruit]
marjolaine oregano; marjoram
marmande farci tomato filled with a variety of savories such as tuna or lamb
marmelade marmalade; jam [of stewed fruit, not limited to citrus]
marmitako ragout of tuna [chunks of tuna stewed with onions, potatoes, chilies and garlic]

marmite dieppoise fish stew [typically: turbot, sole, mullet or monkfish, with scallops and mussels, cooked with onion, celery and leek, butter, cream and cider or white wine]
marocaine/à la marocaine Moroccan-style [typically: with sweet peppers, eggplant/courgettes, tomatoes and saffron rice]
Marolles/Maroilles AOC cheese [commercial trademark (pasteurized cow's milk) or artisanal (raw cow's milk); brick-red, smooth, salt-washed rind; strong pungent aroma of fermented fruit; creamy smooth soft cheese and strongly flavored: sweet-salty, mushrooms, nuts, lemons]
   sauce Maroilles Maroilles cheese sauce [Maroilles cheese and cream; may be flavored with shallots, parsley and olive oil; typically served with steak or chicken]
   tarte au Maroilles Maroilles cheese tart/pie
marquis/Sauce marquis Marquis sauce [a variation of hollandaise sauce]
marquise a mousse-like dessert [made with dark chocolate, eggs, sugar, cream and butter]
marquisette alcoholic beverage with many variations according to where it is produced [typically includes lemonade, champagne, white wine, sugar, mandarin liqueur and pieces of lemon]
marron edible chestnut
   purée de marrons chestnut purée [may contain sugar and/or vanilla]
marrons glacé sweet preserve of chestnut in sugar syrup
marrons Mont Blanc chestnut purée topped with whipped cream
marrons plombières iced custard with chestnuts, kirsch, vanilla and rum
marseillaise/à la marseillaise Marseilles-style [typically: with anchovies, tomatoes and olives]
mascotte/à la mascotte garnished with potatoes, artichoke hearts and truffles [chicken or roast joints]
mascotte sponge cake soaked in kirsch or rum, filled with praline or coffee-flavored butter cream, then coated with the butter cream and sprinkled with almonds
   beignet mascotte fritter; ball of fried dough, sweet or savory
massacanat large meat-filled omelet
massepain marzipan [a kind of confectionary dough made with 2/3 blanched ground almonds and 1/3 egg whites and sugar]
massepain marzipan cake
massepain de St-Léonard macaroon made with marzipan
Masséna/à la Masséna typically: garnished with artichoke hearts, Béarnaise sauce and bone marrow
massillon small cake made with marzipan and kirsch
matafan/matefaim a large, thick *crêpe* [sweet or savory]
matelote sailor
matelote alsacienne Alsatian fish stew [typically: made with pieces of fresh water fish cooked in a stock of heavy cream, butter (and maybe eggs), white wine, onion, leeks, carrots and/or celery and *bouquet garni*]
matelote au cidre fish stew with cider
matelote au Riesling freshwater fish stew with Riesling wine

matière matter; substance
  sans matières grasses fat-free
matignon mixture of carrots, celery and onions or shallots plus fresh herbs cooked in butter and Madeira and reduced [served with meat or fish]
matouille a fondue of Tome de Bauges (cheese) baked with garlic and wine until melted [for dipping cooked potatoes]
matza matzo; matzah [dumpling]
mauve mallow
mauviette lark
mayonnaise mayonnaise [egg yolks, oil, vinegar, and *often with mustard*]
  sauce mayonnaise mayonnaise with mustard
mayonnaise à l'ail garlic mayonnaise
mayonnaise à l'americaine American mayonnaise [mayonnaise with tomato paste, harissa sauce (hot peppers and spices) or tabasco sauce]
mayonnaise à l'indienne Indian mayonnaise [mayonnaise with chopped green onions and curry powder]
mayonnaise à la mangue mango mayonnaise
mayonnaise à la russe Russian mayonnaise [frothy mayonnaise with aspic jelly, tarragon vinegar and horseradish]
mayonnaise aux anchois mayonnaise with anchovies [consists of eggs, olive oil, mustard, anchovy fillets, lemon juice, salt and pepper]
mayonnaise chantilly chantilly sauce [mayonnaise thickened with lemon juice and fluffed up with whipped cream]
mayonnaise collée jellied mayonnaise [mayonnaise with aspic jelly]
mayonnaise onctueuse creamy mayonnaise [made with egg yolk, mustard, oil, vinegar or lemon juice, salt and pepper]
mayonnaise rémoulade mustard mayonnaise [mayonnaise with the addition of finely chopped parsley, mustard, lemon juice and creamy horseradish]
mayonnaise verte green mayonnaise [with purée of greens such as watercress, parsley, spinach or tarragon]
mazagran iced coffee
mazarin a cake made with two layers of sponge cake with a layer of praline mousse
mazarin a thick sponge cake filled with candied fruit and topped with candied fruit icing
méchoui North-African style spit- or pit-roasted lamb
Médidi/à la Médici steak with artichoke hearts, peas, carrots, turnips (and sometimes carrots)
mélange a mixture
mélangé mixed or blended
Melba refers to desserts made with whipped cream
  crêpe Melba sweet crêpe with whipped cream and fruit
  fraises Melba strawberries, ice cream and whipped cream
  pêche Melba peaches, ice cream and cream or whipped cream
mêlé-casse blackcurrant syrup and brandy drink
méli-mélo an assortment

méli-mélo de légumes assortment of vegetables
méli-mélo de mer seafood platter
méli-mélo de poissons assortment of fish
mélisse lemon balm [an herb with a lemony flavor]
melon melon
melon de Cavaillon sweet melon or cantaloup
melon de Cavaillon au Beaumes-de-Venise Cavaillon melon soaked in Muscat wine
melon de Lectoure a *charentais*-type sweet melon
melon du haut-poitou IGP sweet melon from Poitou Charentes
melon du Quercy IGP sweet melon from Quercy
melonnée a type of squash or pumpkin
melsát large pork sausage made from spleen, liver, bread and spices and sometimes eggs and tripe
menacé threatened, endangered
   non-menacé not threatened
mendiant dry cake with nuts, preserved fruit and cinnamon
mendiant name given to an assortment of four dried fruits: almonds, figs, hazelnuts and raisins
menoun Easter lamb or kid
menthe mint
menthe bergamote bergamot mint
menthe crépue curly mint
menthe des champs field mint
menthe frisée curly mint
menthe poivrée peppermint
menthe pouliot pennyroyal
menthe suave sweet mint
menthe sylvestre Scots mint
menthe verte spearmint
menu a limited list of dishes offered at a restaurant at fixed prices, as opposed to the *à la carte* listing, which includes everything on offer [typically, a *menu* displays a short selection consisting of *entrée* + *plat* (starter and main dish) or *entrée* + *plat* + *dessert* (starter, main dish and dessert) or *entrée* + *plat* + *boisson* + *dessert* (starter, main dish, drink and dessert)]
mer sea
   amande de mer dog cockle [sweet, almond-like flavor]
   araignée de mer spider crab [any of a variety of long-legged crabs]
   fruits de mer shellfish
   poule de mer lumpfish; John Dory fish; ocean pout; sea hen
Mercredi Wednesday
merguez sausage [spicy; does not contain pork]
meringue meringue [baked stiffly beaten egg whites with sugar]
meringué with meringue
meringue cuit stiff, white, powderey meringue
meringue suisse firm, glossy meringue
merise wild cherry
merlan whiting
merle blackbird
merle/labre merle brown wrasse [soft, tender, tasty]

merlu hake
merluche dried cod
merluche blanche white hake [thin fish with white flesh, said to have more fat and be more delicious than cod]
merluche écureuil squirrel hake; red hake; ling cod
merluche rouge red hake; ling cod
méron grouper
mérou Mediterranean grouper; monkfish
merveille **fritter** [fried sweet dough of various shapes and sizes, served hot, warm or cold and sprinkled with sugar]
mesclun a mix of young lettuces
mets dish
mets délicat delicacy
mets gras fatty food
meule wheel (of cheese)
meunière/à la meunière miller's wife style [typically: cooked in browned butter with parsley and lemon juice]
    sole meunière skinless sole dusted with flour and fried in butter and served with browned butter and lemon juice
meurette freshwater fish, chicken or veal stew [typically: prepared with red wine, and traditionally with bacon, onions and mushrooms]
meurotte vinaigrette made with vinegar and warm bacon fat
    pissenlits à la chaude meurotte dandelion salad with warm *meurotte vinaigrette*
Mexicaine/à la Mexicaine Mexican-style [typically: with tomatoes, mushrooms, sweet peppers and rice]
miche round loaf; cob loaf
mi-cuit partially cooked
miel honey
    gâteau de miel honey cake
    moutarde au miel honey mustard [a sweet mustard made with whole mustard grains and honey]
    sauce au miel honey sauce
    tartine de miel slice of bread and honey
miel d'acacia acacia honey [clear liquid, with a subtle and sweet scent of the acacia flower]
miel d'aster aster honey [dark, rich flavor]
miel d'aubépine hawthorn honey [ivory to amber color; very fragrant with a mild pleasant flavor]
miel d'avocat/miel d'avocatier avocado honey [from Mexico; fairly dark red, thick; may have hints of coffee and licorice]
miel d'eucalyptus eucalyptus honey [dark yellow ochre; strong, pungent aroma; slightly bitter, rich in minerals]
miel d'oranger orange blossom honey [clear yellow and bright, with an aroma of marmalade or orange liqueur]
miel de bleuet blueberry honey [dark, strong floral flavor]
miel de Bruyère heather honey [reddish in color; strong aroma and tangy, caramel taste but slightly bitter; very nutritious]
miel de Châtaigneraie AOC chestnut honey [dark amber; very aromatic; sweet with some bitterness from tannins]

miel de châtaignier chestnut honey [dark reddish-brown, full-bodied flavor]
miel de citronier citrus honey [clear, almost white; creamy texture; fresh, light aroma and taste of orange]
miel de colza canola honey; rapeseed honey [pale straw-colored; slightly fragrant, delicate; slight smell of cabbage]
miel de coton cotton honey [light, almost white; very high in anti-bacterial attributes]
miel de fleurs sauvages wild flower honey [golden amber, creamy or liquid, taste depends on which wildflower were visited by the bees]
miel de framboise/miel de framboisier raspberry honey [pale yellow; fragrant floral aroma with a subtle and sweet flavor]
miel de jujubier sauvage wild jujube honey [high quality honey; floral, fragrant and bittersweet]
miel de lavande lavender honey [clear to golden yellow, highly aromatic, tangy]
miel de luzerne alfalfa honey [very clear, becoming darker as it crystalizes; soft, light, with fruity hints]
miel de manuka honey from the Australian manuka bush; said to be high in anti-bacterial qualities
miel de Maquis d'automne AOC autumn scrub brush honey [light amber; bitter]
miel de Maquis de Printemps AOC Maquis spring honey [amber; aroma of licorice or coconut; delicate taste of caramel or cocoa; from the spring flowering of white heather, sea lavender and broom]
miel de Maquis d'été AOC summer scrub brush honey [clear, amber and creamy; floral, fruity aroma; delicate caramel flavor from the flowers of thyme, blackberries and germander]
miel de Miellats du maquis AOC scrub brush honeydew honey [very dark, almost black; its mild taste hints of caramel, dried figs, coconut, malt, ripe fruit, gingerbread and licorice]
miel de montagne mountain honey [a generic name for honey from mountain flowers such as clover, raspberry, heather, dandelion, blackberry and rhododendron; generally clear, fragrant, delicate, sweet and woody, though these flavors vary from year to year and according to weather conditions]
miel de myrtille blueberry honey [dark, strong floral flavor]
miel de Narbonne rosemary honey [clear white to pale yellow]
miel de pissenlit dandelion honey [bright yellow, like the flower; a slight whiff of ammonia on the nose, but a fine, sweet flavor]
miel de pommier apple honey [attractive pale gold color; delicate fragrance; subtle flavor]
miel de Printemps AOC spring honey [clear golden color; light and sweet, somewhat floral]
miel de Provence IGP a variety of different honeys (both mono-floral and poly-floral)
miel de romarin rosemary honey [pale, almost white to almost brown in color; smooth, pasty consistency; strong aroma but mild, delicate flavor]

miel de ronce blackberry honey [red, aromatic, persistent on the palate; slow to crystalize]
miel de sapin fir tree honey [almost black, strong and malty, sometimes minty]
miel de sapin des Vosges AOC Vosges fir honey [dark, with a woody aroma and malty, balsamic flavor]
miel de sarrasin buckwheat honey [dense brown color; subtle aroma but powerful flavors hinting of wood and earth]
miel de sauge sage honey [translucent yellow; sweet with a hit of pepper]
miel de soya soy honey
miel de thym thyme honey [lightly colored, brilliant appearance; intense flavor]
miel de tilleul Linden honey [clear amber, highly flavored with a mint taste]
miel de tournesol sunflower honey [bright yellow, has a fresh vegetable flavor, slightly tart, very sweet]
miel de trèfle clover honey [clear, almost white to light gray; subtle floral scent; delicate taste that lingers on the palate]
miel de verge d'or goldenrod honey [has a flavor somewhere between that of clover honey and buckwheat honey]
miel de vinaigrier sumac honey
miel rosat rose honey
miel saufage wild honey
miel toutes fleurs wild flower honey [golden amber, creamy or liquid; taste depends on which wildflowers were visited by the bees]
miel vierge pure honey
miette bread crumb
migliacciu thin, savory bread made with goat or sheep cheese
mignardises after-dinner sweets [little gem-like pastries]
mignon poultry, sweetbreads or small pieces of sautéed beef with artichoke hearts filled with peas, truffle sauce and Madeira
 filet mignon the most tender cut of pork, veal or beef tenderloin [literally: dainty fillet]
mignonette mignonette [a plant with small fragrant flowers]
 sauce mignonette mignonette sauce for oysters [minced shallots, milled peppercorns, red or white wine and lemon juice (or wine vinegar)]
migourée fish stew [typically: in white wine, water, onion, shallot, parsley, tarragon, *bouquet garni* and spices]
mijoté simmered; stewed
mikado/sauce mikado mikado sauce [*hollandaise* sauce with zest and juice of mandarin or other oranges added]
mil cereal
milanais name given to a variety of pastries such as *petits fours* made with almond paste, flavored with lemon or orange and decorated with almonds or candied fruit
Milanaiss/à la Milanaise a topping of macaroni or risotto, with sliced mushrooms, ham and beef tongue with truffle slices
Milanaise/à la Milanaise baked macaroni with breadcrumbs, Parmesan cheese and tomato sauce

Milanaise/à la Milanaise veal cutlets or veal chops coated with egg and breadcrumbs and pan fried
milhàs/milas cold corn porridge that is grilled or fried
milhassou/milhassou corrézien crispy potato "pancake" bound with egg and flavored sometimes with onion, garlic or shallots, and bacon or pork
millas corn flour cake
millassou corn pancake
millassou citrouille pumpkin pancake
millassou de pomme de terre crispy potato cake [made with grated potatoes, egg, bacon, garlic and parsley]
millassou potiron pumpkin pancake
mille-feuille three-layered puff pastry
mille-feuille de pommes de terre Primeur de l'Île de Noirmoutier et oignons layers of thinly-sliced spring potatoes, onions and tomatoes stacked alternately and baked in round metal cylinders
millet millet [cereal grain]
milliard a thick, baked pancake with cherries (or apricot, apple or plum)
mimosa a garnish of chopped, hard-boiled egg yolks, parsley and mayonnaise
mimosa stuffed hard-boiled eggs
minéral mineral
    eau minérale mineral water
mique dough cooked in salt pork broth
miquette de Frontignan small anise bun
mirabeau garnished with anchovies, tarragon, green olives and anchovy butter
mirabelle plum brandy (*eau de vie*)
mirabelle de Lorraine yellow plum speckled with red
mirepoix finely diced celery, onions and carrots
mirepoix au gras finely diced celery, onions and carrots with meat such as ham
mirepoix au maigre finely diced celery, onions and carrots without meat
mirepoix fond blanc finely diced celery, onions and parsnips
mirliton de Pont-Audemer a pastry made of rolled dough filled with a praline mousse and closed at both ends with chocolate
mirlitons de Rouen small tart/puff pastry [made with sugar, almonds, whipping cream, eggs and orange flower water]
mistrelle sweet fortified wine [wine mixed with alcohol, usually brandy (*eau de vie*) during fermentation to stop the fermatation process and preserve the sweetness and aromas of the grapes]
miroton boiled beef baked with vinegar or mustard and onions and bacon (or tomato sauce) and breadcrumbs
mitonné gently stewed; carefully prepared
mode style
    à la mode de in the style of
    boeuf mode beef braised with carrots, onions and red wine
moelle marrow
    sauce à la moelle marrow sauce [typically: made with red wine, shallots, beef marrow, lemon juice, thyme and bay leaf]

mogette/mojette smooth, fine dry white bean
moisissure mold or fungus on ripening cheese
mojettes white beans [cooked or in a salad]
moka/moka café mocha coffee
moka gâteau small sponge cake with layers of coffee butter or chocolate
moléculaire/gastronomie moléculaire culinary achievements based on a scientific study of the chemical and physical properties and processes involved in cooking [there is a reliance on non-traditional tools and utensils such as liquid nitrogen, syringes and tabletop distilleries, as well as food substances such as carrageenan and xanthan; often resulting in unorthodox concoctions such as faux caviar, transparent ravioli and liquid pea spheres]
mollet soft
  oeuf mollet soft-boiled egg
  oeuf poché mollet runny poached egg
  pain mollet milk bread; soft white bread roll
molva ling [marine fish]
mombin tropical fruit [yellow or red; sweet orange-like flavor]
mondé hulled; ball-shaped
monégasque/à la monégasque Monaco-style
  courgettes à la monégasque zucchini/courgettes first boiled, then sliced lengthwise and browned in butter
  tomates à la monégasque tomatoes stuffed with tuna
Mont Blanc chestnut purée with whipped cream on top
montagne mountain
  fromage de montagne artisanal sheep's milk cheese from the Pyrénées
  jambon de montagne cured ham
montmorency sour-tart cherry
  gâteau montmorency cake topped with pitted cherries
montmorency/à la montmorency dishes and cakes containing montmorency cherries
montmorency/à la montmorency garnished with artichokes, carrots and potatoes
montpensier garnished with artichokes, potatoes, asparagus and truffles
Morbier AOC artisanal cheese [raw cow's milk; pressed, uncooked cheese with a layer of sweet, edible wood ash in the middle (originally, this layer of ash was put on the first layer of the cheese to protect it from insects until the next day when enough milk was gathered to create the second layer]
morbiflette small tart made with potatoes, sausage and Morbier cheese
morceau piece; morsel; a small portion
morceau de choix choice cut
morceau de gâteau piece of cake
morceau de pain piece of bread
morceau de sucre sugar cube
morceaux de viande cuts of meats

morille morel mushroom [distinctly honeycomb-like or sponge-like shape; unique flavor is highly prized; often sautéed in butter or lightly breaded and then fried; sometimes added to soup]

morille des pins cauliflower mushroom [sweet-smelling; edible when young; brown, deeply crinkled, resembling cauliflower]

mornay/sauce mornay mornay sauce [made with butter, flour, milk, cheese, egg yolk, salt, pepper and nutmeg or other aromatic garnishes such as thyme, shallots, parsley, peppercorns, bay leaf or garlic]

Mortadelle smoked sausage [Italian *Mortadella*]

morue cod
>**brandade de morue** salt cod purée [a purée of salt cod and olive oil; typically served with bread or potatoes]
>
>**raïto de morue** cod in a sauce made from minced onions, flour, olive oil, garlic, tomatoes and red wine

morue barbeuse white hake [thin fish with white flesh, said to have more fat and be more delicious than cod]

morue ognac Greenland cod

morue salé salt cod

morvandelle Morvan (or other) ham in a sauce made with white wine, shallots, cream, tomato concentrate and Gruyère cheese

mosaïque mosaic

mostelle rockling; stone loach [marine fish; excellent flesh]

mou organ meat

mouclade seasoned mussles pot; mussels in a white wine sauce

mouclade vendéenne mussels in a curry sauce [mussels cooked in butter and white wine and served with a creamy curry sauce]

mouillette a "tongue" of bread, fresh or toasted, for dipping into the runny yolk of an egg

moulé molded

moule mussel
>**sauce aux moules** mussel sauce [a generic name for a sauce to accompany mussels (or a sauce with mussels as an ingredient to accompany cod or other seafood)]

moules à la crème mussels in a cream sauce

moules à la provençale mussels with tomatoes, olive oil, white wine, garlic, basil and parsley

moules de bouchot de la Baie du Mont-Saint-Michel AOC farmed mussels raised on logs of oak or chestnut half buried vertically in the sand in the Bay of Mont Saint Michel

moules de Barfleur Barfleur mussel [most mussels are farm raised; Barfleur mussels, in contrast, are harvested from the sea; as such, they tend to be larger and meatier than farmed mussels]

moules en mouclade mussels in a mild curry sauce

moules farcies stuffed mussels

moules farcies à la sétoise Sète-style stuffed mussels [typically: stuffed with chopped sausage meat mixed with garlic, parsley, bread and egg, then cooked in a tomato sauce]

moules marinière mussels in white wine [mussels cooked with white wine, parsley, shallots, thyme, garlic and maybe celery or lovage]

moulu ground
    cannelle moulue ground cinnamon
    épice moulue ground spice
    poivre moulu ground pepper
mounassou crispy potato pancake [bound with egg and flavored sometimes with onion, garlic or shallots, and bacon or pork]
mounjetado a rich, rustic casserole [typically: pork or ham, lamb or duck, sausage, bacon, white beans, tomatoes and root vegetables]
mourone red bell pepper [a Basque term]
mourtayrol/mourtaïrol a stew with saffron [typically: ham and chicken or beef with leeks, carrots, turnips, onions and celery]
mouseau de boeuf head cheese
mousse a frothy, airy dish, sweet or savory
mousse de foie gras a reduced *pâté de foie gras*, containing a minimum of 55% goose liver
mousse perlée d'Irlande carragheen [Irish moss; edible red seaweed]
mousseron Scotch bonnet mushroom [smooth tan or buff colored; sweet tasting]
mousseux effervescent; sparkling [said of wine]
moutarde mustard
    sauce moutarde mustard cream sauce [usually made with shallots, mustard, white wine, chicken broth and cream]
moutarde à l'ancienne grain mustard [coarse mustard made with whole black and brown mustard grains, somewhat sweet]
moutarde à l'estragon tarragon mustard [a variant of Dijon mustard]
moutarde à la tomate tomato mustard [a sweet mustard, made with whole mustard grains, spices, dried tomatoes, wine vinegar and sugar]
moutarde à la violette violet mustard [a sweet mustard made with spices, juice of violets]
moutarde allemande German mustard [a light, weak mustard; made with spices, turmeric and sugar]
moutarde au cassis blackcurrant mustard [a variant of Dijon mustard]
moutarde au miel honey mustard [a sweet mustard made with whole mustard grains and honey]
moutarde aux aromates (sweet) mustard with aromatic herbs
moutarde aux fines herbes mustard with sweet herbs [made with whole mustard grains, white wine, sugar, parsley, coriander and *fines herbes* (sweet herbs: parsley, chives, tarragon and chervil)]
moutarde brune mustard greens
moutarde brune douce aux aromates sweet brown mustard with sugar and spices
moutarde chinoise mustard greens
moutarde de Bénichon Bénichon mustard [more like jam than mustard; made of mustard flour, sugar, cinnamon, anise, cloves, white wine, mulled wine]
moutarde de Charroux Charroux mustard [stone-ground mustard seed, vinegar and St. Pouçain wine]

moutarde de Dijon Dijon mustard
moutarde de grains à l'ancienne grain mustard
moutarde de meaux Meaux mustard ["king of mustards" made with stone-ground mustard seeds]
moutarde des Allemands horseradish
moutarde douce sweet mustard [made with sugar, caramel and *fines herbes* (sweet herbs: parsley, chives, tarragon and chervil]
moutarde en grains pimentée whole grain mustard [a strong mustard made with whole mustard grains and chili pepper]
moutarde extra forte very hot mustard
moutarde forte hot mustard
moutarde italienne Italian mustard [sweet mustard made with cinnamon and preserved fruit]
moutarde Provencale Provencal mustard [a strong mustard made with whole mustard grains, red pepper, garlic, white wine, oil and herbs]
moutarde violette de Brive violet mustard from Brive [made with mustard grains and unfermented grape juice and pomace]
mouton sheep
    carré de mouton rack of mutton
    cuisse de mouton leg of mutton
    gigot de mouton leg of mutton
    haricot de mouton mutton stew
    ragoût de mouton mutton stew
    selle de mouton saddle of mutton
    viande de mouton mutton meat
mouton de pré-salé mutton raised on the salt marsh meadows
moutounesse lamb meat ham [a block of deboned lamb meat that is salted, rolled and covered with skin, then smoked and dried; the dark red ham is sliced very thin and served both as a starter (entrée) and with dishes such as cheese melt, pizza and salads]
mufle organ meat
muge mullet
mulard hybrid duck [lean and meaty; bred for meat and liver]
mulet doré golden gray mullet
mulet gris gray mullet
Munster AOC cheese [raw cow's milk, brine-washed brick-colored rind; strong, penetrating aroma; semi-soft cheese with a very strong taste]
mûr/mûre ripe
mûre blackberry
    confiture de mûre blackberry jam
mûre sauvage wild blackberry; blackberry bramble
mûre mulberry
mûre de ronce blackberry
mûre sauvage wild blackberry
muscade mace
    fleur de muscade mace spice
    noix de muscade nutmeg
museau organ meat
musqué musk
    courge musquée de Provence musk squash of Provence

fraisier musquée musk strawberry
muxu almond macaroon
myro cocktail made with one part blueberry cream and seven parts rosé wine
myrte myrtle
myrte piment myrtle spice; allspice
myrtille blueberry
nage/à la nage/en nage de fish or seafood cooked in its own juices or in juices of other ingredients such as vegetables and herbs
nantais soft butter biscuit
nantais/à la nantaise Nantes-style [garnished with potatoes, peas and turnips]
    canard nantais Nantes duck [small duck with a delicate taste]
nantua/à la nantua Nantua-style [with crayfish tails and truffles]
napé covered or coated with a sauce
Napoléon Royal Ann cherry [sweet white-fleshed cherry; red and pale yellow in color]
Napoléon two layers of puff pastry with a filling of cream and sometimes berries
napolitain cylindrical or hexagonal almond-dough pastry with fruit preserve filling and topped with almonds and/or candied fruit
napolitain small, thin square of bitter chocolate
napolitaine/à la napolitaine garnished with pasta, grated cheese and tomato sauce
nappage coating
nappage de caramel fudge topping
nappé uniformly covered with a sauce, cream or jelly
narbonnaise/à la narbonnaise Narbonne-style [typically with eggplant/aubergine, beans, and tomatoes]
nature simple, unadorned preparation; plain
naturel natural
    au naturel in brine; in its own juices
navaraise/à la navaraise Navarre style [usually with sweet peppers, onion and garlic]
navarin lamb or mutton stew with onions and potatoes
navarin d'agneau lamb stew
navel navel orange
navel jaune rutabaga turnip
navet turnip
    abatis aux navets poulty giblets (minus the liver) with chopped turnips, chopped onions, garlic, diced bacon and button onions added to raw sliced livers
    purée de navet turnip soup
navet boule d'or golden turnip
navet boulette de Bussy an heirloom variety of turnip with a sweet flavor
nectar nectar
nectar d'abricot apricot nectar
nectarine nectarine [smooth peach]
nedungo hot chili pepper [extremely hot pepper with a distinct flavor; for flavoring meat; native to Africa and Brazil]

nedungo piri-piri hot chili pepper [extremely hot pepper with a distinct flavor; for flavoring meat; native to Africa and Brazil]
nèfle medlar [a winter fruit, brown with large seeds]
nèfle du Japon/nèfle Japonaise a yellow-orange fruit from warm countries [ripens in spring; the large seed is poisonous, but the flesh, when thoroughly ripe, is juicy and lightly tart]
négus chocolate caramel candy with a sugar coating
neige snow [refers to whisked egg whites]
   oeufs à la neige snow eggs; floating island [stiffly beaten egg whites floating in a milky custard sauce]
   oeufs en neige stiffly beaten egg whites
neige sorbet made with red fruit juice with added sugar
neige de Florence very light white pasta flakes used to decorate clear soups
nélusko *petit four* pastry with a cherry stuffed with redcurrant jam and soaked in brandy
nem spring roll
Neufchâtel AOC cheese [mostly raw, some pasteurized cow's milk; dry, edible white rind; mushroom aroma; soft white, grainy cheese]
niçoise/à la niçoise Nice-style [typically: with garlic, olives, anchovies, tomatoes and green beans]
   salade niçoise tomatoes, cucumbers, fresh cooked dry beans, artichokes, green peppers, onion, boiled eggs, anchovies or tuna, black olives, olive oil, garlic and basil
nid nest
   au nid small birds, such as quail, presented in a nest of potato "straws" or wafers or pancakes, often accompanied by a garnish and sauce
   concombre au nid stuffed cucumber
   oeufs au nid hollowed out cucumber or tomato stuffed with soft-boiled or poached egg with cheese and mayonnaise
nid d'hirondelle swallow's nest [white, sometimes tinged with yellow, translucent lattice-like dried mucus; rare, expensive delicacy from southeast Asia; usually used in soup]
niflette puff pastry toped with custard
nigelle nigella [the black seeds are peppery]
niôle brandy
noir black
   beurre noir browned butter
noisette a small, choice piece of lean meat; medallion
noisette hazelnut; filbert
   beurre de noisette hazelnut butter
   chocolat aux noisettes hazelnut chocolate
noisette nutty; nut-brown in color
   beurre noisette browned butter
   café noisette coffee with milk
   pommes noisettes peeled potatoes cut into small balls and lightly sautéed in butter
noisette de beurre knob of butter
noisettine du Médoc caramel coated hazelnut

noissette d'agneau knuckle/medallion of lamb [choice cut of meat]
noix round "nut" of meat [from the inner thigh muscle; very tender with a fine texture]
   sous noix sub-knuckle (posterior thigh muscle, medium-grained, often used for cutlets]
noix walnut; nut
noix d'arec betel nut
noix de beurre knob of butter
noix de cajou cashew nut
noix de coco coconut
noix de coquilles saint-jacques scallops
noix de jambon round (cushion) of ham
noix de mer slipper limpet; sea walnut [said to have a nutty flavor]
noix de muscade nutmeg
noix de saint-jacques au pineau des charentes scallops in a white wine sauce
noix de veau round fillet of veal [from the inner thigh muscle; very tender and fine-textured]
noix d'entrecôte round (cushion) of rib steak
noix du Brésil Brazil nut
noix du Périgord AOC Périgord walnut
noix pâtissière knuckle of meat [from the front thigh of veal or pork; very tender]
noix pâtissière de porc round cushion or knuckle of pork [choice cut of meat]
noix pâtissière de veau round cushion or knuckle of veal [choice cut of meat]
non compris not included in the price
   service non compris service not included [it means you should leave a tip]
non potable not for drinking; unsafe to drink
nonnat sardine-like fish
nonette spiced bun
nonpareille caper
nonpareille tiny sugar pearls of many colors used for decorating cakes, pastries and ice cream
normande/à la normande Normandy style
norvegiènne Norwegian
   omelette norvegiènne Norwegian omelet; Baked Alaska [ice cream rolled inside cake, topped with meringue and then flambéed]
nougat nougat [made with egg whites, sugar, honey and almonds]
nougat de Limoux almond nougat [made with whole roasted almonds, honey, egg whites, sugar and vanilla]
nougat de Sault almond nougat [made with egg whites, lavender honey and whole almond]
nougat de Montélimar almond-pistachio nougat
nougatine de Nevers sponge cake filled with praline ice cream and fudge
nouilles noodles
   potage aux nouilles noodle soup

nouilles chinoises Chinese noodles
nouilles sautées crispy noodles
nouillettes small noodles
nourrain suckling pig
nouveau/nouvelle new
   pomme de terre nouveau new potato
   vin nouveau young wine
noyau kernel, stone, pit
   fruit à noyau stone fruit
   liqueur de noyau liqueur flavored with apricot and cherry kernels
Noyau de Poissy liqueur based on apricot kernels macerated or distilled in brandy with herbs; aromas of vanilla or orange blossom
Noyau de Vernon liqueur based on apricot kernels macerated or distilled in cognac; aromas of cherries and almonds
oeil d'anchois an appetizer consisting of a raw egg yolk encircled by anchovies and chopped onion
oeuf egg
oeuf à cheval egg on horseback [fried egg on top of grilled steak or hamburger]
oeuf à la coque boiled egg
oeuf à la moelle poached egg with marrow sauce [a brown sauce made with bone marrow and white wine]
oeuf à la poêle fried egg
oeuf au lait simple custard made with egg added to warmed milk and sugar and baked
oeuf au mirroir lightly fried egg [the yolk is still runny]
oeuf au plat fried egg
oeuf dur hard-boiled egg
oeuf en gelée hard-boiled/poached egg molded in aspic
oeuf filé raw whisked egg drizzled into hot soup to form "strings"
oeuf frit fried egg
oeuf mirror sunny-side-up egg
oeuf mollet soft boiled egg
oeuf moulé coddled egg [egg cooked in a mold with other ingredients, such as asparagus, ham, mushrooms, truffles]
oeuf poché poached egg
oeuf poché au champagne egg poached in champagne
oeufs à la bénédictine poached egg on creamed salt cod
oeufs à la/en neige snow eggs; floating island [stiffly beaten egg whites floating in a milky custard sauce]
oeufs à la causalade fried eggs and bacon
oeufs à la tripe chopped hard boiled eggs with onions (no tripe)
oeufs au chausseur scrambled eggs with chicken livers
oeufs au lait egg custard
oeufs au nid hollowed out cucumber or tomato stuffed with soft-boiled or poached eggs with cheese and mayonnaise
oeufs brayons eggs baked in ramekins with sour cream and served on toasted canapés with fresh cream and parsley
oeufs brouillés scrambled eggs

oeufs brouillés d'Argenteuil scrambled eggs gently cooked at a low heat so that they remain soft and creamy
oeufs bûcheronés oven-baked toast covered with ham and beaten eggs
oeufs cocottes eggs baked in ramekins with eggplant/aubergine, tomatoes, onion and olive oil
oeufs cocottes à la normande eggs baked in ramekins with mussels, cream and cheese
oeufs de lump lumpfish roe
oeufs de poisson fish eggs; roe
oeufs durs à la normande hard-boiled eggs with mussels and mushrooms
oeufs en cocotte eggs baked in ramekins [sometimes with eggplant/aubergine, tomatoes, onion and olive oil]
oeufs en gelée poached eggs in aspic
oeufs en gelée Stendhal poached eggs in aspic with bits of ham
oeufs en meurette poached eggs in a rich red wine sauce with bacon, onions and shallots and served with toasted garlic bread
oeufs farcis stuffed eggs [hard-boiled eggs; the yolks are mixed with mayonnaise and mustard or other ingredients]
oeufs florentine poached eggs on spinach with a cheese sauce
oeufs Justine hard boiled eggs stuffed with mushrooms and thick cream sauce
oeufs montés/oeufs montés en neige stiffly beaten egg whites
oeufs Rossini poached egg yolks baked on a bed of stiffly beaten egg whites, or on a bed of chicken livers, or on a bed of *foie gras*
oeufs sur plat fried eggs
offert with the compliments of the house; free
oie goose
  confit d'oie potted goose/canned goose [preserved in fat]
  foie gras d'oie goose foie gras [fat goose liver]
oie à l'instar de Visé roast goose in a garlicky cream sauce
oie cendrée graylag/greylag goose
oie en daube d'Alençon goose stew
oie rôtie roast goose
oie sauvage wild goose
oignon onion
  aux petits oignons with pickling onions
  petit oignon blanc scallion; spring onion
  purée d'oignon white onion soup
  sauce aux onions finely diced onions, butter and flour
  soupe à l'oignon onion soup
  soupe aux oignons onion soup
oignon doux des Cévennes sweet onion from Cévennes
oignon frais fresh onion
oignon jaune yellow onion
oignon rouge red onion
oignonade a dish that includes onions
oiseau bird
oiseau sans tête veal bird [thin slice of meat rolled with a filling and made to look like a small bird]
oliu di Corsica AOC olive oil of Corsica

olive olive
olive de Lucques gourmet green olive [said to taste meaty and sweet with hints of almonds and avocados]
olive de mer edible mollusk
olive de Nice AOC olives from Nice [the AOC includes olives and olive pastes from Nice]
olive de Nîmes AOC olives from the area around Nîmes
olive noire black olive
olive noire de Nyons AOC black olive from Nyons
olive verte green olive
olives cassées de la vallée des Baux-de-Provence, **AOC** crushed olives from the Valley of Baux-de-Provence
olives noires de la vallée des Baux-de-Provence, **AOC** black olives from the Valley of Baux-de-Provence
omble/omble chevalier char [from freshwater arctic lakes]
ombre freshwater grayling [small freshwater fish; somewhat endangered]
omelette omelet/omelette
omelette à la pipérade pepper omelet; Basque omelet [made with chilies, preferably Espelette, onion, tomato and ham]
omelette aux cèpes omelet with *cèpe* mushrooms
omelette aux piments doux de Gascogne omelet with sweet peppers from Gascogne
omelette basquaise Basque omelet [omelet with chilies (preferably *espelette* chilies), onion, tomato and ham (preferably Bayonne ham)]
omelette baveuse runny omelet
omelette de la mère Poulard omelet made by beating the egg whites and yolks separately
omelette fourrée filled omelet
omelette nature plain omelet
omelette landaise omelet with gently browned pine nuts
omelette norvégienne Baked Alaska [a dessert made with sponge cake, ice cream and meringue; may be flambéed with Grand Marnier]
omelette salée savory omelet
omelette sucrée sweet omelet
omelette surprise/omelette soufflé en surprise baked Alaska [a dessert made with sponge cake, ice cream and meringue; may be flambéed with Grand Marnier]
omelette vallée d'Auge sweet omelet topped with browned diced apples in butter and cream and flambéed with Calvados
onctueux unctuous; creamy [often said of cheese]
onglet hanger steak; skirt steak
opaline opaline [sugar is melted with water and glucose in a non-stick pan in a thin layer and cooked until it becomes a solid sheet or lace-like sheet; it is then chilled until solid and brittle]
opéra dessert made with layers of light almond biscuits, coffee-flavored butter cream and chocolate *ganache* (buttery chocolate cream), topped with chocolate icing
opéra/à l'opera opera-style [with chicken livers, duchesse potatoes and asparagus tips]

orange orange
orange amère Seville orange
orange bigarde Seville orange
orange sanguine blood orange
oreille ear [usually pig's ear]
oreille de mer abalone
oreiller pillow
oreilles d'âne literally: donkey's ears [a lasagna made with layers of lasagna pasta a wild spinach called donkey's ears]
oreilles de cochon pig's ears [boiled with vegetables, or breaded and fried]
oreilles de cochon pig's ears fritters [sweet fritter shaped like a pig's ear]
oreillette a sweet, flat fried pastry (fritter)
orge barley
   crème d'orge barley soup
orge perlé pearl barley
orgue/morue orgue Greenland cod
orientale/à l'orientale Eastern Mediterranean style or Balkan style [with tomatoes, garlic and saffron]
origan oregano; wild marjoram
orléanaise/a l'orléanaise Orleans-style [typically: with braised chicory and potatoes]
orloff/veau orloff haunch of veal with cheese and mushrooms
ormeau/ormet/ormier abalone
oronge Caesar's mushroom [rare and highly valued type of agaric mushroom; has an orange cap and yellow gills; firm white flesh; has a pleasant aroma and a sweet, nutty flavor]
orphie marine garfish
ortie nettle
ortie de mer sea anemone
os bone
os à moelle marrow bone
osciètre caviar [small, firm and golden with hints of hazelnut; from the Black Sea, Caspian Sea, and Azov Sea]
oseille sorrel
   feuille d'oseille sorrel leaf
ossiètre caviar [true caviar, smaller than beluga eggs; color ranges from brown to golden (the golden variety is rare and has a very rich flavor); highly prized, almost as much as Beluga]
osso buco veal shank slowly simmered in white wine broth with aromatic herbs and vegetables
ouillade garlicky bean and vegetable soup
oursin sea urchin
   langues d'oursin the sexual glands of the sea urchin, said to be comparable to caviar
oursin violet violet sea urchin
oursinade sea urchin soup
oursinade the eating of sea urchins [the term refers to an array of ways to eat sea urchins: raw on bread with a drop of lemon juice; in a fish stew; with a cream sauce or on boiled eggs; the taste and texture do not appeal to everyone, but connoisseurs

say that the flavor is salty with both sweet and bitter nuances, with hints of smoke, hazelnut, honey and even blood; the texture is creamv]
ourson en guimauve a milk chocolate in the shape of a little bear
ouvert open
pacane pecan nut
pachade thick crêpe [made simply with flour, egg and milk; traditionally eaten by farmers at breakfast "after soup and before cheese"]
paella paella [a Spanish dish consisting of flavored rice (usually with saffron) garnished with any of a variety of meats (fish, seafood, foul, ham, sausage, rabbit, etc.) and vegetables (tomatoes, peppers, beans, peas, artichoke, etc.)
pageot porgy [marine fish in the sea bream family]
pagre red porgy; sea bream
paillasson literally: straw mat [a dish made with fried grated potatoes or fried grated zucchini/courgettes which form a kind of "mat" (thin pancake)]
paillard de veau thin slice of veal, grilled or fried
paille straw; stick; bread stick
  vin de paille/vin paillé golden-colored wine made from grapes partially dried on beds of straw, thus concentrating the sugar and making the wine sweeter
paille/pommes paille fried potato sticks
paille au fromage cheese bread stick
paille aux framboises raspberry straw [a gooey "sandwich" made of baked puff pastry or pasta pastry and jam; the layers of pastry are rolled, baked, then cut into cross sections that look like coiled rope or straws, then spread with raspberry jam]
paillet/vin paillet pale red wine
paillette flake; flaky pastry or thin lacy crêpe
pailleté feuillantine thin crunchy "cake" made with melted chocolate mixed with crushed thin lacy crêpe and spread between two paper sheets to harden; when cooled, the pastry is cut into pieces
paillettes thin rings or strips of potatoes, onions or pastry
paillettes dorées cheese straws
paillettes d'oignons frits fried onion rings
paillettes framboises two layers of crunchy flaky pastry with raspberry jam filling
pain bread
pain à cacheter wafer
pain à l'ail garlic bread
pain à la grecque small rectangular cake of bread pudding, brown sugar and cinnamon
pain à la tôle bread baked in a rectangular mold; weighs about one kilo (2.2 pounds)
pain à soupe twice-baked bread [very dry disc of bread with a dark brown crust; pieces are cut off to be dipped into soup]
pain au chocolat chocolate pastry [similar to a croissant, but rectangular, and containing one or two bars of chocolate]

pain au lait literally "milk bread" [small bun or dinner roll made with butter and milk, but no eggs (as would be the case with *brioche*)]
pain au levain sourdough bread
pain au sucre toast with maple syrup
pain aux graines seeded bread
pain aux noix walnut bread
pain aux raisins raisin bread; raisin roll
pain azyme unleavened bread [usually baked at Passover]
pain bis brown bread; whole meal bread
pain blanc white bread
pain brié heavy, oblong loaf of white bread with a tight crumb
pain brioché sweet egg bread
pain complet granary bread; whole meal bread
pain cordon wheat or wheat/rye bread loaf baked with a braided or unbraided strip of dough (*cordon*) on top
pain crestou whole grain bread made with sesame seeds
pain d'Aix a small, slightly oblong loaf with a lengthwise slit resulting from the baking process; may also be a fancifully shaped sourdough loaf (linked rounds, flower petals, etc.)
pain d'épices spicy gingerbread
pain de Beaucaire bread of Beaucaire [a kind of sourdough bread characterized by a lengthwise split in the light, thin crust]
pain de campagne farmhouse bread
pain de froment wheat bread
pain de Gênes almond sponge cake
pain de la Mecque sweet puff pastry [large oval shape with a golden crust decorated with granulated sugar and almond flakes]
pain de légumes vegetable loaf [puréed vegetables baked in a mold]
pain de maïs corn bread
pain de ménage home made bread
pain de Nantes small round cake made with lemon or orange scented dough and baked in a pan lined with almond flakes, covered with icing and a powdering of sugar
pain de poisson fish loaf; fish terrine
pain de sarrasin buckwheat bread
pain de seigle rye bread
pain de son whole meal bread; bran bread
pain de sucre sugar loaf
pain de veau/pain de viande meatloaf [minced veal and pork baked in a mold]
pain de volaille finely minced chicken meatloaf
pain d'épeautre spelt bread
pain d'épice gingerbread
pain des paysans chestnut flour bread
pain doré French toast [stale bread coated with egg and crisply fried]
pain entier wholemeal bread
pain épi bread stick about the size of an ear of corn
pain garrot du Cotentin bagel-like bun

pain grillé toast
pain integral wholemeal bread
pain mollet soft white bread roll
pain noir brown bread; wholemeal bread
pain non levé unleavened bread; matzo
pain parisien large baguette
pain perdu egg-coated fried bread; French toast
pain pidé Turkish bread [soft, light bread made during Ramadan; decorated with sesame seeds, black cumin (nigella seeds), poppy seeds or cumin; may be filled with cheese, ground meat, onions]
pain pistolet small baguette used for sandwiches
pain plat flat bread
pain plié folded bread [the dough is folded back on itself and then baked]
pain polka round, flattish bread with a cross-hatch pattern incised on top
pain rôti toast
pain tranché sliced bread
pain trouvé French toast topped with white sauce, chopped ham and grated cheese
pain viennois milk bread
pain-coing quince bread
paiper fier a winter dish consisting of potatoes and sausages usually cooked with butter, onion, garlic and savory
Pajaro/fraises Pajaro high-quality strawberry
palais/palais de boeuf beef pallet [fleshy membrane of the inner, upper part of the mouth; a type of red tripe]
palamos/gambas de palamos king prawn from Palamós, Spain
paleron cut of beef from the area above the shoulder near the neck [usually braised, poached or stewed]
palet puck biscuit/cookie [dry biscuit that looks like a shuffleboard puck; rich in butter and flavored (rum, anise, vanilla, etc.) and dusted with almond powder; traditionally made with currants]
palet d'or rich chocolate cake or cookie decorated on top with "gold leaf" (bits of golden thin lacy crêpe)
palette cut of pork just below the shoulder or just below the ham
palette à la diable a traditional dish in Alsace consisting of roasted pork (the portion just below the shoulder or just below the ham) in a mustard (and sometimes beer) sauce
palme palm
palmier palm tree
   coeur de palmier palm heart
palmier palm tree-shaped flaky pastry dusted with powdered sugar
palois two-layer cake, with a filling of chocolate or sliced apples or other fruit
palombe pigeon; wood pigeon
   salmi de palombe wood pigeon stew [made with red wine, olive oil, bacon or cured ham, onion, garlic, bay leaf, thyme, flour salt and pepper]
palourde clam
   porc aux palourdes pork with clams

soupe épaisse de palourdes clam chowder
pamplemousse grapefruit; pummelo
panade bread soup
panaché mixture [of ingredients, such as salads, fruits]
panaché shandy [mixture of beer and lemonade]
pan bagnat tuna sandwich [typically: a round loaf of bread sliced in half, the two sides drizzled with olive oil and filled with tuna, hard boiled eggs, lettuce, peppers, tomatoes, olives]
panaché garnished with flageolet and green beans
panaché multicolored mixtures or layers
panade rustic soup made with water, milk and bread
pancake pancake
panais parsnip
pané coated with (seasoned) flour or breadcrumbs prior to frying
panisse fried chickpea dough; chickpea pancake
panisse aux cébettes fried chickpea pancake with small spring onions
pannacotta Italian baked cream dessert [thick cream, honey or sugar and egg white baked in a low oven]
pannequet twice-folded *crêpe* or pancake with sweet or savory filling
pantin/pâté pantin savory crusty pastry filled with pork, veal, sausage, etc.
panure coating of breadcrumbs
panzerottu beignet/fritter/donut [made with a dough of rice flour, wheat flour and chickpea four; may be stuffed with chopped chard and raisins; sprinkled with sugar while warm
papaline d'Avignon chocolate candy resembling a thistle flower, filled with *origan du Comtat* (a liqueur made with oregano and other herbs)
papaye papaya
papet stew/hot pot of leeks and potatoes, often served with smoked ham or sausage
papeton d'aubergine aubergine/eggplant flan [a flan made with aubergine/eggplant caviar and eggs; cooked in a mold the shape of the pope's tiara and served with a tomato sauce]
papillion literally: butterfly [small flake pastry cake dusted with sugar]
papillon oyster
papillote parchment
   en papillote baked in a parchment wrap (or aluminum foil) as a way to hold in moisture, thus steaming the food
paprika paprika; paprika powder
paquette dark green lobster roe; the lobster that yields the roe
parfait rich iced mousse made with fresh cream [various flavors]
parfumé flavored; scented
Paris-Brest a circle of choux pastry sliced to make two rounds which are filled with praline cream
Parisien cream pastry with lemon marzipan, candied fruit and topped with Italian meringue

Parisien/à la Parisien vegetable accompaniment [potato, artichoke bottoms, and sometimes half-braised lettuce, in a deglazed wine sauce]
parlementin de Rennes pastry consisting of almonds, apples and cider
parmentier a name applied to various dishes containing potatoes [potato cream soup, omelet or scrambled eggs with fried potatoes, or a meat filling with potatoes]
    purée parmentier purée of potatoes, leeks and onions
parmentier shepherd's pie
    hachis parmentier cottage pie, shepherd's pie
pascade a pancake/galette made with walnut oil, eggs, milk and wheat flour fried in plenty of oil
pasilla chili pepper [several varieties; true pasilla is the dried *chilaca* pepper; mildly hot with a rich flavor]
passe-crassane pear [round pear with thick, rough skin, gold with red veins; grainy flesh which is creamy and tangy]
pastèque watermelon
    pastèque à confiture watermelon with pale green flesh used for making preserves
pastèque avec pépins watermelon with seeds
pastèque sans pépins seedless watermelon
pastis anise liqueur
pastis landais a cake-like bread containing much butter and flavored with rum, orange flower water and vanilla
pâtisson pattypan squash
pastizzu pastry [a generic word used in Corsica to refer to a dessert made with stale bread, caramelized sugar, milk and eggs baked in a mold and sometimes served with a coating of caramel sauce]
patate/patate douce sweet potato
pâte dough [for bread or pastry]
pâte cheese/pate [the part of the cheese that is inside the rind or crust]
pâte pastry; pie pastry
pâte à choux a light pastry dough for puff pastry
pâte à foncé shortcrust pastry; pie pastry
pâte à pain dough; bread dough
pâte à sucre sugar pastry
pâte à tarte pastry
pâte brisée pie pastry; pie crust
pâte croquante crisp almond and sugar pastry
pâte d'amandes almond paste; marzipan
pâte de coing crystalized quince [quince pulp cooked with an equal amount of sugar; can be cut into squares]
pâte de fruits crystalized fruit; fruit jelly
pâte de guimauve marsh-mallow
pâte de Pâques veal and pork pie
pâte fueillletée pastry; flaky pastry
pâte sablée short pastry; sugar pastry
pâte sucrée sweet pie pastry
pâté meat pie or pasty

pâté pâté [minced or chopped meat cooked in a mold and allowed to cool; sliced and served as an appetizer]
pâté aux pommes de terre potato pie, sometimes with meat or cream added
pâté aux tartoufes potato pie, sometimes with meat or cream added
pâté d'alouettes à l'ancienne pie made with minced lark and truffles
pâté de campagne farmhouse pâté [a rustic terrine (a coarse meatloaf) typically containing containing pork, chicken or pork liver, onion, parsley, garlic, cream and brandy, and seasonings]
pâté de canard chopped duck meat, liver, heart and gizzards baked in a pastry shell
pâté de foie liver pâté
pâté de foie gras fat liver pâté [duck or goose liver paste; made from birds that have been fattened by force-feeding them corn with a gavage (tube); outside of France, the ducks/geese are fed naturally; the flavor of the pâté should be rich, buttery and delicate]
pâté de fromage cheese pâté
pâté de Houdan chicken breast, chicken liver and sausage baked in a pastry casing
pâté de lapin de garenne à la mode de Gisors wild rabbit, veal and pork tenderloin baked in a pastry shell
pâté de tête head cheese; pâté of pig's head meat; jellied pork brawn; potted head
pâté en croûte dense meat pâté baked in a crust/pastry shell
pâté en terrine dense meat pâté baked in a terrine or other mold
pâté grandmère grandmother's pâté [a rustic terrine (a coarse meatloaf) typically made with pork and either beef or rabbit, white wine, shallots, garlic, cream, cognac and seasoned with cinnamon, ginger, cloves and nutmeg]
pâté lorrain a pâté of pork and veal marinated in wine with shallots and parsley and cooked in a flaky pastry shell
paté maison house-made pâte served as an appetizer
pâté pantin savory meat pâté in a pastry shell, baked without a mold; served warm
pâtes pasta
  plat de pâtes pasta plate
  salade de pâtes pasta salad
pâtes à potage soup noodles
pâtes de fruits pieces of crystallized fruit
pâtes fraîches fresh pasta
pâtes vegetarienne vegetarian pasta
patelle limpet [barnacle-like shellfish]
patience fraxinoise sugar cookie scented with orange flower
pâtisserie cake; pastry
pâtissière/crème pâtissière thick pastry cream [milk, egg yolks, sugar and flour and usually flavored with vanilla]
pâtisson summer squash; pattypan squash [small and flat with scalloped edges]
patte foot

patte noir literally: black foot
   poulet pattes noirs black footed chicken
   volaille pattes noirs black footed foul/poultry
patranque a rustic dish made of stale bread soaked in milk or broth and fresh tome or *Cantal* cheese; drained and worked in a pan with onions and garlic or chopped parsley
patudo a type of tuna
pauchouse a fish dish made with two kinds of lean fish (such as pike and perch) and two kinds of fatty fish (such as eel, tench or salmon) cooked in a white wine sauce
paupiette thin slice or fillet of meat or fish stuffed and rolled and shaped to look like a bird]
paupiette d'anchois anchovy roulade appetizer [flattened anchovy fillet rolled with a stuffing of minced fish]
paupiette de boeuf beef roulade [thin fillet of beef rolled with a stuffing of pâté, mousse, or other filling]
paupiette de dinde turkey roulade [thin fillet of turkey rolled with a variety of fillings such as bacon, mushrooms, parsley, thyme, bay leaf, onion and white wine]
paupiette de poisson fish roulade [thin fillet of fish rolled with a stuffing of pâté, mousse, or other filling]
paupiette de veau veal roulade [thin fillet of veal rolled with a stuffing of mushrooms, vegetables, bacon, or other filling]
pavé literally: cobble stone [paver; thick slice or slab of meat, cheese, cake, etc.]
pavé thick rectangular cheese
pavé thick rectangular pastry or dessert
pavé de boeuf slab of beef
pavé de cabillaud slab of cod; cod paver
pavé de rumsteak slab of rump steak
pavé de saumon slab of salmon
pavé nantais almond-sugar cake [made with butter, powdered sugar, almond powder, flour, eggs and rum; with a light sugar icing; good with a nice cup of tea]
pavie a variety of peach
pavot poppy
   graines de pavot poppy seeds
paysanne/à la paysanne peasant-style [rustic dish, usually with onions, carrots and bacon]
peau skin; peel
   grillé sur sa peau grilled with its skin still on
pèbre d'ai/pèbre d'ase savory [herb]
pêche peach
pêche-abricot yellow peach
pêche de vigne red peach [ripens late; sometimes grown between rows of *vigne* (grape vines)]
pêche Melba peach Melba [vanilla ice cream with peaches and raspberry sauce]
pêcheur/du pêcheur in the style of the fisherman
peigne the family of shellfish that includes scallops
pela savoyarde potatoes and onions with melted Reblochon cheese

pélamide bonita; small tuna
Pélardon AOC goat cheese [raw goat's milk; natural crust; soft, runny cheese with a hint of hazelnuts; may have a natural crust, a crust covered with ashes or with olive oil and herbs, or may be consumed as sweet curds with jam, honey or chestnuts; may be breaded and fried and served warm in a dandelion salad]
pella potatoes and onions with melted Reblochon cheese
pensées brouillées fried pastries
pépin pip; seed
pépin de courge squash seed; pumpkin seed
pépon/péponide squash; gourd
perche perch [freshwater fish]
perche de mer sea perch; sea bass
perche-soleil butterfish
perche-truit largemouth bass
perdreau young partridge
perdreau à la normande partridge with potatoes and cream
perdrix partridge
perdu/pain perdu French toast
Périgourdine/à la Périgourdine in the style Périgord [typically includes truffles or *foie gras*]
Périgueux/sauce Périgueux in the style Périgord [typically includes truffles or *foie gras*]
perlé literally: like a pearl [pearl-shaped; polished]
perlot small oyster
perroquet peppermint and *pastis* alcoholic beverage
pérouille pear [a variety which ripens in summer]
persil parsley
persil frisé curly parsley
persil plat flat-leaf parsley
persillade a mixture of chopped parsley and chopped shallots and/or garlic, sometimes with the addition of breadcrumbs
persillé with finely-chopped parsley
persillé marbled with fat (beef, ham)
   jambon persillé ham with parsley [typically: ham and pork shoulder cut into small cubes, coated with aspic flavored with parsley, onion, shallot, thyme and garlic; cooked in a broth of white wine, mustard and wine vinegar]
persillé blue-veined cheese
pet de nonne light, fluffy fritter
pétéram offal stew [tripe and sheep's trotters]
pétillant sparkling; fizzy; bubbly
   eau pétillante sparkling water
   vin pétillant sparkling wine
petit small
petit déjeuner breakfast
petit beurre butter biscuit
petit carré de Nice sweet bell pepper
petit four small pastry/delicacy
petit duc/au petit duc small duke style [typically: creamed chicken in small pastry shells with truffles, asparagus tips and sometimes mushrooms]

petit gris little gray mushroom [white flesh, fragile, very fine]
petit gris little gray snail [fine, delicate snail; can be farmed]
petit gris de Rennes heirloom variety of melon cultivated near Rennes [small fruit with a gray-green skin, very sweet]
petit hochet mildly hot pepper
petit lait buttermilk; milk whey
petit noir strong espresso, no milk
petit pain small baguette; bread roll
petit pain fourré filled bread roll [small baguette with a filling such as cheese or minced meat]
petit pâté de Nîmes tiny pastry filled with veal or pork, or sometimes salt cod
petit pâté de Pézenas tiny pastry with a sweet and savory filling of lamb and raisins
petit pois pea
  canard aux petits pois duck with peas
petit pois en conserve canned peas
petit salé salt pork; salted pork sausage
petit salé aux lentilles salt pork and lentils
petit vert marseillais chili pepper
petite crêpe épaisse crumpet; pancake; griddle cake [literally "thick little crêpe"]
petites tripe of sheep or calf
petits fours small desserts such as chocolates, sweetmeats or decorated cakes to accompany coffee after a meal
petits pois à la française peas, scallions and lettuce cooked in a creamy sauce: sometimes with bacon
petits pois en boîte canned/tinned peas
petits secs small cream biscuits
pétoncle small scallop; variegated scallop
pettanmamia a dessert consisting of cooked apple slices with fresh cheese curd and black cherry jam
pézize edible wild mushroom [bright orange or brown]
pholade piddock or angel wing [edible mollusk]
piadina thin Italian flatbread
pibale elver; eel
picatta meat that is sliced, breaded and sautéed, served with a sauce
pichade a kind of pizza dressed with a tomato sauce, anchovies and black olives
pichet small pitcher; jug
pichet d'eau pitcher of water
pichet de 25cl quarter-liter pitcher [about one pint]
pichet de 50cl half-liter pitcher [about one quart]
pichet de rosé a pitcher of rosé wine
pichet de vin pitcher of wine
  grand pichet a one liter pitcher
pichet de vin blanc pitcher of white wine
pichet de vin rouge pitcher of red wine
picholine green table olive
picoussel chopped chard, sausage (or pork) and onion with prunes baked in a batter of eggs, milk and flour

pièce piece; portion
pièce de boeuf portion of beef
pie/à la pie like a magpie [and arrangement in black and white; a white cheese with dry black herbs]
pied foot; trotter
pied-de-cheval large oyster
pied de mouton mutton's foot mushroom; hedgehog mushroom; sweet tooth mushroom [yellow to light orange to brown in color; pleasant odor; mild, sweet, nutty and peppery]
pieds cendrillons literally: Cinderella's feet [minced pigs' trotters, mushrooms and truffles wrapped in pastry or wrapped in paper and cooked in hot ashes]
pieds de porc pig's feet
pieds de mouton à la rouennaise sheep's feet stuffed with pork, breaded and fried]
pieds de porc Sainte-Ménehould Sainte-Ménehould pigs feet [pigs feet cooked slowly for a very long time and served with Sainte-Ménehould sauce (made with onion, butter, white champagne and white wine, herbs and mustard); gourmands crack the bones to savor the fragrant, luscious marrow]
pieds paquets/pieds et paquets a dish of sheep offal (tripe and feet) simmered in white wine and tomato sauce; the tripe is formed into packets and filled with parsley, garlic and pepper
piémontaise/à la piémontaise Italian piedmont style [typically: with risotto or polenta, white truffles and maybe tomato sauce]
　risotto à la piémontaise rice with tomatoes, onions, and bacon or chopped cooked chicken
　salade piémontaise salad with tomatoes, hard boiled eggs, potatoes, ham and pickles with mayonnaise
pieuvre octopus
pigeon pigeon
pigeon en crapaudine grilled pigeon splayed out to resemble a toad (*crapaud*)
pigeonneau squab; young pigeon
pignatelle ham and cheese fritter
pignon pine nut
pignolat de Nostradamus pastry containing pine nuts, sugar, rose water and fennel
pilaf spicy rice
pilchard herring; sardine
pilet pintail duck
pili-pili African bird's eye chili [extremely hot red pepper]
pilon drumstick; leg of poultry
pilon de cuisse chicken drumstick
piment pimento; pepper; capsicum
　feuille de piment leaf of the allspice tree; strong flavor of cloves
　poudre de piment chili powder
piment antillais hot pepper [fire-engine red; one of the hottest peppers in the world]
piment banane jaune yellow banana pepper
piment d'Anglet Anglet pepper [a sweet pepper]

piment d'espelette mildly hot pepper [a widely used and highly regarded pepper]
piment de Cayenne cayenne pepper [hot red pepper]
piment de la Bresse small hot red pepper [medium hot; used in sauces, *coulis* (bisque; thick sauce) or to accompany cold meat]
piment de Jamaïque allspice
piment doux mild pepper; sweet pepper
piment doux de Gascogne sweet pepper of Gascogne
piment doux des Landes sweet pepper of Landes
piment fort hot pepper; chilli pepper
piment fort Gorria pepper [a type of red *espelette* pepper; somewhat hot]
piment jaune yellow pepper
piment Kabyle Kabyle pepper [a pepper from the Kabylie region in the north of Algeria]
piment lampion hot pepper [fire-engine red; one of the hottest peppers in the world]
piment langue de oiseau hot bird-tongue chili pepper [extremely hot pepper with a distinct flavor]
piment martin bird pepper or martin pepper [slightly hotter than cayenne pepper]
piment Naga Viper extremely hot pepper [said to be one of the hottest]
piment orange orange pepper
piment rouge red pepper; chili pepper
piment végétarien vegetarian chili pepper [mild sweet pepper]
piment vert green chili pepper
piment zozio hot chili pepper [extremely hot pepper with a distinct flavor]
pimenté spicy; piquant
pimiento del piquillo piquillo pepper
pimiento morrón sweet bell pepper [of any color: red, green, yellow, purple]
pimprenelle salad burnet [pungent, slightly bitter tasting leaves]
pintade guinea fowl
    blanc de pintade guinea fowl breast
    blanc de pintade farci stuffed breast of guinea fowl
pintade au cidre guinea fowl prepared with cider
pintade vallée d'Auge guinea fowl prepared with cider, Calvados, cream and apples
pintadeau young guinea fowl
pipérade a typical Basque dish made with the colors of the Basque flag: red tomatoes, green peppers and white onions; flavored with the *Espelette* pepper
pipérade omelet made with *espelette* peppers, onion, tomatoes and ham
piquant hot; spicy
    sauce piquante hot sauce [many variations exist]
piquenchâgne a pie-like dessert made with flaky pastry, custard and pears (or sometimes quinces)
Piquette a dairy dessert made with partially drained cheese curd, sometimes with milk or cream, sugar or fruit added

piquillo/pimiento del piquillo piquillo pepper
piri-piri hot chili pepper [extremely hot pepper with a distinct flavor]
pissaladière a type of pizza topped with onion and black olives and often with anchovies [traditionally without tomatoes or tomato sauce]
pissaladière Provençale a kind of pizza dressed with tomato sauce, anchovies and black olives
pissalat anchovy purée with olive oil
pissenlit dandelion
    salade de pissenlit wild herb salad [typically: seasonal wild herbs, especially dandelion, with *lardons* (bacon) and sometimes hard-boiled eggs; a vinaigrette is made in the pan with the bacon fat and then drizzled over the salad]

pistache pistachio
pistache de mouton a l'ail shoulder of mutton simmered with diced ham and fifty cloves of garlic
pistoles flattened seedless prunes
pistolet milk bread roll
pistou basil sauce [with tomatoes, garlic and olive oil (never with cheese)]
    soupe au pistou soup with summer vegetables and pasta, served with *pistou* sauce
pithiviers pastry-pie [usually sweet with a filling of almond paste or possibly chocolate and cream; may be savory, with fillings such as ham and leeks, onions, duck liver, cheese, etc.]
pithiviers/pithiviers Parisien almond pastry-pie [made with a frangipane paste and rum or kirsch between two layers of flaky pastry]
plancha metal slab on which food is grilled over a flame
plat flat
    eau plate literally: flat water [still water; non-carbonated water]
plantain/plantain aromatique pig weed; plantain
    banane plantain plantain; banana for cooking
plantain potagère buck's horn plantain [salad herb]
plat/plat principal main dish [in the US, it is called the entrée; however, *entrée* in French is the "opening" dish, or starter]
plat de côtes de boeuf beef ribs
plat de côtes de porc pork ribs
plat de côtes d'agneau lamb ribs
plat de côtes de veau veal ribs
plateau tray
plateau de fromages cheese platter
plateau de fruits de mer seafood platter
pleurote oyster mushroom [a flat, white mushroom that grows on tree trunks; used in stir-fry or sautéed in butter]
pleurote corne d'abondance cornucopia mushroom
pleurote en coquille oyster mushroom
plie flounder; plaice
plie au cidre flounder in a creamy cider sauce

plombières/glace plombières ice cream made with milk, cream, sugar, eggs and candied fruit
plum pudding plum pudding
pluvier plover
pochade stew of freshwater fish with raisins and carrots
poché poached
pocheteau/pocheteau gris skate [ray-like fish, once common but now endangered]
pôchouse a fish dish made with two kinds of lean fish such as pike, perch, trout or pike-perch (*sandre*) and two kinds of fatty fish such as eel, tench, carp or salmon, cooked in a white wine sauce (generally *Bourgogne aligoté*) and accompanied with potatoes, bacon and croutons
poêlé pan fried; seared
poêlée de legumes mixed fried vegetables
poids/selon poids according to weight
point point [as in "to reach a certain point"]
   à point medium; medium rare
pointe de filet pork tenderloin; pork fillet
pointe d'ail touch of garlic
pointes d'asperges asparagus tips
poiré perry [a sparkling beer-like alcoholic beverage made from fermented pear juice; usually made with *Plant de Blanc* pears]
poire pear
   alcool de poire pear brandy
   eau de poire pear brandy
poire à poiré a variety of pear used for making *poiré* (a sparkling beer-like alcoholic beverage made from fermented pear juice)
poire à rissoles pear [a cooking pear]
poire de fisée pear [ripens in autumn]
poire de septembre pear [autumn pear; sweet, fragrant, juicy flesh; tangy and slightly musky]
poire Douillard pear
poire Doyenné pear [more than a dozen varieties of pear have *Doyenné* in their name]
poire duchesse Duchess pear
poire Louise pear [elongated fruit, green skin with a yellow blush; firm flesh; ripens in autumn]
poire Louise Bonne d'Avranches sweet pear [green with a red blush]
poire Passe-Crassane de Rouen large winter pear
poireau leek
   blanc de poireau white portion of the leek
   purée de poioreaux leek soup
   soupe aux poireaux leek soup
poireau de Créances IGP leek; tender, with a light, sweet taste
poires Alma pears poached in port wine
poires Belle Hèlene pears poached in syrup and served with vanilla ice cream and chocolate sauce
pois pea
petits pois peas; petit pois
pois à la francaise peas braised with lettuce

pois cassés split peas
pois chiche chickpea
pois écossés shelled peas
pois gourmands sugar peas; edible-pod peas
poisson fish
   brochette de poisson fish kebab
   filet de poisson fillet of fish
   pain de poisson fish loaf [minced fish baked in a mold]
poisson brun browned fish in a wine sauce
poisson-chat catfish
poisson de Loire au beurre blanc fish such as pike, perch or salmon in white sauce
poisson frit fried fish
poisson fumé smoked fish
poisson loup wolffish; sea wolf; ocean catfish; devil fish
poisson meunière aux amandes fish browned in butter and topped with almonds
poitrine beef brisket; pork, lamb, veal or mutton breast
poitrine de porc pork belly
poitrine fumée smoked streaky bacon
poivrade butter sauce, white sauce or vinaigrette with pepper
poivrade small, young purple artichoke, eaten raw or cooked
poivrade/sauce poivrade a pepper sauce made from diced carrots, onions and celery with wine, vinegar and pepper
poivre pepper
   filet de maquereau au poivre peppered mackerel fillet
   steak au poivre pepper steak
poivré peppery
poivre blanc white pepper
poivre concassé coarse ground pepper
poivre d'âne savory/savoury [wild herb]
poivre de cayenne cayenne pepper
poivre de Jamaïque allspice
poivre en graines peppercorns
poivre giroflée allspice
poivre gris black pepper
poivre noir black pepper
poivre rose pink pepper [from Reunion and Madagascar; mild flavor, almost sweet at first, then aromatic, spicy and hot]
poivre vert green pepper [from immature (green) pepper corns]
   sauce au poivre vert green pepper sauce
poivron sweet pepper; capsicum [mild/sweet pepper]
poivron Ariane sweet pepper [very tasty bright orange pepper]
poivron aristocrat sweet pepper [dark red when fully ripe]
poivron Carré d'Asti sweet pepper
poivron corno di toro rosso sweet pepper [literally: red bull horn pepper]
poivron doux d'Espagne sweet Spanish pepper
poivron farci stuffed pepper
poivron grillé grilled pepper
poivron gypsy sweet pepper
poivron rôti au four oven roasted pepper

poivron rouge sweet red pepper
poivron tequila sweet pepper [square purple fruits with soft flesh]
poivron vert green pepper
poivrote pear brandy (*eau de vie*)
pojarski minced meat (veal, poultry or fish) in the shape of a cutlet, breaded and fried
polenta boiled chestnut flour; may be cut into squares and fried, or used in place of rice or pasta
polonaise/à la polonaise Polish-style [typically: with cabbage or beet and sour cream, or vegetables with chopped egg, parsley and breadcrumbs]
pomelo pomelo [a sweet, grapefruit-like citrus]
pommé a kind of jam made with apple cider an apples
pomme apple
    compote de pommes apple sauce; stewed apples
    pomme de terre potato
pomme à cidre cider apple
pomme a l'ail garlic potato
pomme cannelle cinnamon apple; custard apple
pomme cuit cooked apple; baked apple
pomme d'or squash [looks like a very small pumpkin; spherical in shape, orange in color; very fine flavored, reminiscent of artichoke]
pomme de Risoul apple [fragrant and tart]
pomme de terre potato
    chips de pomme de terre potato chips/crisps
    gratin de pomme de terre sliced potatoes baked in milk until a crust forms on top; cheese and/or bread crumbs may be added
    mouseline de pommes de terre potato mousse [puréed potatoes whipped with egg whites and/or cream]
    purée de pommes de terre mashed potatoes
    salade de pommes de terre potato salad
pomme de terre à la braytoise cheese-stuffed baked potato
pomme de terre au lard potato with bacon
pomme de terre farcie stuffed baked potato
pomme de terre farcie à la chair à saucisse potato stuffed with sausage meat
pommes de terre sous la cendre potatoes roasted in wood coals
pomme du Limousin AOC golden Limousin apple
pomme sautée à l'ail garlic roasted potato
pomme Calville blanc white Calville apple [tender, juicy, sweet]
pomme surette jujube [tropical fruit; smooth skin, green turning to yellow, then orange, then brown; crunchy, tart and sweet]
Pommeau de Bretagne AOC cider brandy
pommée/laitue pommée head lettuce; cabbage lettuce
pommes à la grivette a dessert made with sliced apples in sweetened cheese curd, drizzled with Calvados
pommes à l'anglais plain boiled potatoes
pommes allumettes very thin potato chips
pommes amandine potato breaded with crushed almonds and deep fried
pommes Anna thinly sliced potatoes baked until golden

pommes boulangère roasted potatoes
pommes chips potato chips
pommes dauphine deep fried potato croquette and puff pastry mixture
pommes dauphinoises sliced potatoes layered with milk and cheese and baked
pommes de terre à l'anglaise boiled potatoes
pommes de terre à l'eau boiled potatoes
pommes de terre à l'huile potato salad made with oil
pommes de terre à la boulangère baked sliced potatoes and onions
pommes de terre à la crème potatoes in a creamy sauce
pommes de terre à la dauphinoise sliced potatoes baked in a cream sauce until golden
pommes de terre à la lyonnaise potatoes sautéed with onions
pommes de terre à la sarladaise sliced potatoes cooked in goose fat [truffles may be added]
pommes de terre à la vapeur steamed potatoes
pommes de terre allumettes fried matchstick potatoes
pommes de terre Anna thinly sliced potatoes cooked in butter
pommes de terre au beurre potatoes with butter
pommes de terre au four roasted or baked potatoes
pommes de terre au lait Ribot potatoes with buttermilk
pommes de terre bouillies boiled potatoes
pommes de terre campagnardes cuites au diable a rustic dish of small potatoes slowly simmered with shallots and garlic in an earthenware pan
pommes de terre château little potatoes sautéed in butter [bacon may be added]
pommes de terre chips potato chips/crisps
pommes de terre Darphin baked or pan-fried shredded potato pancake
pommes de terre dauphin fried croquette made of potato purée and puff pastry
pommes de terre duchesse potato pancake [potato purée, egg, butter formed into a thin cake, breaded and fried or baked
pommes de terre en chemise unpeeled potatoes [usually baked, but may be boiled]
pommes de terre en papillote potatoes cooked in aluminum foil
pommes de terre en robe des champs/de chambre unpeeled potatoes [boiled, baked, cooked on coals, steamed or cooked in the microwave]
pommes de terre noisette little balls of potato fried in oil or butter
pommes de terre paillassons baked or pan fried shredded potato pancake
pommes de terre paille potato straws [thin strips of fried potatoes]
pommes de terre persillées parsley potatoes
pommes de terre pont-neuf twice-fried thick French fries
pommes de terre rôties roasted potatoes; baked potatoes
pommes de terre sautées sautéed potatoes
pommes de terre vapeur steamed potatoes

pommes de terre-céleri celery root
pommes duchesses duchesse potatoes [riced or mashed potatoes with butter, egg yolks and seasonings piped into interesting shapes and baked until browned]
pommes en copeaux grated potatoes
pommes en robe de chambre steamed or boiled unpeeled potatoes
pommes en robe de champs steamed or boiled unpeeled potatoes
pommes frites French fries; chips
pommes mouselines mashed potatoes
pommes pailles straw potatoes; deep fried julienne potatoes
pommes reinettes reinette apples [a name given to scores of varieties of apples, most of which are heirloom varieties]
pommes sauvages crab apples
pommes savoyarde sliced potatoes layered with cheese and baked
pompe a generic term for certain breads or pastries in the south and center of France
pompe à l'huile a sweet, somewhat flat bread made with olive oil, orange flower water and sometimes orange zest
pompe aux grattons a rustic bread made with chunks of meat and fat trimmings
pompe aux pommes a dessert made with flaky pastry covered with pieces of apple
poncirus trifoliate orange; Chinese bitter orange
porc pork
   carré de porc pork loin
   côte de porc pork chop
   côtelette de porc pork chop
   jarret de porc knuckle of pork; pork shank [tender, choice cut]
porc du Limousin IGP, **Label Rouge** pork from pigs raised according to strict regulations
porc du Ventoux pork from pigs raised outdoors at elevations 800 to 100 meters around Mont Ventoux in Provence
porc d'Auvergne IGP pork from pigs raised outdoors according to strict regulations
porcelet suckling pig
porché stewed pigs' ears and trotters
porchetta niçoise roast of piglet stuffed with pig giblets
porreau leek [Belgian name; *poireau* in French]
porto port wine
portugaise/à la portugaise Portuguese-style [with tomatoes, garlic and onions]
   crème portugaise cream of tomato soup with rice
portugaise oyster
portune crab; velvet swimming crab [small crab with thin meat, but quite delicious]
pot jug
pot au feu beef stew; hot pot [typically: a rustic dish of seared meat (usually beef) poached with root vegetables in broth; traditionally the broth is served first as the first course (*entrée*) and the meat and vegetables are served later as the main dish]

pot bouilli beef stew; hot pot [typically: a rustic dish of seared meat (usually beef) poached with root vegetables in broth; traditionally the broth is served as the first course (*entrée*) and the meat and vegetables are served later as the main dish]
potable drinkable; safe to drink
  non potable undrinkable; unsafe to drink
potage soup
potage à la crème cream-based soup
potage a l'abigeoise beef stock soup with preserved goose, ham, sausage, calves feet and vegetables
potage à la bressane pumpkin soup
potage à la tortue turtle soup [many variations exist, but basically, this is a clear soup (not creamy) made with turtle meat seasoned with vegetables such as carrots, celery, leeks, and onions, along with perhaps red wine and various pungent herbs]
potage au riz rice soup
potage au vermicelle noodle soup
potage aux haricots bean soup [dried beans, not green beans]
potage aux légumes vegetable soup
potage aux lentilles lentil soup
potage aux nids d'hirondelles birds' nest soup
potage aux nouilles noodle soup
potage aux petits pois green pea soup
potage aux pois cassés split pea soup
potage aux tomates tomato soup
potage aveugle fat-free soup
potage bonne femme leek and potato soup
potage crème faubonne creamy white bean soup
potage crécy carrot soup [with potatoes and leeks or onions]
potage de tomate tomato soup
potage en sache packet soup
potage paysanne mixed vegetable soup
potage Saint-Germain split pea soup
potage tête de veau veal head soup [sometimes considered a substitute for turtle soup]
potage velouté velvety smooth soup
potée meat and vegetable stew
potée alsacienne Alsatian stew/hot pot [typically: cabbage, potatoes, lean bacon, pork knuckle and sausages]
potée auvergnate Auvergne stew/hot pot [typically: cabbage, potatoes, lean bacon, pork knuckle and sausages]
potée bourguignonne Burgundy salt pork and cabbage stew/hot pot [typically: with winter vegetables, such as kale, potato, carrot, turnip and onion]
potée champenoise Champagne stew/hot pot [typically: lean bacon, salt pork, sausage, ham, cabbage, carrots, turnips and potatoes]
potée limousine Limousin stew/hot pot [typically: smoked bacon, salt pork, cabbage, leeks, turnips, carrots and potatoes]
potée lorraine Lorraine stew/hot pot [typically: smoked pork shoulder, sausage, smoked bacon, cabbage, turnips, carrots, potatoes and onions]

potimarron squash [pear shaped; red, brick red, pink, bronze or green in color; said to taste a bit like chestnuts]
potiron squash; pumpkin [flatter than a pumpkin; reddish or dark green]
potiron another name for the edible parasol mushroom
potiron doux d'Hokkaido sweet Hokkaido squash
potjevleesch pieces of meat (chicken, rabbit, pork and veal) preserved in aspic [literally: little pot of meat; often served cold with hot French fries or fried potato wedges which melt the aspic]
potji pâté
pot-pourri stew [a mixture of different meats and vegetables]
pouce pied barnacle
pouding pudding
pouding au pain bread pudding
pouding de colombo curry paste made with garlic, red chili peppers, turmeric, coriander and mustard
pouding Nesselrode chilled sweet chestnut purée with egg custard, raisins, currants, maraschino liqueur and cream
poudre powder
    sucre en poudre superfine sugar; castor sugar
poudre d'amande almond powder
poularde young female chicken
poularde demi-deuil poached chicken in a mushroom sauce with braised calves' or lambs' sweetbreads and topped with sliced truffles
poule stewing hen
    lait de poule eggnog
poule au blanc chicken slowly cooked with carrots, turnips, leeks, and clove-studded onions in a white sauce with cider
poule au pot boiled stuffed chicken [possible ingredients are carrots, turnips, leeks, onions and cloves; stuffed with ham and bread pudding]
poule d'Inde turkey hen
poule de neige grouse
poule faisane pheasant hen
poulet chicken; broiler
    aiguillette de poulet chicken fillet
    aile de poulet chicken wing
    blanc de poulet chicken breast
    brochette de poulet chicken brochette
    cuisse de poulet chicken leg
    curry de poulet chicken curry
    fricassée de poulet chicken fricassee
    manchon de poulet chicken wing
    nugget de poulet chicken nugget
    poitrine de poulet chicken breast
    roulade de poulet chicken roulade [flat piece of chicken rolled with a filling]
    tarte au poulet chicken tart
    tourte au poulet chicken pie
    viande de poulet chicken meat

waterzooi de poulet chicken waterzooi [chicken simmered in broth with carrots, onions, celery and leeks, served with a cream sauce]
poulet à la crapaudine spatchcock [a pair of attached chicken breasts splayed flat to resemble a toad]
poulet au Meursault chicken in white wine sauce
poulet au Riesling chicken and mushrooms in a white wine sauce
poulet au vinaigre chicken and shallots in wine vinegar and cream
poulet comtoise chicken baked in a creamy casserole with Comté cheese
poulet de Bresse free range Bresse chicken [said to be uniquely flavorful; this breed is raised on small farms in small flocks and allowed to free range until they are fattened on grains and milk; with their red combs, white feathers and blue legs, they have the colors of the French flag]
poulet de graine grain-fed chicken
poulet de Loué free range Loué chicken [white, yellow or black chickens raised on pasture until they are fattened on grain for the market]
poulet fermier free-range chicken
poulet frit fried chicken
poulet Gaston Gérard chicken (usually *poulet de Bresse*) cooked with a sauce made with pan juices, grated *comté* cheese, white Burgundy wine, Dijon mustard, paprika and cream [often served with potatoes and white wine]
poulet noir a breed of black chicken with a slightly gamey flavor
poulet préparé dressed chicken
poulet rôti roast chicken
poulet sauce rouilleuse chicken cooked with a wine and blood sauce
poulet sauté d'Yvetot aux pommes pieces of chicken and pieces of apple cooked in layers with a splash of Calvados
poulet sauté Marengo chicken with wild mushrooms, crayfish, eggs, garlic and brandy
poulet vallée d'Auge chicken flambéed with Calvados [typically: with mushrooms and fresh cream, accompanied by apples simmered in cream with bacon]
poulette pullet
pouliot pennyroyal
poulpe octopus
poulpe en daube octopus stew
pounti chopped chard, sausage (or pork) and onion with prunes baked in a batter of eggs, milk and flour
poupart crab
poupeton fish pudding [made from fish leftovers]
poupeton veal slices with minced meat
pourprier purslane [thick, fleshy, slightly sour leaves used in salads, stir fried or cooked]
pousse de bambou bamboo shoot
pousse-café alcohol served with or after coffee at the end of a meal as a *digestif*

pousse-café cocktail of differently colored liqueurs layered in a drink
pousse-pied goose neck barnacle [considered a delicacy]
pousse-pierre samphire; sea fennel [an edible seaweed]
pousse-pierre sea asparagus; sea bean, sea pickle
pousses de salades young salad leaves; lettuce seedlings
poussin very young chicken [four to six weeks old]
poutargue dried fish roe
poutargue de Martigues caviar of Martigues [a delicacy made from dried egg mullet]
pouteille du Gévaudan a dish typically made with pig's feet, pieces of beef, potatoes, onion and red wine
poutine young sardine or young anchovy [eaten in soup, in fritters, in omelets, or raw with lemon juice and olive oil]
praire warty venus clam
pralin pulverized praline (caramelized nuts) used as a topping or ingredient in desserts
praliné a dessert topped or coated with crushed praline (nut brittle)
praline nut brittle [in France, this is a candy made with nuts (usually a whole almond) and caramelized sugar to which coloring and flavors are added, although many variations exist]
praline chocolate candy [in Belgium, a praline is a candy with a hard chocolate shell with a softer filling]
  brioche aux pralines sweet bun with chocolate
praline belge Belgian chocolate candy [hard chocolate shell filled with softer chocolate or a flavorful liquid]
praline rose pink praline [almond coated with caramelized sugar tinted pink]
  tarte aux pralines roses cake made with crushed pink pralines
préparé prepared
préparé par nos soins prepared by us
pré-salé salt-marsh; mutton or lamb raised in salt marsh pastures [said to improve the flavor of the meat]
  agneau (de) **pré-salé** salt meadow lamb
  mouton (de) **pré-salé** salt meadow mutton
pressé pressed; squeezed
pression draft beer
  demi-pression glass of draft beer (25 cl/8 oz)
prêtre smelt; silverside [small marine fish]
primeur young wine
primeurs early spring vegetables or fruits
primevère edible flowers of the primrose
princesse/à la princesse princess-style [with truffles and asparagus tips, *noisette* potatoes and maybe a white sauce]
prisuttu AOP raw cured ham [dried for twelve to eighteen months]
prix price
prix fixe fixed-price menu
prix hors boisson price not including drinks
prix net service included [no tip required, though if you are very pleased with the service, you may add a tip of about 10%]

profiterole profiterole; cream puff [a small, light cake made with puff pastry and filled with whipped cream, ice cream or *crème patissière* (pastry cream)]
provençale/à la provençale of Provence [typically with tomatoes, garlic and olive oil]
prune plum
    eau de prune plum brandy
    eau-de-vie de prune plum brandy; plum spirit
pruneau prune
pruneau d'Agen IGP Agen prune
prunelle small purple plum
prunelle sloe liqueur [brownish-red liqueur made with gin or neutral grain spirits and the fruits of the blackthorn tree, a relative of the plum]
psalliote champêtre edible common field mushroom
puit d'amour literally: well of love [puff pastry with a sweet vanilla cream custard filling]
pulenda round bread made with chestnut flour
pulpe pulp; fruit pulp
punch punch made with rum [may be flavored with lemons, cinnamon or other]
punch à l'ananas pineapple-rum punch
purée purée
Pyrénées the Pyrenees mountains
Pyrénées cheese [a generic name for cheese from the Pyrenees mountains; may be made from either cow's milk or sheep's milk]
quart one quarter; one fourth
quasi beef or veal round/loin
quasi de boeuf beef round/loin
quasi de veau veal round/loin
quasi de veau bourgeoise veal round/loin casserole with pork, calf's foot and vegetables
quatre fruits the four traditional summer fruits: strawberries, raspberries, cherries and red currants
quatre-quarts literally: four fourths [a cake made of equal parts of four ingredients: flour, sugar, butter and eggs, each component therefore being one of the four fourths]
quenelle poached dumpling [the torpedo-shaped dough may filled with minced savories such as chicken, salmon, pike, whiting, pork liver, etc.; usually boiled in a broth and served with a sauce]
quenelle à la farine wheat flour dumpling [typically made with just flour and eggs]
quenelle au fromage blanc white cheese dumpling
quenelle de foie pork or beef liver dumpling
quenelle de Lyon Lyon-style cheese dumpling [flour, butter, eggs, Gruyère cheese and nutmeg]
quenelle de pommes de terre écrasées et de farine mashed potato and flour dumpling
quenelle de pommes de terre râpées et de farine grated potato and flour dumpling
quenelle nature unfilled dumpling [a dough of flour, water, eggs and butter is boiled in a broth and served with a sauce]

quéniole Christmas brioche
quetsche plum [dark purple skin, green flesh]
queue tail
queues de merlan à la mode de Cherbourg Cherbourg-style whiting tails [posterior half of the fish poached with oysters in white wine with mushrooms]
quiche de Honfleur quiche with mussels or shrimp or oysters or all three
quiche lorraine originally, a quiche made with eggs, cream and smoked bacon [numerous variations exist]
quignon crust; hunk
quignon de pain crust/hunk of bread
quinoa quinoa [high-protein seed (pseudocereal)]
rabasse en Provençal truffle [*Tuber melanosporum*; said to be the queen of truffles in terms of taste; the aroma is strong, with hints of strawberries or a fine old red wine; black inside and out and finely marbled]
râble saddle (lower back) of rabbit
rabot/rabotte apple or pear hollowed out and filled with nuts and raisins or caramel and then baked in a pastry shell
rachel/à la rachel Rachel-style [steak garnished with artichokes, bone marrow and parsley]
racine root vegetable
Raclette cheese [cow's milk; pressed, uncooked cheese; the cheese is heated gently so that the melted part can be scraped onto bread or a dish of various foods]
raclette a dish of various foods onto which melted cheese is scraped [traditionally, the foods are potatoes, dried meat, gherkins and onions; other vegetables and mushrooms may also be used]
radeau d'asperges asparagus raft [asparagus spears side-by-side; as a bed for fish, ham or other]
radis radish (red)
radis de cheval horseradish
radis noir black radish
raffiné refined (sugar)
raffiné fine, delicate (taste)
rafraîchi brightened up; refreshed
ragoût thick stew [more meat than vegetables]
ragoût de truffes truffle stew [a rare and expensive dish consisting of 200 to 300 grams of truffles (seven to ten ounces) cooked in wine with olive oil or butter, shallots or onions, and served with toasted or fried bread]
ragoût de lieu noir Pollock stew
rahmkueche cream cheese cake
raie skate; ray [a fish, similar to a sting ray]
    aile de raie wing of skate
raie au beurre noir ray cooked in browned butter
raie blanche white skate
raie bouclée thronback ray
raifort horseradish
raiponce rampion [white roots are eaten in salads]

raisiné bourguignon jam made with very ripe grapes, quinces, pears and sugar
raïto sauce made with tomatoes, onions, red wine, olives and capers
raïto de morue salt cod in a sauce made of tomatoes, onions, red wine, olives and capers
raisin grape
raisin de caisse raisin from southern France
raisin de Corinthe very small raisin from Greece; currant
raisin de Smyrne sultana; golden raisin from Smyrna
raisin de Málaga large, red-violet raisin
raisin de table table grape; dessert grape
raisin sec raisin
rasiné jam made with grapes and other fruits
râle rail [a game bird prepared in the manner of quail]
ramboutan tropical fruit similar to the litchi
ramequin small tart or cake baked in a ramekin
ramequin/ramequin au fromage cheese fritter
ramequin bugiste au Comté a mixture of two cheeses, *Comté* and *Ramequin de Lagnieu*, melted in white wine and flavored with kirsch and served in the manner of a fondue
ramereau young wood pigeon
ramier ring dove; wood pigeon
râpé grated
    beignets râpés grated potato pancake [traditionally, prepared with no other ingredients, though flour and egg may be added]
    carottes râpées grated carrots
    fromage râpé grated cheese
râpé de pommes de terre grated potato pancake [traditionally, prepared with no other ingredients, though flour and egg may be added]
râpé morvandelle potato pancake made with grated potatoes, cheese, eggs and cream
rascasse scorpion fish
    petite rascasse brown scorpion fish [a rare delicacy]
rascasse du fond bluemouth rockfish; blackbelly rosefish; bluemouth seaperch [a type of scorpion fish; very delicate]
rascasse rouge red scorpion fish
rassis stale
    pain rassis stale bread
ratafia fortified wine or fruit-based beverage
ratafia de Champagne fortified wine made with unfermented grape juice and neutral alcohol or fine brandy
ratafia de Bourgogne fortified wine made with unfermented grape juice and *marc de Bourgogne* (Burgundy grape residue brandy)
ratafia de cidre fortified aperitif made with apple cider and apple brandy
ratatouille vegetable stew [tomatoes, onions, zucchini, eggplant/aubergine, peppers and garlic; served cold or hot]
raton literally: young rat [refers to a kind of cheesecake made with cottage cheese]
ratte yellow potato

ravigote/sauce ravigote ravigote sauce [based on a velvety sauce to which are added lemon or white wine vinegar, shallots, and sometimes mustard]
rave turnip; radish; rape
   céleri rave celeriac
   chou rave kohlrabi
raviolis ravioli [squares of pastry filled with meat, vegetables or cheese]
ravioles ravioli from the areas of Drôme and Savoie
Reblochon AOC cheese [raw cow's milk; whitish-yellow crust tinged orange; pressed, un-cooked semi-soft ivory-colored cheese, mildly fruity with a persistent hazelnut flavor; it is the main ingredient in the *tartiflette*, a rustic dish consisting of potatoes, *reblochon*, bacon and onions]
reblochonade a dish of various meats and vegetabels onto which melted *Reblochon* cheese is scraped
réforme/à la réforme Reform club style [typically: with strips of ham and carrots, and gherkins, egg whites, truffles and mushrooms]
régence/sauce régence Regency sauce [made from a *demi-glace*, white wine, finely diced carrots, onion and celery and truffle shavings or from a velvety chicken roux with cream and mushrooms, white wine and truffle shavings]
reglisse licorice
reine/à la reine queen-style [with chicken, especially chicken coated with a sauce, mushrooms and truffles]
   crème reine chicken soup
reine-claude greengage plum
reine de Saba chocolate cake
reinette apple [ripens in late autumn, early winter]
reinette gris russet apple
relevé seasoned
   sauce relevé ketchup
religieuse *éclair*-type dessert made of a small puff pastry sitting on top of a larger puff pastry; both are filled with chocolate-, vanilla- or coffee-flavored custard with a layer of chocolate, vanilla or coffee icing between and on top
rémoulade mayonnaise with mustard
   sauce rémoulade tartare sauce with anchovy essence
repas meal
requin shark
requin marteau hammerhead shark
reverchon large dark red sweet cherry
revesset green bouillabaisse [fish stew with spinach, chard and a bit of sorrel in place of potatoes]
rhubarbe rhubarb
rhum rum
rich rich
rigodon a rustic pudding typically made with bread soaked in boiled milk, then mixed with eggs, walnuts and hazelnuts and baked; served with fruit marmalade

rillette potted meat paste [tender, heavily salted, slowly cooked shredded meat (usually pork) mashed with fat to make spreadable paste which can be a bit chunky or more smooth, similar to pâté; usually served at room temperature on toast or bread]
rillons fried pork rinds
riquette wild rocket [salad green with a mild pungent flavor]
ris sweetbreads [culinary term for the thymus or pancreas of calf or lamb; other glands, such as the parotid, sublingual glands and testicles may also be considered sweetbreads]
rissole flaky pastry pocket filled with sweet or savory ingredients, pan fried or oven baked
riz rice
riz à l'imperatrice cold rice dessert made with rice, red jelly, vanilla, cherries and meringue or heavy cream
riz au blanc plain rice
riz au gras fried rice
riz complet whole rice; brown rice
riz de Camargue long grain rice from the Camargue area of Languedoc Rousillon
riz gluant sticky rice
riz rouge wild red Camargue rice
riz sauvage wild rice
robe/en robe de champs unpeeled cooked potatoes
robinet tap
    eau de robinet tap water
Rocamadour AOC goat cheese [raw goat's milk; fine bluish rind; light aroma of goat; a type of soft or lightly firm *Cabécou* cheese with a milky sweetness hinting of hazelnuts]
rocambole mild red garlic
rocambole rolled cake with sweet or savory filling [Brazilian roll; the filling may be guava marmalade or other sweet, or minced chicken, tuna, etc.]
rocambole carne a layer of minced meat with a layer of ham and cheese rolled into a log and baked
rocambole carne a pastry shell filled with savories such as mushrooms, ham, minced meat or cheese
rocambole de filets de poulet a layer of chicken fillet with a layer of ham rolled into a log and baked
rocher small cake in the shape of a rock
rocotillo mildly piquant but sweet-tasting pepper
rognon de Pont l'Abbé white bean
rognon kidney
rognons en chemise veal kidneys roasted with their own suet and served with their juices deglazed in a red wine sauce
rognons turbigo sautéed kidneys in a white wine and tomato sauce garnished with mushrooms and sausages
rognonnade saddle of veal with kidneys
rognons blancs testicles [bull, veal or sheep]
rollmops herring fillets marinated in vinegar with a little sugar, then rolled around onion, pickle or sauerkraut
romaine romaine (cos) lettuce

romanof fruit soaked in *curaçao* liqueur; served with whipped cream
romarin rosemary
Roquefort blue sheep cheese [raw sheep's milk; aged in natural caves which provide the precise temperature and humidity to produce the blue mold; cream or ivory colored surface (no rind); ivory colored semi-firm tangy cheese with blue, gray or green veins; the flavor evolves from mild to sweet, smoky and then slightly salty]
ronce blackberry (brambles)
rond round house; round rump of beef [tender; usually roasted]
rond de boeuf round rump of beef
rond de gigot thick cut of leg of lamb or mutton steak
rond de gîte à la noix cut of horse meat from the middle thigh [lean, tender; usually roasted, but may be served thinly sliced en carpaccio (raw)]
roquette rocket [pungent young leaves are used in salads]
rosbif roast beef [usually cooked rare]
rose pink
rosé pinkish
rosé cooked rare (pink)
rosé pink wine
rosé des prés pink meadowsweet mushroom
rosette cured pork sausage/salami [a famous sausage of Lyon]
rosette du Morvan pork salami [up to two feet long; lean pork (shoulder, ham), pork fat, plus herbs and spices; steamed, then left to dry and cure for three months; fine textured with a fine flavor]
roseval red-skinned potato
rosette de Lyon dried pork sausage [similar to salami; slowly cured; eaten raw]
rosquille baked biscuit flavored with vanilla, citrus and anise and coated with a sugar glaze
rosquille/rosquilla light golden doughnut/fritter made with a dough of flour, oil, white wine, sugar and eggs
rossbif roast horse meat
Rossini refers to dishes made with *foie gras* (fat liver paste) and truffles
    tournedos Rossini medallions of beef in a sauce made with butter, red wine, cream, *foie gras* and truffles
rotengle rudd [freshwater fish]
rôti roasted
rôti a roast; a joint
rôti braisé pot roast
rôtie toast
rouelle de veau veal steak (cut across the leg)
rouennaise Rouen-style
    canard/canneton à la rouennaise duck stuffed with puréed duck liver in a sauce made with red wine thickened with blood
rougail hot sauce [diced tomatoes, crushed ginger and chopped onions]
rougail au combawa hot sauce with kaffir lime

rouge red
    Label Rouge red label [an official agricultural label awarded only to products of recognized quality]
rouget mullet
rouget barbet red mullet
rouget à la sauce verte de Chausey striped red mullet in a green sauce made of shallots, garlic and parsley lightly cooked in butter with mustard and vinegar; cream and tarragon are added
rouget grondin gurnard; sea robin [marine fish]
rougette lettuce with red-tinged leaves
rouille spicy sauce served with fish soup or bouillabaisse [composed of monkfish liver, red peppers, potatoes or bread, tomatoes, garlic and olive oil]
roulade rolled meat [a slice of meat rolled around a filling of cheese, vegetables or other meat]
roulade de porc pork roulade [a slice of pork rolled around a filling of cheese, vegetables or other meat]
roulade de poulet chicken roulade [a slice of chicken rolled around a filling of cheese, vegetables or other meat]
roulade de veau veal roulade [a slice of veal rolled around a filling of cheese, vegetables or other meat]
roulade Sévigné guinea fowl roulade stuffed with mushrooms, walnuts and apples
roulé Swiss roll; rolled meat
rouleau roll [meat, cake or other food rolled into a log shape]
rousseau pandora, roach; sea bream [marine fish]
roussette small shark; spotted dogfish
roux roux [a smooth, creamy binding or thickening agent for sauces made by heating equal parts fat (usually clarified butter) and flour]
roux blanc white roux
roux blond blond roux
roux brun brown roux
royale/à la royale prepared with truffles or *foie gras* (fat liver paste)
    lièvre à la royale rabbit stuffed with its giblets and stewed with carrots, garlic, onions and shallots in red wine sometimes thickened with blood]
royan pilchard [small, oily herring]
rubis de groseille redcurrant liqueur [apéritif or with desserts]
rubis de cassis blackcurrant liqueur [apéritif or with desserts]
rue odorante rue [a bitter herb]
rumpsteck rump steak
sabardin pork and offal sausage [very spicy; cooked in red wine; dried for three months; eaten cold with a salad or warm with potatoes or lentils]
sabayon a kind of sweet mousse or sauce [can be a dessert or a beverage; usually made with egg yolks, sugar, and sweet wine (or champagne) and sometimes Grand Marnier]
sablé any food (pastry, cheese, etc.) that has a crumbly texture
sablé crumbly cookie or biscuit
sablé au fromage crumbly cheese biscuit

sabodet pork and offal sausage
sacristain twisted strips of flaky pastry with a caramelized sugar coating and sometimes almond flakes
sabre cutlassfish; scabbard fish
sabre noir black scabbard fish
sadrée savory [pungent herb]
safran saffron
sagou sago starch [from the sago palm tree]
saiblinge several types of salmonid fish, including arctic char and various lake trout
saignant cooked very rare [literally "bloody"]
saindoux pig lard
Saint Germain soups and purées made with green peas
Saint Honoré a dessert consisting of a base of flake pastry on which is arranged a circle of small puff pastries surrounding a center of thick pastry cream and whipped cream; the puff pastries are drizzled with caramel
saint jacques scallop
   coquille saint-jacques scallop
   terrine de coquille saint-jacques à la ciboulette scallop terrine with chives
Saint Nectaire AOC cheese [cow's milk; thick rind with white, yellow or red mold depending on age; aromas of straw and mushroom; pressed, un-cooked creamy, supple cheese with a flavor of hazelnuts]
Saint Nicolas au pain d'épice gingerbread cookie
Saint-Pierre John dory [marine fish]
Sainte Alliance/à la Sainte Alliance dishes made with truffles and *foie gras*
   faisan Sainte Alliance pheasant with a stuffing of chopped woodcock and truffles
saisi picked; gathered; harvested
   juste saisi freshly harvested
saison season
   de saison in season
   fruits de saison in season fruit
   légumes de saison in season vegetables
   salade de saison in season salad
salade salad
salade au lard potato salad with bacon, onion and greens
salade aux fruits fruit salad
salade cauchoise potato salad typically with endive, ham, Gruyère cheese and walnuts with a cream sauce and lemon
salade comtoise a salad typically of lettuce, smoked ham or bacon, sausages, potatoes, tomatoes, nuts, grated cabbage, croutons and a vinaigrette dressing
salade de barabans wild herb salad [typically: seasonal wild herbs, especially dandelion, with lardons (bacon) and sometimes hard-boiled eggs; a vinaigrette is made in the pan with the bacon fat and then drizzled over the salad]
salade de cramaillots wild herb salad [typically: seasonal wild herbs, especially dandelion, with lardons (bacon) and sometimes

hard-boiled eggs; a vinaigrette is made in the pan with the bacon fat and then drizzled over the salad]
salade de cramias wild herb salad [typically: seasonal wild herbs, especially dandelion, with lardons (bacon) and sometimes hard-boiled eggs; a vinaigrette is made in the pan with the bacon fat and then drizzled over the salad]
salade de dents-de-lion wild herb salad [typically: seasonal wild herbs, especially dandelion, with lardons (bacon) and sometimes hard-boiled eggs; a vinaigrette is made in the pan with the bacon fat and then drizzled over the salad]
salade de fruits fruit salad
salade de groin d'ane wild herb salad [typically: seasonal wild herbs, especially dandelion, with lardons (bacon) and sometimes hard-boiled eggs; a vinaigrette is made in the pan with the bacon fat and then drizzled over the salad]
salade de pissenlit wild herb salad [typically: seasonal wild herbs, especially dandelion, with *lardons* (bacon) and sometimes hard-boiled eggs; a vinaigrette is made in the pan with the bacon fat and then drizzled over the salad]
salade de pomme de terre à la lorraine potato salad traditionally made with boiled potatoes with skins, smoked bacon and hard boiled eggs [may also include ham or sausage, pickles, red onion or chives; usually with a vinaigrette dressing]
salade de saison in season salad
salade des chalutiers fécampois dandelion salad with smoked herring and a vinaigrette dressing
salade folle savory salad (duck meat, quail eggs, or other fine ingredients) with *foie gras*
salade landaise a plate of hot items such as gizzards, meat fillets and duck combined with cold items such as lettuce, tomatoes, cucumber, apples and asparagus
salad lyonnaise a salad of dandelion leaves or frisée lettuce, smoked or unsmoked bacon, garlic or shallots, poached or soft boiled eggs and maybe croutons; with warm bacon-fat vinaigrette dressing and bread
salade mixte sausage and cheese salad [*cervelas* sausages, Gruyère cheese, lettuce, onion, and parsley with a mustard vinaigrette dressing]
salade niçoise salad traditionally made with scallions, tomatoes, hard boiled eggs, black olives, basil leaves and anchovies or tuna flakes; sometimes embellished with fava beans, celery, artichokes, green and red peppers
salade normande potato salad with ham and apples; with cider and mayonnaise dressing or a creamy dressing
salade panachée mixed salad
salade parisienne Parisian salad [somewhat like chef's salad; made in a variety of ways, but usually including cooked potatoes, browned chicken, ham, hard-boiled eggs, cheese, lettuces and perhaps celery, bell peppers, etc., with a vinaigrette dressing]
salade russe Russian salad [chopped vegetables bound with mayonnaise]

salade simple plain salad
salade tiède lukewarm salad with a hot salad dressing
salaison food that is salted [sausages, hams]
salamandre salamander
salami salami
salambo/salammbô pastry similar to a round *éclair* [puff pastry filled with liqueur-flavored pastry cream and topped with icing which is colored to indicate the type of liqueur in the pastry cream: green for rum (*rhum*), pink for *Grand-Marnier*; may otherwise be topped with caramel and chopped pistachios or sliced almonds]
salé savory, salted; corned
sale à manger dining room
Salers AOC cheese [raw milk from cows on natural pastures; thick dry crust dotted with red and orange mold; pressed, un-cooked firm cheese with fragrances of the local flora (the cheese is made only while the cows are on pasture); 30% fat]
salicorne sea asparagus; sea pickle; samphire; glasswort
salmigondis stew made with meat (Bayonne ham, duck, squab, etc.) that has been browned prior to being cooked again in a sauce or broth; the dish often contains truffles and *foie gras*
salmis a dish made with roasted wild fowl (woodcock, duck, pheasant, partridge) or domestic fowl (pigeon, guinea fowl, duck) which is stewed in a well-seasoned sauce
salmis de palombe pigeon stew [roasted pigeon simmered with various ingredients such as ham, pork belly, onion and sweet peppers or onions, shallots and garlic in a wine broth]
salpicon diced fish, meat, fowl, mushrooms, truffles, etc. to accompany meat or to garnish vol-au-vent (small round, hollow puff pastry)
salsifis salsify; oyster plant
Samdi Saturday
sandre/sandre doré pike-perch [freshwater and brackish water fish; light, tender flesh with few bones]
sandwich sandwich
sandwich au jambon ham sandwich
sandwich mixte club sandwich
sang blood
    canard au sang duck cooked in a wine sauce thickened with the duck's blood
sanglier wild boar
    carré de sanglier rack of wild boar
    cuissot de sanglier haunch of wild boar
sanguette fried blood [coagulated blood of poultry, usually duck, which is seasoned and combined with bacon, then cut into strips and fried]
sanguine/orange sanguine blood orange
sanquette fried blood cake [the blood of freshly butchered poultry or lamb is collected and mixed with vinegar to slow coagulation, and garlic, sweet onions, parsley, pieces of belly, salt and pepper; when it finally coagulates, the "cake" is fried and eaten hot]

sans without
sans matières grasses fat-free
sans colorant without coloring/colouring
sapotille sapotilla [tropical fruit with brown skin and sweet flesh tasting of caramel]
sarcelle teal [wild duck, similar to the mallard]
sard sea bream
sardine sardine; young pilchard
sargue sea bream
sardinade fresh grilled sardines [typically: whole fish, un-gutted, served with a dash of olive oil and seasoned with thyme or *herbes de Provence*]
sarladaise/sauce sarladaise sarladaise sauce [diced hard boiled eggs, thick cream, truffles, olive oil, lemon and cognac]
   pommes de terre sarladaise thick slices of potatoes cooked in goose or duck fat with a bit of garlic (and sometimes diced smoked bacon)
sarrasin buckwheat; buckwheat flour
sarriette savory [herb with a pungent flavor]
saté satay [usually: skewered and grilled meats with peanut or other sauce]
sauce sauce
sauce à l'ail garlic sauce
saucisson à l'ail garlic sausage
sauce au vin muscat muscat wine sauce
sauce au kari curry sauce
sauce poivrade a brown sauce [the strained broth produced by cooking together giblets (or smoked bacon or veal broth) with white wine, carrots, onions, celery, vinegar, juniper seeds, bouquet garni, salt, pepper]
sauce soya soy sauce
saucisse sausage [any cooked, uncooked or cured sausage eaten hot]
saucisse à la catalane ring of fried sausage in a garlicky white wine and tomato sauce
saucisse à la languedocienne typically: sausage sweated in good fat and garlic, then served with a tomato, wine vinegar and caper sauce
saucisse au champagne fresh gourmet pork sausage [typically: seasoned with peppercorns, nutmeg, cloves, ginger and champagne; deep fried before serving]
saucisse au fenouil fennel sausage, poached and grilled
saucisse au paprika short Frankfurter (hot dog) seasoned with paprika
saucisse bretonne pork and pork fat sausage with peppercorns, nutmeg, cloves and ginger
saucisse chaude warm sausage
saucisse d'Ajoie smoked pork sausage [air dried or boiled]
saucisse d'Alsace-Lorraine pork sausage [flavored with peppercorns, nutmeg, cloves and ginger]
saucisse d'Arosa pork and beef sausage
saucisse d'Auvergne small dry sausage

saucisse de campagne air dried sausage [pork, fat bacon, red wine, spices; sometimes smoked]
saucisse de choux pork and cabbage sausage [one third pork and two thirds white cabbage, encased in pork gut]
saucisse de Davos pork and beef sausage
saucisse de Droie smoked lean pork sausage [resembles a hot dog]
saucisse de Francfort hot dog
saucisse de gruau boiled and dried sausage made with chitterling, groats or wheatmeal, spices and lemon zest
saucisse d'herbe pork and herbs sausage [equal parts pork and greens such as chard, spinach and cabbage, seasoned with garlic, onion, salt and pepper]
saucisse de Montbéliard smoked lean pork sausage [resembles a hot dog]
saucisse de Morteau IGP thick smoked pork sausage
saucisse de Schaffhouse pork and beef sausage
saucisse de Strasbourg cold-smoked sausage [thin finely-minced pork and pork fat seasoned with coriander and mace]
saucisse de Thann smoked lean pork sausage [resembles a hot dog]
saucisse de Toulouse pork sausage [keeps fresh for one week, or can be dried to keep longer]
saucisse du Périgord pork and pork fat sausage [with truffles and white wine, peppercorns, nutmeg, cloves and ginger]
saucisse en brioche sausage roll [sausage baked in brioche dough]
saucisse juives calves' liver sausage
saucisse madrilène sausage made with chopped veal, pork fat and sardines, poached in veal stock; fried in butter
saucisse sèche dried sausage [small sausage, eaten cold]
saucisse viennoise lightly smoked sausage made with finely minced lean pork, veal and fillet steak, cayenne pepper and coriander
saucisson large sausage [boiled, dried or smoked; eaten hot or cold]
saucisson au foie de porc sausage made with pork liver, pork and pork fat, onions, peppercorns, nutmeg, cloves, ginger, cayenne pepper and kirsch; air dried, then boiled and served cold
saucission au poivre vert pure pork sausage made with green peppercorns
saucission chausseur air dried pork sausage
saucisson-cervelas sausage made with pork, or pork and other meats and bacon, garlic and shallots [sometimes brined and lightly smoked]
saucission cuit au madère cooked sausage made with pork fillet and pork fat, peppercorns, nutmeg, cloves and ginger, Madeira wine, truffes and/or pistachios
saucission de campagne air dried pork and pork fat sausage seasoned with garlic, peppercorns, nutmeg, cloves and ginger
saucission de Paris small lean pork sausage
saucisson d'Italie smoked sausage made with pork, pork fat, nutmeg, cinnamon, ginger, pigs' blood and white wine

saucisson d'Arles pinkish-gray salami-sausage made with a lean mixture of pork, beef and donkey meat with pork fat and spices
saucisson de Bourgogne air dried pork and pork fat sausage seasoned with peppercorns, nutmeg, cloves, ginger and brandy or kirsch
saucisson de cheval pork and horse meat sausage [25% horse meat]
saucisson de jambon ham sausage
saucisson de lièvre hare meat sausage
saucisson de Lyon dried sausage made with lean pork leg and pork fat
saucisson de ménage air dried pork and pork fat sausage seasoned with garlic, peppercorns, nutmeg, cloves and ginger
saucisson de montagne dried coarsely chopped pork sausage
saucisson de Morteau smoke-dried pork sausage [dense; strongly flavored]
saucisson en croute sausage cooked in a pastry shell
saucisson gris dried sausage made with lean pork, pork fat, lean beef, peppercorns, nutmeg, cloves, ginger and garlic
saucisson lorrain dried sausage made with lean pork, pork fat, lean beef, peppercorns, nutmeg, cloves, ginger and garlic
saucisson provençal dried and lightly smoked sausage made with pork leg or shoulder, little fat, nutmeg, peppercorns, cinnamon and ginger
saucisson sec thick dry salt-cured sausage [pork, or a mixture of pork and other meats plus spices; similar to salami]
saucisson sec aux herbs dry pork sausage with *herbs de Provence*
saucisson vaudois dried smoked sausage made with pork and pork fat
sauge sage
saugrené a warm salad of mixed cooked vegetables herbs
saugrené seasoning made from herbs such as savory, marjoram, thyme, bay laurel, and salt in olive oil or butter
saumon salmon
    darne de saumon salmon steak
    filet de saumon salmon fillet
    medaillon de saumon salmon medallion
    rose saumon pink salmon
    tartare de saumon salmon tartar [fresh raw salmon with seasonings; usually eaten on crackers or bread as an appetizer]
    tarte au saumon salmon tart
    tourte au saumon salmon pie
    tranche de saumon slice of salmon
saumon à l'aneth salmon with dill
saumon au cidre salmon served with a creamy cider sauce
saumon blanc hake [marine fish]
saumon d'élevage farmed salmon
saumon fumé smoked salmon
saumon lomi-lomi lomi-lomi salmon salad [typically: raw diced and salted salmon with tomatoes, Maui onions or green onions, and sometimes cucumbers or hot chili peppers; eaten cold]

saumonnette term used for several species of small sharks and dogfish
saumuré brined
saupe salema porgy [a type of sea bream]
saupiquet thick, pungent sauce for rabbit or hare made with bread, salt and vinegar or ginger
saupoudré powdered (for example, with sugar)
saur salted and smoked herring
sauté a technique by which food is cooked quickly in a shallow amount of hot fat in order to brown it
sauté de boeuf et rognons en croûte steal and kidney pudding
sauté de veau marengo veal sautéed with onions, carrots, garlic, tomatoes and white wine
sauterelle de mer mantis shrimp
sautoir sauté pan
   doré au sautoir browned in a sauté pan
sauvage wild
savarin ring-shaped sponge cake soaked in sweet rum syrup and topped with various fruits or cream
savarin à la chantilly small sponge cake in the form of a ring, soaked in a flavored syrup and filled with whipped cream
savarin au rhum rum sponge cake
saveur flavor
Savoie Savoy
   biscuit de Savoie/gâteau de Savoie molded sponge cake
scampi scampi [prawn or shrimp]
scarole frizzy lettuce; chicory; endive; escarole
schnaps/schnàps clear brandy (*eau de vie*) made from grains, roots or fruits, especially cherries (*kirschwasser*), apples (*pommes*), pears (*poires*), peaches (*pêches*), plums (*prunes* or *quetsches*), apricots (*abricots*) or blueberries (*mirabelles*)
sébaste/sébaste chèvre blue-mouth rockfish; blackbelly rosefish; bluemouth seaperch [marine fish similar to the scorpion fish, but more delicate]
sébaste atlantique deepwater redfish; beaked redfish; ocean perch; Norway haddock
sec/seche dry
   vin sec dry wine
sec straight up; a drink served without ice (literally, "dry")
Secca d'Entrevaux salt-dried beef ham
Seccu farmer's sheep or goat cheese [raw sheep's milk (or sometimes raw goat's milk); fresh and soft, it is called *brocciu* (with a mild, sweet flavor); when salted and semi-dry, it is *passu*, and when dry, it is *seccu;* considered to be the national cheese of Corsica]
sedum sedum; stonecrop [raw in salads or cooked in soups]
seiche squid; cuttlefish
   blanc de seiche squid fillet
   encre de seiche squid ink
   risotto à l'encre de seiche squid ink risotto
seigle rye
   pain de seigle rye bread

sel salt
   demi-sel lightly salted
sel de Guérande sea salt from Guérande, Bretagne
sel de mer sea salt
sel marin sea salt
sel naturel natural salt
selle d'agneau saddle of lamb
selle de mouton saddle of mutton
selon according to
selon arrivage according to arrival/availability
selon grosseur according to size
selon le marché according to market/availability
selon poids according to weight
seltz/eau de seltz seltzer; soda water
semoule semolina [coarsely ground wheat; wheat granules]
seranno Serrano ham ["mountain" ham; less expensive than *jamon ibérique* (but still a delicacy); hams are salted for about two weeks, then dried for about six months, then hung for an additional 6 to 18 months, usually in sheds found at higher elevations]
serran comber [marine fish]
serpolet thyme
servise service charge
servise compris service charge/tip included [in France, the tip is normally included in the bill; if you feel you have had superior service, you may tip an additional amount, usually about 10%]
servise en sus service charge/tip *not* included [in this case, you may wish to tip 10% to 15%]
service non compris service charge/tip *not* included [in this case, you may wish to tip 10% to 15%]
sésame sesame
Sétchoun Sichuan
setchouanaise/à la setchouanaise Sichuan-style
Sétoise/à la Sétoise Sète-style [a way to prepare seafood, especially in a stew with tomatoes, onions, carrots and garlic]
   bourride à la Sétoise a ragout of fish similar to bouillabaisse, but with white fish only and with *aïoli* (garlic mayonnaise)
sevruga caviar [true caviar; small eggs, gray in color]
Siesskaes Munster cream cheese with kirsch
silure glande large freshwater catfish [firm white flesh]
singapour sponge cake with fruit preserves and fresh or candied fruit (pineapple, cherries, etc.)
sirop syrup; cordial
sirop de menthe mint syrup; mint cordial
Sichuan Sichuan
smout lard [used for cooking, in pastries, or spread on bread
sobacha roasted buckwheat tea
Socca chickpea biscuit [thin, flat golden biscuit made with chickpea flour, olive oil, water and a dash of pepper; served hot]
soda soda water
soissonaise/à la soissonaise with white kidney beans
soissonaise/purée soissonaise white kidney bean soup

soissons white kidney bean
soja soy
    farine de soja soy flour
    huile de soya soy oil
    sauce soja soy sauce
sole sole; Dover sole
sole au cidre fillet of sole with cider [often cooked with apples slices]
sole belle normande fillet of sole [typically: with mussels, oysters, crayfish or scallops, mushrooms in a creamy white sauce]
sole Bercy poached sole [typically: in stock with white wine, lemon juice and shallots]
sole bonne femme poached sole [typically: in stock with white wine, lemon juice and shallots and topped with sliced mushrooms]
sole Colbert butterflied sole fillets [typically: breaded and deep fried and served with parsley butter]
sole dieppoise/sole à la dieppoise poached sole [typically: in white wine and mussel liquor and garnished with shrimp or crayfish and white wine sauce; may include mushrooms]
sole Dugléré poached sole [typically: in stock with white wine, lemon juice, shallots and tomato purée]
sole limande lemon sole
sole Marguery fillet of sole [typically: with shrimp and mussels covered in a white wine sauce]
sole normande poached sole [typically: with truffle cream sauce and garnished with oysters and mussels]
sole Walewska poached sole [typically: in fish stock and topped with cooked lobster and truffles then coated with a creamy white sauce and grated cheese]
solette small sole
solferino/crème solferino half cream of tomato and half puréed leak, onion and potato
solferino/sauce solferino sauce made with tomato juice, meat glaze, lemon juice, parsley butter, shallots and tarragon
son bran
son de moutarde mustard seed
sommités tops [leafy tops of vegetables]
sorbet sorbet [a frozen dessert made with water flavored with fruit juice and sometimes extra sugar, but usually not with with egg whites or milk]
sorbet à l'orange orange sorbet
sorbet au citron lemon sorbet
sorgho sorghum: Indian millet
sot-l'y-laisse chicken's oyster [tender morsel of chicken meat at the base of the tail; literally means "you'd be a fool to leave it"]
soubise with puréed onions
sauce soubise soubise sauce [made from a white sauce to which onions, butter and fresh cream; often white truffles are added]
souchet wild spoonbill duck
souchet galingale; rush; tiger nuts [sweet pulp of the tubers is eaten raw or grilled]

souchet/sauce souchet sauce made with the poaching liquor from fish reduced and mixed with white wine sauce, butter, flour and julienned carrots, leeks and celery
souci marigold
soufflé soufflé [*souffler* means "to puff up"; therefore, this is a light, fluffy cake made with egg yolks and whipped egg whites]
soufflé à la Bénédictine soufflé made with Bénédictine, eggs, sugar, butter and lemon
soufflé au fromage cheese soufflé
soufflé de crevettes shrimp soufflé
soufflé normand apple soufflé
soufflé pomme de terre potato soufflé [made with puffed-up sautéed potato slices (and sometimes cheese) rather than egg and is traditionally served with steak]
soupe soup [thick soup or broth with chunks of meat and or vegetables]
soupe du jour soup of the day
soupe à l'ail garlic soup
soupe à l'oignon/aux onions brown onion soup [nearly caramelized thinly sliced onions in broth with grated Gruyère cheese browned on top]
soupe à la graisse fat vegetable soup [fresh vegetables such as potatoes, onions, carrots, leeks, turnips and green beans plus fat; may also be prepared using rice, peas, corn or dried beans]
soupe à l'échalote d'Avranches shallot soup [shallots, potatoes broth and cream: served over croutons]
soupe angevine sparkling wine cocktail [made with Crémant (sparkling wine), lemon juice, cane sugar and orange liqueur]
soupe au cresson watercress soup [with or without potatoes]
soupe au fromage cheese soup [typically made with either Laguiole or Cantal cheese, plus onions, bread, dry white wine, butter, flour and broth; may also include garlic, cabbage or tomato]
soupe au pistou red, white and green bean soup with basil sauce [red cranberry beans, white cannellini beans, green beans with other vegetables such as zucchini (courgettes), potatoes, leeks, carrots and onions, plus noodles/macaroni and possibly smoked ham; a pesto-like sauce made with tomatoes, basil, garlic and olive oil is added after the beans and vegetables have cooked]
soupe au vermicelle noodle soup
soupe aux choux cabbage soup
soupe aux choux verts à la vendéenne green cabbage soup [cabbage, potatoes and ham]
soupe aux poireaux leek soup [leeks and potatoes in broth]
soupe aux rognons kidney soup
soupe de crustacés seafood soup
soupe de légumes vegetable soup
soupe de lentilles lentil soup
soupe de moules d'Étretat Étretat-style mussel soup [typically: cooked mussels removed from shells in a soup of tomatoes, vermicelli, leeks, parsley, and curry served with grated cheese]
soupe de nouilles noodle soup

soupe de poisson fish soup, sometimes with saffron
soupe de poisson à la sétoise Sète style fish soup [typically: horse mackerel, conger, hake, scorpion fish, gurnard, and monkfish cooked in dry white wine, olive oil, leek, garlic, carrots, onion, tomatoes, hot pepper, parsley, thyme and saffron; typically served with croutons and grated cheese]
soupe de riz rice soup
soupe de saumon du Mont-Saint-Michel salmon soup [typically: salmon in a soup of carrots, onions, garlic, oil, butter, and saffron with a purée of tomatoes]
soupe gardiane tomato soup [typically: tomatoes, potatoes, celery, leeks, basel and garlic]
soupe germou vegetable soup with pumpkin
soupe miso miso soup
soupe paysanne de Mortain vegetable soup [typically: potatoes, leeks, cabbage, celery, white beans, lard]
soupir de nonne fried puff pastry dusted with confectioners' sugar
souple supple [said of cheese that is not firm; said of wine]
souris knuckle [delicate oval-shaped morsel of meat that surrounds the tibia near the knuckle joint of mutton or lamb]
souris d'agneau knuckle of lamb [delicate oval-shaped morsel of meat that surrounds the tibia near the knuckle joint of lamb]
sous-noix undercushion of veal or beef [posterior thigh muscle; very lean]
spaghetti végétal spaghetti squash
sparassis crépu cauliflower mushroom [edible when young; brown, deeply crinkled, resembling cauliflower or coral; sweet-smelling]
spéculos/spéculoos spice cookie; gingerbread cookie
spisules surf clam; trough shell [spisula ovalis]
spoom fruit sorbet [made with foamy beaten egg whites with sweet wine and spirits such as Calvados or champagne]
spritz de Noël stick-like cakes or biscuits made with flour, butter, eggs, sugar and sometimes cocoa
squille/squille de mer mantis shrimp
sprat sprat; brisling [small fish, similar to herring]
spuma foam
spunchade fruit sherbet
St. Germain/à la St. Germain St. Germain-style [with peas]
  purée St. Germain green pea soup [split peas, carrot, leek, onion, ham]
steak de boeuf beef steak
steak haché ground beef; minced steak
steak tartare seasoned, chopped raw beef [sometimes prepared with the addition of ingredients such as mustard, chopped capers, Tabasco sauce, wine vinegar, egg yolk, shallots]
sterlet caviar [a true caviar; small eggs with a golden color]
sterlet small sturgeon [noted for its caviar and its delicate flesh]
stockfisch air-dried cod [usually salted; used in fish stew]
stollen small almond-flour cake with nuts and dried fruits
stroganov/boeuf stroganov slices of beef in a creamy sauce with onions and mushrooms

subrics minced meat and mashed potatoes bound with egg, formed, and deep fried
succédané substitute
succédané de café coffee extender [chicory]
succédané de lait non-dairy coffee lightener
succédané de thé tea substitute
succédané de caviar caviar substitute [eggs from fish other than sturgeon; not the true caviar]
succès layered cake consisting of two layers of almond meringue and two layers of praline butter cream
sucre sugar
    beignet au sucre sugar doughnut
    canne à sucre sugar cane
    gauffre au sucre waffle with sugar
    pain de sucre sugar loaf
    tarte au sucre sugar pie
sucré sweet; sweetened
sucre brun brown sugar
sucre de pomme apple sugar candy
sucre vergeoise brown sugar
sucrine sucrine lettuce [small Romaine lettuce; sweet and buttery]
sucrine du Berry du Berry squash [clear orange flesh, sweet and fragrant; used grated, puréed, in soups, pies, flan and jam]
sueri Ruewe salted turnips
supion squid, calamari, cuttlefish
suprême supreme
sauce suprême supreme sauce [a sauce based on a velvety sauce (*velouté*) made from chicken stock to which is added heavy cream or *crème fraîche*; lemon juice is sometimes added]
suprême de volaille the white breast meat and adjoining first wing joint of poultry (chicken, turkey or other)
suprême de volaille poultry fillet in white sauce
sureau/baie de sureau elderberry
surgelé frozen
surimi white fish processed to imitate crab meat
surprise/en surprise surprise
sus/en sus extra charge
    service en sus service *not* included [you are expected to leave a tip for the service rendered]
suzette/crêpe suzette thin pancake with orange or lemon butter and Grand-Marnier or Curaçao
table d'hôte fixed-price menu [a set number of courses, sometimes with the opportunity for substitutions with subsequent price alteration]
taboulé tabouli salad [cold crushed cooked wheat typically with chopped tomatoes, onions, mint and mint; sometimes with added couscous or bulgur]
tacaud whiting pout [marine fish; similar to cod]
tacon young salmon; parr
tafia molasses rum
tagliatelles tagliatelli pasta [flat, ribbon-like]

tagine/tajine meat stew cooked in an earthenware pot [beef, chicken or fish]
takifugu pufferfish [highly toxic internal organs, small amounts of which create a sensation on the tongue that is sought after by connoiseurs]
talibur apple baked in a pastry sleeve
Tallyrand/à la Talleyrand Tallyrand-style [typically: with macaroni, cheese, *foie gras*, and mushrooms or truffles]
talmouse a kind of cheese cake [flake pastry filled with *béchamel* sauce (white sauce made with butter and flour) and Emmental cheese]
talo/taloa thick corn flour crêpe which is filled and folded to form a sort of sandwich [similar to a fajita]
tamarin tamarind; Indian date [tropical leguminous, pod-like fruit; sweet-sour taste]
taminoise/crêpe à la taminoise thick beer pancake [flour, eggs, oil, beer and milk]
tanaisie tansy [pungent herb]
tanche tench; doctor fish [freshwater and brackish water fish; used in place of carp in some recipes]
tangelo tangelo [hybrid of grapefruit and tangerine/mandarin orange]
tangerine tangerine/mandarin orange
tangor hybrid between the mandarin orange (tangerine) and the sweet orange
tapas tapas [small dishes, snacks or appetizers]
tantimolle thick *crêpe*
tapenade minced olives, anchovies and capers, sometimes with garlic
tapioca tapioca [cassava starch; used as a thickener in puddings and doughs]
tarif price list
tarif des consommations price list
taro taro root
tartare raw beef (or sometimes fish) with raw egg yolk, capers, onion and parsley
   à la tartare served with a spicy sauce usually containing horseradish, anchovies, peppers
   sauce tartare tartare sauce [typically: made with mashed hard-boiled egg yolks, vinegar, oil, mayonnaise and puréed spring onions]
   sauce tartare tartar sauce [typically: made with mayonnaise, capers, pickles, onion, parsley, chervil, tarragon, and sometimes mustard, chives, espelette pepper]**steak tartare** raw lean beef, minced and garnished with capers, onions and parsley and sometimes raw egg yolk
tartare fresh cream cheese with herbs
tartare aller-retour raw *steak tartare* patty which is lightly seared on one side
tartare de cheval raw horse meat [minced and garnished with capers, onions, parsley and raw egg yolk]
tarte tart; open pie [sweet or savory; no top crust]

tarte à l'onion onion pie
tarte à la crème custard tart
tarte à la rhubarbe rhubarb tart
tarte à la tomme pastry made with fresh cottage cheese or *tomme* cheese; baked and slightly caramelized
tarte al djote/tarte al'djote cheese and chard tart
tarte au citron lemon pie
tarte au comté tart garnished with Comté cheese, potatoes and smoked bacon with a white sauce
tarte au Maroilles tart made with stinky Maroilles cheese baked in a pie shell with an egg and cream mixture
tarte au me'gin cheese tart made with white cheese and cream in a pie crust
tarte au papin tart with egg custard (flan) which is made with eggs, milk, sugar, flour and vanilla, and garnished with brown sugar [sometimes with prunes added]
tarte au Quemeu de Brévoines cheese tart [made with fresh Langres cheese which is beaten with eggs, cream and either sugar or salt and pepper]
tarte au riz sweet rice pie [dessert rice, raisins or sultanas, chopped almonds, nutmeg]
tarte au sucre sugar pie
tarte au Camembert Camembert cheese tart
tarte aux brimbelles blueberry tart/pie
tarte aux cerises de Duclair Duclair cherry tart/pie
tarte aux cerises noires black cherry tart/pie
tarte aux mirabelles plum tart/pie
tarte aux myrtilles blueberry tart/pie
tarte aux pommes apple pie
tarte aux pommes chaudes warm apple pie [typically with cream and Calvados]
tarte aux pêches de vigne tart/pie made with "peach of the grapevine" or "blood peach" [peaches which taste like a cross between raspberries and white peaches]
tarte aux quetsches plum tart/pie [damson plum; large purple plum]
tarte bourdaloue aux poires tart/pie made with pears in almond cream
tarte d'Yport apple tart/pie
tarte de boudin noir aux pommes black pudding/sausage pie with potatoes and apples
tarte de ménage comptois a thick puff-pastry pie or cake [made with flour and yeast, milk, orange flower, eggs and cream; sprinkled with white or brown sugar after baking]
tarte de Mur cheese tart
tarte de Raulhac cheese tart
tarte de Vic cheese tart
tarte du Champsaur/tarte à la confiture du Champsaur tarte made with fruit preserves
tarte fine aux pommes normande apple tart/pie
tarte flambée pizza-like; covered with cottage cheese or *crème fraîche*, onions and bacon

tarte jausiereine a thin cake with a filling of raspberries or blueberries
tarte limousin clafoutis a pie filled with a thick pancake-like batter and fruit such as cherries
tarte lorraine quiche-like pie with onions and spicy pork or veal
tarte Polonaise sweet tart/pie with cottage cheese and raisins
tarte tatin upside-down fruit tart [the fruit, usually apples, is caramelized in butter and sugar before the tart is baked]
tarte tropézienne tart/pie made with butter cream and pastry cream
tartiflette a dish made with potatoes, *Reblochon* cheese, smoked bacon or smoked salmon and onions
tartine slice of bread and butter
tartine suisse puff pastry with thick vanilla cream
tartouillat thick sweet baked pancake embedded with fruit such as cherries, apples or pears [a rustic dessert, somewhere between a *clafoutis* and a *flan*]
tasse cup
   en tasse served in a cup
tasse à thé tea cup; cup of tea; cuppa
tasse de café cup of coffee
tataki de saumon salmon quickly seared to make the surface crunchy while the interior remains warm but raw
tatin/tarte tatin upside-down fruit tart [the fruit, usually apples, is caramelized in butter and sugar before the tart is baked]
taupe porbeagle shark [marine fish; type of mackerel shark]
taureau bull [meat of young bull is traditionally eaten in southern France]
telline wedge shells [small, triangular shellfish]
tende-de-tranche rump steak; topside of beef
teewurst spreadable raw smoked spicy sausage made from two parts meat (beef and pork or just pork) and one part fat; smoked over beech wood and ripened for a week to ten days
téméraire cake made with dried fruit, apples and hazelnuts
terre earth
   la terre et le mer surf and turf [fish and meat dish]
terrine meat loaf; fish loaf; vegetable loaf; fruit loaf [made with coarsely chopped ingredients covered in fat or gelatin; usually served cold or at room temperature]
terrine de coquille saint-jacques à la ciboulette scallop terrine with chives
terrine de foie gras au sauternes liver terrine with pepper and wine
terrine de lapin de garenne rabbit terrine [rabbit meat mixed with pork lard and seasonings]
terrine normande apples baked with sweetened beaten eggs and flavored with Calvados
terrinée normande cooked sweet rice milk with cinnamon
terroir sense of place [a term used to indicate that an agricultural product has characteristics based on interactions with specific soil profiles, the geology and climate of a specific locale as well

as farming techniques; applied especially to wines, cheeses, hams, olive oils, honeys and a few other agricultural products]
tête head
tête de veau veal head meat [brains and tongue, usually rolled, tied and blanched then poached with vinegar or lemon and served hot with a sauce]
tête de veau sauce gribiche veal head with *gribiche* sauce [cold egg sauce made with hard-boiled egg yolks, mustard, oil, chopped pickles, capers, parsley, chervil, tarragon and sliced boiled egg whites]
tête de veau de Rambervillers veal head [poached in water with carrots, onion, garlic and vinegar; typically served with a sauce and steamed potatoes]
tête de violon fiddlehead [the edible unfurled fronds of ferns]
tétine udder
tétragone New Zealand spinach
tétras grouse
teurgoule cooked sweet rice milk with cinnamon
Thaï Thai
thé tea
   mélange de thé assortment of teas
thé au citron tea with lemon
thé au lait tea with milk
thé glacé iced tea
thé nature tea without milk
thé noir black tea
thé vert green tea
thermidor thermidor **homard thermidor** lobster thermidor [lobster meat baked in the shell with egg yolks, mustard, brandy and cheese; sometimes with mushrooms and truffles]
   sole thermidor poached sole with grated cheese, served with mustard sauce
thon tuna
thon albacore albacore or yellowfin tuna
thon blanc white tuna
thon germon white tuna
thon kaskarote tuna with tomatoes, peppers, onions and pimentos
thon listao bonita; Boston mackerel
thon obèse big-eye tuna
thon rouge Bluefin tuna; red tuna
thonine bonito [marine fish in the tuna family]
thym thyme
tiède warm
tian a dish of baked sliced vegetables such as eggplant/aubergine and zucchini/courgettes and onions and/or tomatoes [the slices are alternated and arranged vertically in a baking dish, sprinkled with chopped garlic and rosemary and drizzled with olive oil]
tilleul linden [sweet, dried blossoms are used for tea]
tielle de Sète squid or octopus pie [finely chopped squid or octopus mixed with a spicy tomato sauce]

timbale timbale [a mold filled with a mixture of cooked meat or vegetables, sometimes in a pastry shell]
timbale de langouste lobster timbale [a creamy mixture baked in a pastry shell]
tisane infusion of herbal tea
Tivoli/à la Tivoli Tivoli-style [with asparagus tips and mushrooms]
toast toasted bread
toastatis toasted bread sandwich
tofailles/tofôlles des Hautes-Vosges alternate layers of potato, bacon and onion simmered until the potatoes make a thick puree
tomate tomato
    coulis de tomate tomato coulis [a *coulis* is a thick sauce]
    crème de tomate cream of tomato soup
    farce à tomate tomato stuffing
    jus de tomate tomato juice
    potage aux tomates tomato soup
    salade de tomates tomato salad
tomate/sauce tomate tomato sauce [considered to be one of the five "mother" sauces; many variations exist]
tomate cerise cherry tomato
tomate confite sun-dried tomato
tomate de mer beadlet [sea anenome]
tomate farcie stuffed tomato
tomate verde tomatillo; ground tomato
tomate verte green tomato
tomates à la provençale baked tomato halves topped with garlic, parsley and basil
tombé literally: fell or fallen
tombée d'epinards cascade of spinach
tome/tomme cheese [a generic name for pressed, uncooked cheeses that are generally made from skim (low-fat) cow's, goat's or sheep's milk; generally fresh and used melted in a fondue or mixed with potatoes (*aligot*); sometimes aged for weeks or months; generally found in mountainous regions such as the French Alps, French Pyrénées, the Massif Central and Switzerland]
Tome fraîche fresh cheese [a generic name for fresh pressed, uncooked cheeses that are generally made from skim milk; similar to *Mozzarella*; used melted in a fondue or mixed with potatoes (*aligot*) or other cooked dishes, or cold in salads]
tonic tonic water
tonkinois chocolate cake [often with rum-cream filling and sometimes with almonds]
topinambour Jerusalem artichoke
torche aux marrons a cupcake-shaped pastry made of chestnut purée and meringue
torchon/au torchon cooked while tied up in a cloth [a way of steeping ham or foie gras in brine]
torréfié roasted
torteau crab
torteau sweet cornmeal pancake

tortellini tortellini [small stuffed pasta]
tortillon short strips of flake pastry twisted together [garnished in various ways and served as small cookies]
torton buckwheat pancake
tortue turtle
  potage à la tortue turtle soup [many variations exist, but basically this is a clear soup (not creamy) made with turtle meat seasoned with vegetables such as carrots, celery, leeks, and onions, along with perhaps red wine and various pungent herbs; calf's head is sometimes substituted for the turtle meat]
  sauce tortue white wine and tomato sauce
tortue/en tortue calf's head soup [typically: made with calf's head meat, tongue and brains, olives, mushrooms and gherkins in a white wine and tomato sauce]
tosazu Japanese vinegar
  sauce tosazu vinegar and soy sauce [and possibly other ingredients]
toscane/à la toscane Tuscany-style [with pasta, foie gras and truffles]
tôt-fait sponge cake [*tôt-fait* means "quickly made"]
touffaye gaumaise potatoes with onions and bacon [seasoned with thyme and bay laurel; slowly cooked for two hours]
tougnol bread scented with anise [breakfast or dessert]
toulonnaise/à la toulonnaise Toulon-style [typically: with a sauce of eggplant/aubergine, tomatoes and garlic]
toulousaine/à la toulousaine [typically: chicken with kidneys, cockscombs, mushrooms, truffles and a creamy white sauce]
tourangelle/à la tourangelle Touraine style [typically: with green beans and flageolet beans in a creamy white sauce]
tourin onion-garlic soup [typically: onions, garlic, goose or duck fat or lard, flour, water, salt, pepper, egg and vinegar]
tournedos medallion of beef
tournedos rossini medallion of beef topped with *foie gras*, truffles and a red wine sauce
tournesol sunflower
touron almond nougat [honey, sugar, egg whites and almonds]
tourte covered flake-pastry pie [with bottom and top crust; savory, usually served hot; or sweet, served warm or cold]
tourte Lorraine pork, veal and onion pie
tourte à la biére pie of beef marinated in beer, with onions, potatoes, carrots and peas
tourte à la biére et au boeuf steak and ale pie
tourte à la citrouille pumpkin pie
tourte à la tartiflette a potato pie made with potatoes, Reblochon cheese, smoked bacon and onions
tourteau cake
tourteau crab; sleeper crab
tourteau fromagé baked cheesecake
tourterelle turtle dove
tourtière/tourtière de pommes de terre flake pastry potato pie with cream
tourtière de viande flake pastry potato pie with meat

tourtière large flat tart, sometimes with apples or prunes
tourtière meat pie [finely diced pork, veal or beef, sometimes with wild game]
tourtière de Gascogne tart/cake with apples or plums with very delicate, fine layers of sweet buttery flake pastry
tourtons aux pommes de terre small fried ravioli with leeks and potatoes
tourtou buckwheat pancake
tourtou wheat or buckwheat pancake [with savory garnishes such as *foie gras* or mushrooms, or with sweet garnishes such as jam, sweet cheese or honey]
toute-épice peppery seeds of nigella
toutché sweet custard tart/pie [sometimes made with apples]
train de côtes beef ribs
train de lièvre saddle of rabbit
tramousse seeds of the white lupin cooked in brine
tranche slice; rasher
   bacon en tranche slice of bacon
   grosse tranche slab; big slice
tranché sliced
   finement tranché thinly sliced
tranche de boeuf beef steak
tranche de jambon fumé slab of smoked ham; gammon steak
tranche de lard rasher; thin slice of bacon
tranche de pain slice of bread; piece of bread
tranche de saumon slice of salmon
tranche grasse sirloin tip steak; silverside of beef
tranche napolitaine multi-layered, multi-flavored ice cream
tranche napolitaine aux petits-beurres Neapolitan ice cream sandwich [ice cream between two layers of cookies]
tranche plombières slice of tutti frutti ice cream
travers de porc pork spare ribs
treipaïs triangular cake [chocolate, hazelnuts, chestnut cream]
trémellodon gélatineux edible wild mushroom [raw or cooked; used in salads, risottos and soups; a gelatinous mushroom]
trenèls/tripous trenèls pouches made from sheep rumen [filled with ham, tripe, garlic and cloves and simmered in a broth of water, white wine, rind, carrots, celery, leek and onion]
trescat flat braided sheep tripe bound with egg yolk
trévise radicchio [a reddish form of chicory and is sometimes called red endive or red chicory; has a bitter and spicy taste when used raw in salads, but is more mellow when cooked]
trianon garnished with three colors
tricandilles tripe cooked in their own fat until golden brown, then doused with vinegar and garlic
tricholome edible mushroom with greenish, yellowish or brownish cap with thick white flesh; strong aroma of soap
tripailles guts; innards
tripe/tripes tripe [offal/stomach of beef, veal, lamb; may also refer to the rumen and feet of these animals]
   à la tripe/oeufs à la tripe sliced hard-boiled eggs in a thick, creamy sauce with puréed onions

tripes à l'Auvergnate beef tripe and pig's feet/pig's trotters
tripes à la crème de Coutances rolled tripe with cream
tripes à l'Djote Christmas sausage [pork and chopped kale, fat, onion, nutmeg and cloves]
tripes à la mode Caen casserole of tripe with calf's foot and vegetables and cider, Calvados or white wine
tripes à la provençale beef tripe, pig's trotters, pork head pieces in tomato sauce
tripes d'Angoulême rumen and calf's foot in white wine, tomatoes, garlic, onions and shallots
tripes d'Authon-du-Perche tripe layered with bacon and cider and simmered with carrots and onions
tripes de Caen beef rumen and foot cooked with sliced carrots in a seasoned broth
tripes de la Ferté-Macé tripe strung in small packets on skewers
tripes de Saint-Malo beef foot, calf's foot, sheep belly and beef with chunks of bacon, shallots and onions
tripes de Vannes tripe with calf's foot baked with cider, onions, carrots and leeks
tripota tripe sausage garnished with a super abundance of onions
tripotxa/tripotcha offal sausage [mutton (or sometimes pork) tripe, lungs and head meat cooked with onion and seasoned with nutmeg, salt and espelette peppers, bound with blood and poached; served hot with tomato sauce]
tripous du Cantal veal and pork forcemeat with onion, garlic and parsley
tripous trenèls pouches made from sheep rumen [filled with ham, tripe, garlic and cloves and simmered in a broth of water, white wine, rind, carrots, celery, leek and onion]
tripoux veal tripe filled with smaller pieces of rumen then rolled in sheep gut and cooked for four hours in veal stock with salt, pepper, white wine, carrots and tomatoes
Tripoux du Massif central tripe cut into small squares to form envelopes which are filled with ham, garlic, clove and pieces of tripe and cooked for seven hours with ham, tomatoes, garlic, onion, celery, carrots, herbs, salt and pepper and white wine
triumph Packam pear [imported from Australia; large pear with thick skin, delicate sweet juicy flesh]
trois frères/gâteau trois frères literally: three brothers' cake [gluten-free ring cake; rice flour and eggs flavored with maraschino cherry liqueur, apricot jam and pieces of angelica preserves]
trompette de la mort trumpet-of-the-dead mushroom; horn of plenty mushroom; black chanterelle; black trumpet [an almost entirely black mushroom; though unattractive, considered to have a good flavor]
tronçon chunk of meat cut off from a piece that is longer than it is wide
troucha omelet stuffed with spinach and chard [served on a plate with tomato sauce (sometimes the tomato sauce includes ground beef or turkey)]

truffade a traditional dish of potatoes, fresh *Cantal* or *Laguiole* cheese and grilled bacon
truffe truffle
truffé with truffles [stuffed with truffles or garnished with shavings or flakes of truffles]
truffe blanche white truffle
truffe blanche d'Alba white truffle [*Tuber magnatum*; very large; yellowish in color; fragrance of garlic, shallots and cheese; very rare and highly esteemed]
truffe blanche d'été white summer truffle [*Tuber aestevum*; about the size of an apricot or larger]
truffe blanche du Piémont white truffle [*Tuber magnatum*; very large; yellowish in color; has a fragrance of garlic, shallots and cheese; very rare and highly esteemed]
truffe de Bourgogne de Champagne Burgundy and Champagne truffle [*Tuber uncinatum*; resembles the summer truffle, *Tuber aestevum*, but with a more pronounced fragrance and flavor; the flesh is brown to chocolate, marbled white]
truffe de Haute-Marne truffle of Haute-Marne [*Tuber uncinatum*; resembles the summer truffle, *Tuber aestevum*, but with a more pronounced fragrance and flavor; the flesh is brown to chocolate, marbled white]
truffe de la Saint-Jean summer truffle [*Tuber aestevum*; about the size of an apricot or larger; resembles the black truffle]
truffe de Lorraine Lorraine truffle [*Tuber mesentericum*; very black on the outside with chocolate-maroon flesh; it has the strong odor of turpentine when young, more like apricot kernel or bitter almond when mature]
truffe d'été summer truffle [*Tuber aestevum*; about the size of an apricot or larger; resembles the black truffle]
truffe fraiche fresh truffle [i.e., not dried]
truffe fraiche noire fresh black truffle
truffe grise gray truffle [*Tuber uncinatum*; resembles the summer truffle, *Tuber aestevum*, but with a more pronounced fragrance and flavor; the flesh is brown to chocolate, marbled white]
truffe grise de Champagne gray truffle of Champagne [*Tuber uncinatum*; round, warty truffle; dark gray outside and chocolate with white veins inside; mild, nutty-woodsy aroma]
truffe musquée musk truffle [*Tuber brumale*; rarely as large as an egg; black on the outside, gray inside with white veins; strong fragrance and very agreeable flavor]
truffe noir de Norcia black truffle of Norcia [*Tuber melanosporum*; said to be the queen of truffles in terms of taste; the fragrance is strong, reminiscent of strawberries or a fine old red wine; black inside and out and finely marbled]
truffe noir du Tricastin black truffle of Tricastin [said to be the queen of truffles in terms of taste; the fragrance is strong, reminiscent of strawberries or a fine old red wine; black inside and out and finely marbled]
truffe noire black truffle

truffe noire d'hiver black winter truffle [*Tuber brumale*; rarely as large as an egg; black on the outside, gray inside with white veins; strong fragrance and very agreeable flavor]
truffe noire du Périgord black truffle of Périgord [*Tuber melanosporum*; has clear white or beige flesh; usually eaten raw in salads or on pasta; said to be the queen of truffles in terms of taste; the fragrance is strong, reminiscent of strawberries or a fine old red wine; black inside and out and finely marbled]
truffe noire Lisse black truffle of Lisse [*Tuber macrosporum*; a small truffle, rarely as large as an egg, that has the strong fragrance of garlic; blackish purple on the outside; pinkish brown flesh, marbled grey]
truffes à la Bénédictine chocolate truffles with Bénédictine
truffes au Calvados chocolate truffles with Calvados
truffiat potato cake
truite trout
truit à la hussarde split trout stuffed with eggplant/augergine
truite à la normande trout (sometimes with mussels) in a creamy white wine sauce
truit arc-en-ciel rainbow trout
truite au bleu very fresh trout cooked in a vinegary broth [the trout is killed minutes before cooking; the vinegar reacts with the fresh fish's coating of mucus to give it a blue color]
truite au vin jaune trout cooked in yellow wine and butter
truite aux amandes trout with almonds
truite de lac lake trout
truite de mer sea trout; speckled trout; brown trout
truite de rivière river trout
truite saumonée salmon with natural light gray flesh [as opposed to salmon that have fed on krill, which causes their flesh to turn orange or farmed salmon whose flesh is tinted with artificial colorants]
trulle black pudding; black sausage [made of pig's blood, pork and pork fat and stuffed with chard and rice; eaten hot or cold]
tsarine/à la tsarine Tsarina-style [chicken breast with cucumber and cream]
Tuber aestevum truffle about the size of an apricot or larger [resembles the black truffle]
Tuber brumale truffle [rarely as large as an egg; black on the outside, gray inside with white veins; strong fragrance and very agreeable flavor]
tubercule root vegetable
Tuber macrosporum truffle [small truffle, rarely as large as an egg; strong fragrance of garlic; blackish purple on the outside; pinkish brown flesh, marbled gray]
Tuber melanosporum truffle [said to be the queen of truffles in terms of taste; clear white or beige flesh; the fragrance is strong, reminiscent of strawberries or a fine old red wine; black inside and out and finely marbled; usually eaten raw in salads or on pasta]
Tuber mesentericum truffle [very black on the outside with chocolate-maroon flesh; strong odor of turpentine when young,

more like apricot kernel or bitter almond when mature; used to great advantage in *terrines* and as a base for sauces]
Tuber uncinatum truffle [resembles the summer truffle, *Tuber aestevum*, but with a more pronounced fragrance and flavor; the flesh is brown to chocolate, marbled white]
tuile thin, delicate biscuit/cookie
tulipe/gâteau tulipe tulip-shaped biscuit cone filled with sorbet or ice cream and fruit
turbot turbot [flat marine fish with fine, flaky flesh]
turbot Greenland halibut
turbotin young turbot
turinois unbaked "cake" made with chestnut purée, rum, chocolate, sugar, vanilla and cream [rich dessert; ingredient in meat sauces, soups or other desserts]
tutti fruitti tutti fruitti [literally: all fruits; refers to desserts with many flavors or fruits]
vache cow
vacherin a frozen dessert made of layers of meringue, whipped cream, ice cream and possibly berries
vah'h thick pancake [made with eggs, flour and milk; may be savory (cooked with diced ham or bacon) or served with fruit (apples, cherries, strawberries)
vanille vanilla
vanillé vanilla flavored
vanneau queen scallop [small shellfish, similar to scallops]
vanneau lapwing; green plover
vapeur steam
   à la vapeur steamed
   pommes vapeur boiled/steamed potatoes
vaute thick pancake [made with eggs, flour and milk; may be savory (cooked with diced ham or bacon) or served with fruit (apples, cherries, strawberries)]
VCC/Vin de Consommation Courante wine for current consumption; young wine
VDL/Vin de Liqueur sweet fortified wine [wine mixed with brandy (eau de vie)]
VDN/Vin Doux Naturel very sweet dessert wine such as Muscadet and Banyuls [grape brandy is added to the fermenting wine which stops the fermentation, thus preserving the sugars]
veau veal
   noix de veau round fillet of veal
   ris de veau calf's sweetbreads [thymus, pancreas]
   rouelle de veau veal steak [cut across the leg]
   tête de veau calf's head
veau de mer porbeagle shark [marine fish; type of mackerel shark]
veau orloff haunch of veal with cheese and mushrooms [typically: cooked veal is sliced and layered with mushroom-onion purée then covered with a white sauce and cheese and browned; truffles or bacon may be added]
végétalien vegan
végétarien vegetarian
velours literally: velvet [refers to carrot soup with tapioca]

velouté/sauce velouté velvet sauce [made from a light stock, such as chicken or fish, and carefully and slowly thickened with a blond *roux* (made with equal parts flour and butter to which a liquid such as milk or broth is added) and a mixture of egg yolks and cream]
veloute soup made with a velvety white sauce (*velouté*)
veloute au vin blanc velvety soup of fish, chicken or veal with white wine added
venaison venison
vendange late harvest wine grapes
vendange a style of sweet dessert wine
Vendredi Friday
vénus American clam
verdure greens; salad greens, green vegetables or green herbs
vergeoise brown sugar
vergeoise brune dark brown sugar
vergeoise blonde light brown sugar
véritable jambon de Luxeuil Luxeuil ham [macerated in wine, lightly smoked over fir wood fire giving it a special flavor]
verjus juice of unripe Verjus raisins
vermicelle vermicelli; noodle
vermouth aromatized aperitif wine [fortified wine flavored with twenty spices and herbs, including wormwood (Artemisia)]
verni/vernis varnished clam; dog cockle [large oval clam]
véronique veronica; water pimpernel
véronique garnished with white seedless grapes
vert/verte green
   anguilles au vert eels cooked with green herbs
   beurre vert green butter [butter with chopped green herbs]
vert-cuit barely cooked; almost raw
vert galant blueberry jam [blueberries, honey and spices]
vert-prè/au vert-prè literally: green meadow [garnished with potatoes and water cress]
vert-prè/au vert-prè literally: green meadow [garnished with green mayonnaise or creamy green sauce and chopped greens or green vegetables]
verte/sauce verte green mayonnaise [mayonnaise with green herbs such as chervil, chives, tarragon or watercress]
verveine lemon verbena; vervain [lemon-flavored herb]
vésiga dried sturgeon marrow
vesse de loup puffball; meadow puffball mushroom [grayish-white in color; eaten when young and still white]
vesse de loup géant giant puffball [the size of a soccer ball; somewhat rare; eaten when young]
vessie bladder
   en vessie meat cooked in a pig's bladder
   poularde/poulet en vessie chicken cooked in pig's bladder
viande meat
viande blanche white meat
viande crue raw meat
viande des grisons cured, dried beef
viande hachée minced meat

viande maigre lean meat
viande rouge red meat
viandes froides cold cuts; cold sliced meats
Vichy sliced carrots cooked in mineral water (*Vichy*) until slightly glazed
Victoria/à la Victoria Victoria-style [typically: with macaroni, tomatoes, lettuce, potatoes and maybe artichokes]
Victoria/sauce Victoria Victoria sauce [lobster sauce (*sauce homard*) with mushrooms]
vieille literally: old woman [refers to several species of wrasse, a kind of bony marine fish]
viennoise/à la viennoise typically: cooked with a coating of breadcrumbs and served with chopped egg, capers and parsley
viennoiserie milkbread pastries such as croissants
vierge literally: virgin [refers to cold-pressed olive oil]
vierge/beurre vierge soft butter whipped with lemon juice
vieux old; aged
vieux garçon old boy
viez cider [similar to English scrumpy; a cloudy cider made with both apples and pears; the level of alcohol is variable]
vigne vine; grapevine
vigneronne/à la vigneronne in the vitner's style [with a wine sauce and garnished with grapes]
villages literally: villages [term reserved for AOC/AOP wines and added after the name of a designation of origin]
vin wine
    coq au vin male chicken/young rooster in wine sauce
vinaigre vinegar
vin blanc white wine
    sauce au vin blanc white wine sauce
vin blanc de blancs literally "white of whites" wine [may be sparkling wine (champagne) or still wine]
vin blanc de noirs white champagne [literally "white of blacks"; champagne made from the juice of pinot noir or pinot meunier grapes; the juice is gently squeezed out of the skins so that the wine stays white]
vin chaud warm wine [usually red wine; spicy]
vin coupé wine cut with water
vin cuit cooked wine [in the tradition of Provence, cooked wine is made with freshly pressed grape must which is heated before fermentation to concentrate the sugar and evaporate the water to produce sweet wines, apéritifs (wine with brandy added) and mulled wine]
vin de Cassis blackcurrant wine
vin de cépage varietal wine
vin de coupage blended wine
vin de dessert dessert wine
vin de fleur wine made when yeast forms a veil (*la fleur*) on the surface of the fermenting wine blocking contact with air; after a few years, the wine develops a bouquet of walnuts, spices or cocoa
vin de fruit fruit wine

vin de glace ice wine [red or white wine made from grapes that have been frozen on the vine, making a more concentrated, very sweet wine; production is limited due to the possibility that the grapes may rot before they freeze or a freeze may not occur]

vin de liqueur sweet fortified wine [wine mixed with alcohol, usually brandy (*eau de vie*) during fermentation to stop the fermatation process and preserve the sweetness and aromas of the grapes]

vin de paille sweet wine [made from clusters of grapes that have been partially dried on beds of straw (*paille*) to concentrate their sugars; 15% to 20% alcohol content]

vin de palm palm wine [fermented sap of palm trees]

vin de pays country wine; ordinary wine of superior quality [wines specific to particular geographic areas; according to French regulations, unlike ordinary table wine, they are labeled with their geographic location, must be tested and analyzed, and must come from specific grapes]

vin de primeur new season's wine [fresh wine, available after October 15 in the case of the IGP wines, or after November 15 for the AOP wines]

vin de table table wine; ordinary wine

vin de voile wine with a fresh, nutty aroma [aged in barrels in which the wine is allowed to evaporate and form a veil of yeast on the surface; vin jaune (yellow wine) and vin de Xérès (sherry) are types of vin de voile]

vin demi-sec semi-dry wine

vin doux/vin doux naturel very sweet dessert wine such as Muscadet and Banyuls [grape brandy is added to the fermenting wine which stops the fermentation process, thus preserving the sugars]

vin effervescent sparkling wine

vin fin literally: fine wine [refers to wines with official designations, as opposed to ordinary table wine]

vin fortifié fortified wine [wine to which alcohol has been added]

vin gazéifie carbonated wine [similar to sparkling wine, but the carbonization is added; it does not come from fermentation]

vin gris very pale rosé wine made from red grapes that yield white juice

vin gris de gris pale rosé wines made from pale red grapes that yield white juice (grenache, cinsault, carignan grapes)

vin jaune yellow wine [from late-harvest savagnin grapes; a strong white wine, similar to sherry, but not fortified; aged for six years and three months; nutty flavor]

vin kasher kosher wine

vin liquoreux fortified wine made with a minimum natural content by volume of 12% alcohol to which alcohol and brandy and/or caramel and/or over-ripe grapes are added

vin moelleux denotes slightly sweet white wines [usually rich in fruits, fats and are low in acidity]

vin mousseux sparkling wine

vin mousseux gazéifié aerated sparkling wine [sparkling wine to which carbonization is added]

vin muté fortified wine [the fermentation process of red or white wine is interrupted by adding alcohol; the white fortified wines may have complex aromas of candied fruit, candied orange peel, white flowers, apricot, peach, spices; the red fortified wines may have aromas of cooked or dried fruit, licorice, fig, plum, fig, violets, mocha or cocoa]
vin nature still wine from the Champagne region
vin nouveau new wine [used after August 31 after the harvest]
vin ordinaire common wine [usually an inexpensive claret; used as table wine]
vin rosé rosé wine; pink wine [not a mixture of red and white wine; wine obtained by allowing red grape skins to remain long enough to tint the fermenting wine]
vin rouge red wine
vin viné wine without residual sugar mixed with brandy (*eau de vie*); only refers to wine having an alcohol content between 18% and 24%]
vinaigre vinegar
vinaigre de cidre cider vinegar
vinaigre Xérès sherry vinegar
vinaigrette/sauce vinaigrette salad dressing [made with oil and vinegar; sometimes with herbs, spices or other ingredients]
violet sea violet; sea fig
violette violet [the flower]
violon guitar fish [marine fish; looks like a cross between a shark and a ray]
viroflay baked chopped spinach with mornay sauce
Viroflay/à la Viroflay Viroflay-style [with spinach, artichokes, potatoes and parsley]
vipérine viper's bugloss; blueweed [edible blue flowers]
visitandine/gâteau visitandine small, light cake [made with egg whites, flour, sugar, butter, almond flour and whipped egg whites]
vitréais caramelized apples and almonds sandwiched between two light biscuits topped with egg whites, confectioner's sugar and sliced almonds and browned before serving
vitelotte blue potato [dark blue to purple skin and blue flesh]
vive weever fish [has poisonous fins; very fine flesh]
VMQ/Vin Mousseux de Qualité quality sparkling wine
volaille poultry
    blanc de volaille chicken breast
    crème de volaille cream of chicken soup
    farce de volaille poultry stuffing
    foie de volaille chicken liver
volailles fermière farm-raised poultry [mostly organic (*bio*) and generally refers to operations where the poultry are allowed to free range for a part of each day]
vol-au-vent light savory pastry, round and bite-sized, with savory filling [served hot or cold as a starter, *canapé* or *hors d'oeuvre*; the filling may be chopped vegetables, mushrooms, fish or meat, usually bound with a sauce]

vol-au-vent régence light savory pastry with foie gras, mushrooms, truffles and minced chicken
vol-au-vent à la toulousaine light savory pastry with sweetbreads, mushrooms and truffles
volière/en volière game birds decorated with their own feathers
volonté/à volonté at your discretion
volpaillère braised chicken fillets with truffle sauce
volvaire soyeuse volvaria mushroom [white flesh; woody aroma]
vôtes thick pancakes [made with eggs, flour and milk; may be savory (cooked with diced ham or bacon) or served with fruit (apples, cherries, strawberries)]
vrai true
vraie tortue real turtle
VSIG/Vin Sans Indication Géographique wines without geographical indication
wagotine nougatine in the shape of a small wagon and filled with colorful sweets such as blueberries in almond paste or various chocolates
wakamé sea mustard [seaweed with a sweet, suble flavor]
waldmeister sweet woodruff
Walewska/à la Walewska Comtesse Walewska style [with lobster, truffles and cheese sauce]
Washington/à la Washington Washington-style [with sweetcorn kernels in a cream sauce]
waterzooï fish or chicken stew [typically: chicken or fish in a creamy sauce flavored with carrots, onions, celery, leeks, tarragon and vermouth]
welsh/welsh rabbit/welsh rarebit cheddar cheese melted in a pot of beer and flavored with mustard and served on toasted bread with a slice of ham
William's pear [yellow skin, slightly granular white flesh, sweet, juicy and slightly acid
Xérès sherry [fortified Spanish wine]
yaourt yogurt
yaourt surgelé frozen yoghurt
ylang-ylang fruit, flowers or essence derived from the flowers of the cananga tree (Cananga odorata) [flowers have a delicate scent of custard and jasmine]
York/Jambon d'York cold York ham
yuzu citrus fruit believed to be a hybrid between a sour mandarine and *Ichang papeda*
zedoaire zedoary; white turmeric [like ginger, but with a bitter aftertaste]
zéphyr literally: light breeze [refers to light frothy preparations which may be sweet or savory, hot or cold]
zeste peel; zest
zeste confit candied peel
zeste de citron lemon peel
zeste d'orange orange peel
zikiro lamb cut into quarters and grilled with white beans, vinegar, garlic and pimentos

zingara/à la zingara gypsy style [typically: garnish made with diced ham, diced tongue, mushrooms and truffles in a tomato sauce with tarragon; may also refer to a paprika tomato sauce]

Notes

Notes

Printed in Great Britain
by Amazon